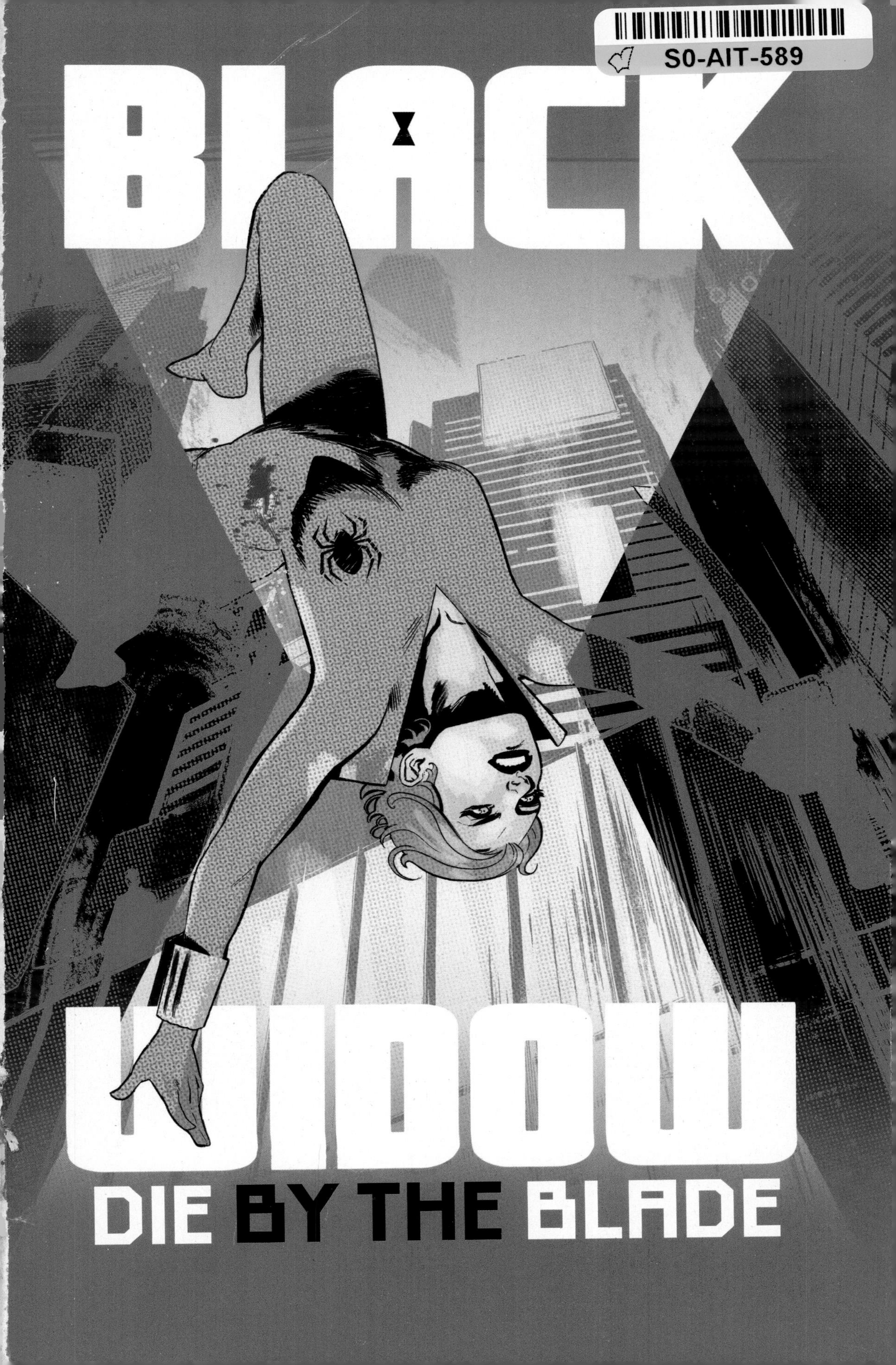
BLACK
WIDOW
DIE BY THE BLADE

Natasha Romanoff, A.K.A. the Black Widow, recently gave up a beautiful husband and perfect baby boy, her actual genetic son, in order to protect them both. With the Winter Soldier's help, she sent James and Stevie far away, where not even she could find them again.

Her fears were justified: A new villain arose in San Francisco and began spreading deadly super-powers to his followers. Natasha and her allies defeated Apogee and his "Olio," but Apogee escaped, and young ally Lucy is now stuck with electrical powers that won't turn off.

The Black Widow's problems are just **beginning.**

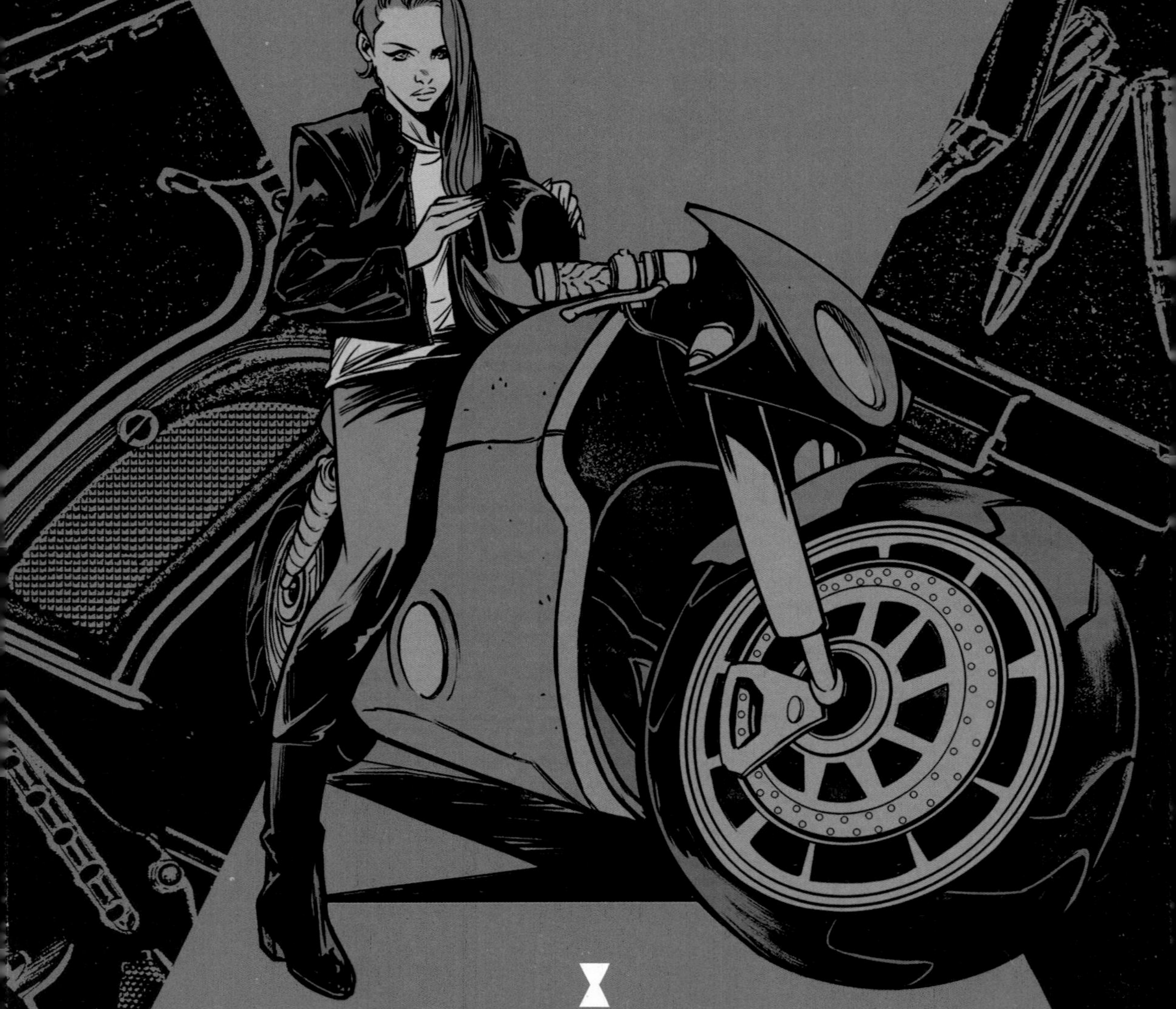

COLLECTION EDITOR **JENNIFER GRÜNWALD**
ASSISTANT MANAGING EDITOR **MAIA LOY**
VP PRODUCTION & SPECIAL PROJECTS **JEFF YOUNGQUIST**
SVP PRINT, SALES & MARKETING **DAVID GABRIEL**

DANIEL KIRCHHOFFER ASSISTANT EDITOR
LISA MONTALBANO ASSOCIATE MANAGER, TALENT RELATIONS
JAY BOWEN BOOK DESIGNER
C.B. CEBULSKI EDITOR IN CHIEF

BLACK WIDOW BY KELLY THOMPSON VOL. 3: DIE BY THE BLADE. Contains material originally published in magazine form as BLACK WIDOW (2020) #11-15. First printing 2022. ISBN 978-1-302-93254-1. *Published by MARVEL WORLDWIDE, INC., a subsidiary of MARVEL ENTERTAINMENT, LLC. OFFICE OF PUBLICATION: 1290 Avenue of the Americas, New York, NY 10104.*

Printed in Canada. KEVIN FEIGE, *Chief Creative Officer;* DAN BUCKLEY, *President, Marvel Entertainment;* JOE QUESADA, EVP & Creative Director; DAVID BOGART, Associate Publisher & SVP of Talent Affairs; TOM BREVOORT, VP, Executive Editor; NICK LOWE, Executive Editor, VP of Content, Digital Publishing; DAVID GABRIEL, VP of Print & Digital Publishing; MARK ANNUNZIATO, VP of Planning & Forecasting; JEFF YOUNGQUIST, VP of Production & Special Projects; ALEX MORALES, Director of Publishing Operations; DAN EDINGTON, Director of Editorial Operations; RICKEY PURDIN, Director of Talent Relations; JENNIFER GRÜNWALD, Director of Production & Special Projects; SUSAN CRESPI, Production Manager; STAN LEE, Chairman Emeritus. For information regarding advertising in Marvel Comics or on Marvel.com, please contact Vit DeBellis, Custom Solutions & Integrated Advertising Manager, at vdebellis@marvel.com. For Marvel subscription inquiries, please call 888-511-5480. **Manufactured between 3/11/2022 and 4/12/2022 by SOLISCO PRINTERS, SCOTT, QC, CANADA.**

10 9 8 7 6 5 4 3 2 1

BLACK

DIE BY THE BLADE

KELLY THOMPSON
WRITER

RAFAEL DE LATORRE (#11),
ELENA CASAGRANDE (#12, #14-15)
& RAFAEL T. PIMENTEL (#13, #15)
PENCILERS

RAFAEL DE LATORRE (#11),
ELISABETTA D'AMICO
(#12, #14-15) &
RAFAEL T. PIMENTEL
(#13, #15)
INKERS

JORDIE BELLAIRE
COLOR ARTIST

VC's CORY PETIT
WITH **CLAYTON COWLES** (#15)
LETTERERS

ADAM HUGHES
COVER ART

KAT GREGOROWICZ & ANITA OKOYE
ASSISTANT EDITORS

SARAH BRUNSTAD
EDITOR

TOM BREVOORT
EXECUTIVE EDITOR

WIDOW

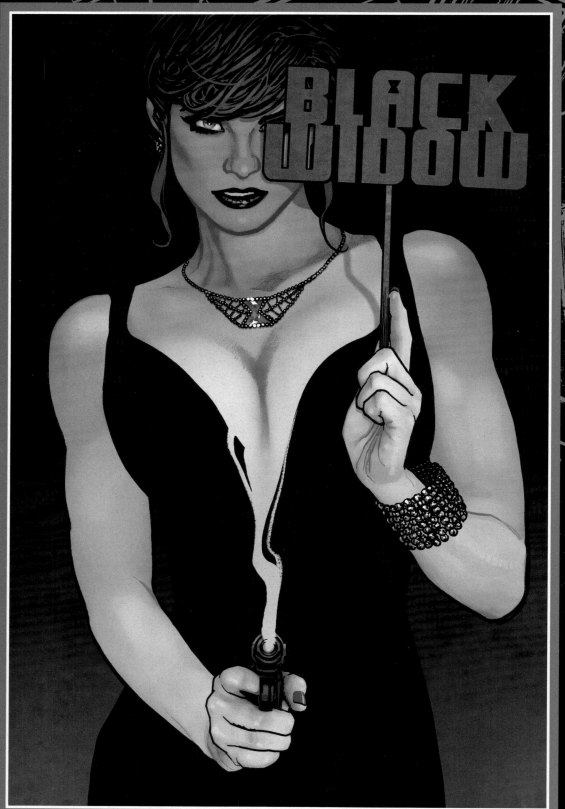

BLACK WIDOW

ELEVEN

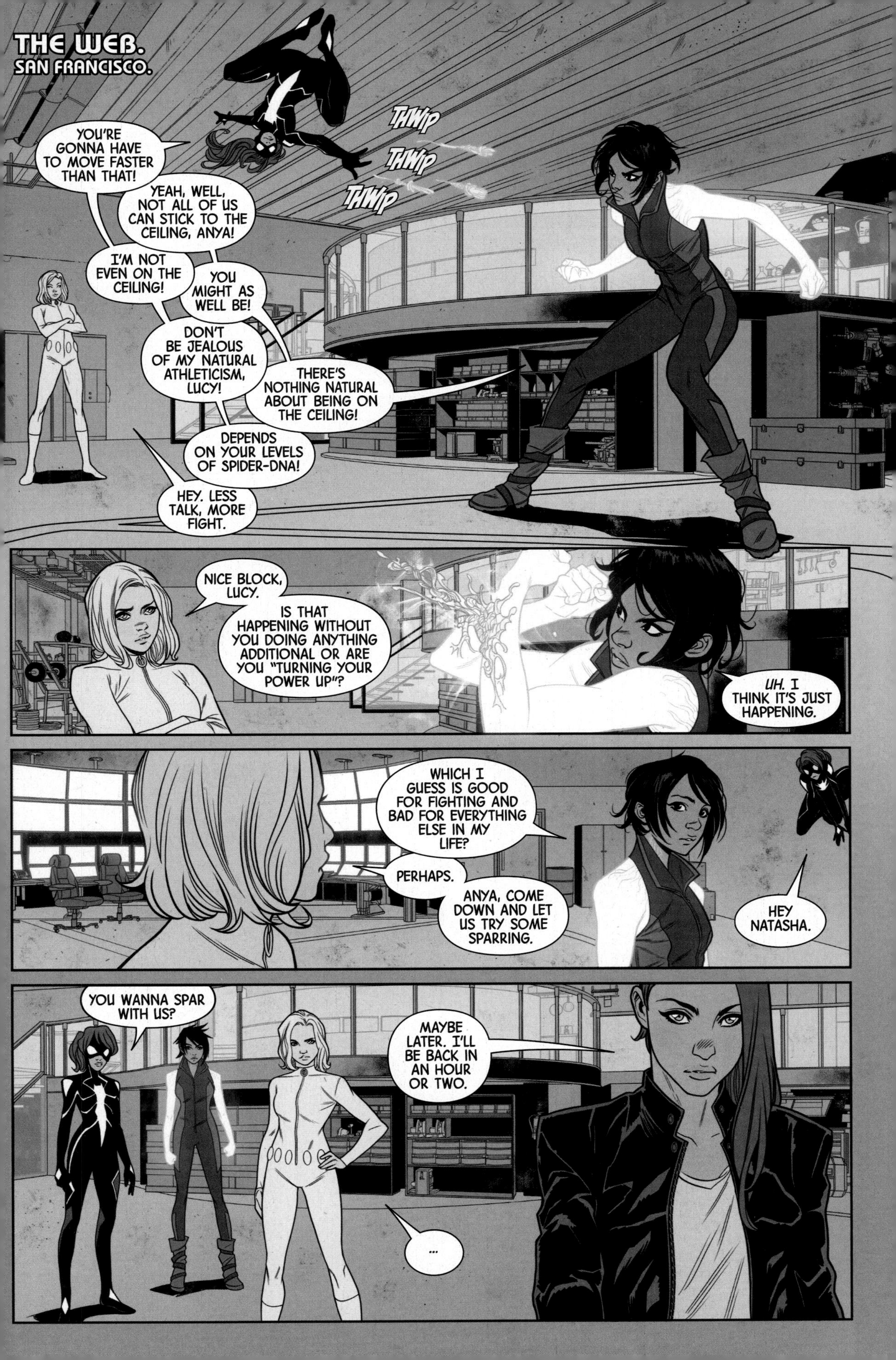
THE WEB. SAN FRANCISCO.
YOU'RE GONNA HAVE TO MOVE FASTER THAN THAT!
THWIP
THWIP
THWIP
YEAH, WELL, NOT ALL OF US CAN STICK TO THE CEILING, ANYA!
I'M NOT EVEN ON THE CEILING!
YOU MIGHT AS WELL BE!
DON'T BE JEALOUS OF MY NATURAL ATHLETICISM, LUCY!
THERE'S NOTHING NATURAL ABOUT BEING ON THE CEILING!
DEPENDS ON YOUR LEVELS OF SPIDER-DNA!
HEY. LESS TALK, MORE FIGHT.
NICE BLOCK, LUCY.
IS THAT HAPPENING WITHOUT YOU DOING ANYTHING ADDITIONAL OR ARE YOU "TURNING YOUR POWER UP"?
UH. I THINK IT'S JUST HAPPENING.
WHICH I GUESS IS GOOD FOR FIGHTING AND BAD FOR EVERYTHING ELSE IN MY LIFE?
PERHAPS.
ANYA, COME DOWN AND LET US TRY SOME SPARRING.
HEY NATASHA.
YOU WANNA SPAR WITH US?
MAYBE LATER. I'LL BE BACK IN AN HOUR OR TWO.
...

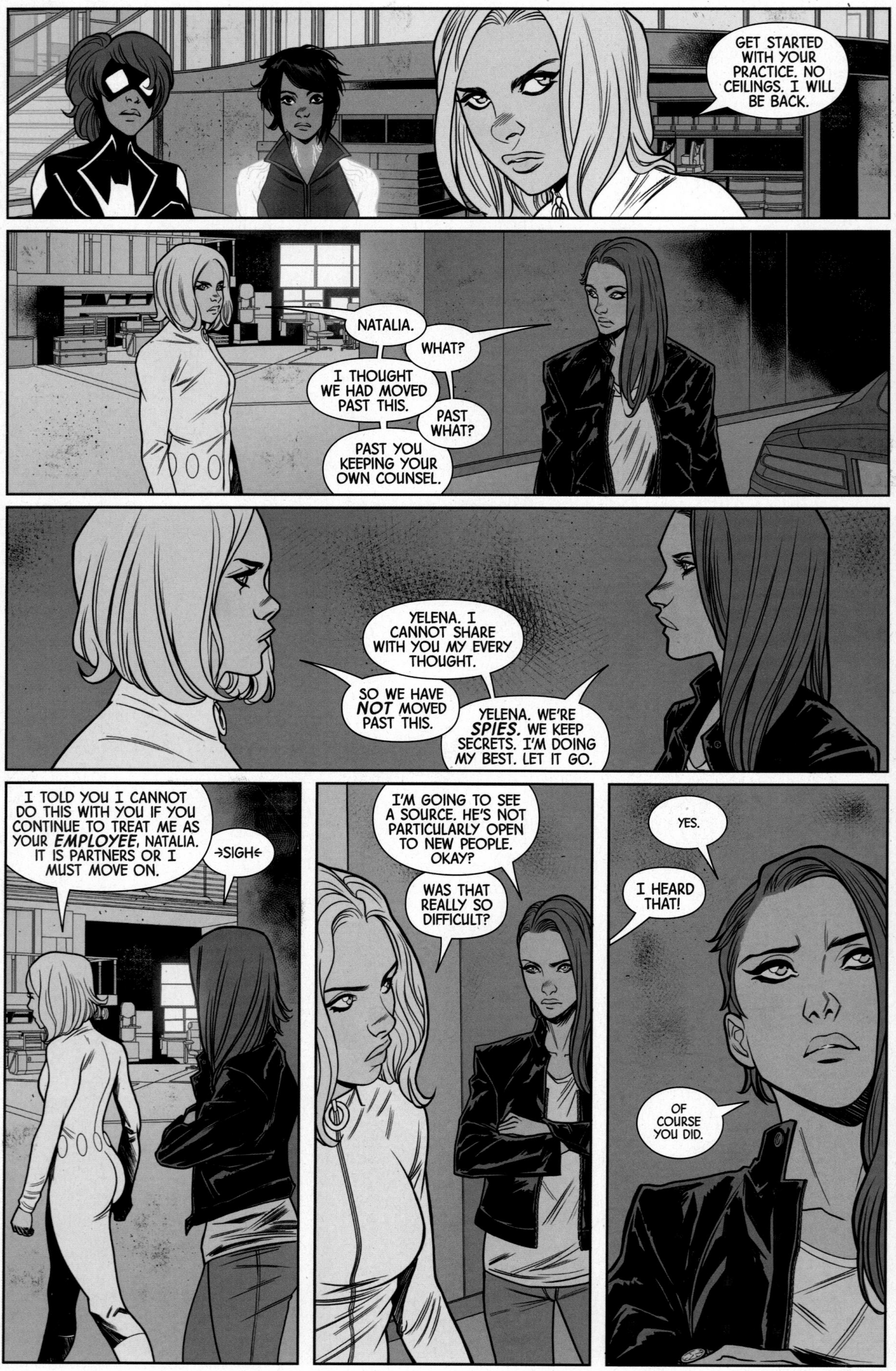
GET STARTED WITH YOUR PRACTICE. NO CEILINGS. I WILL BE BACK.
NATALIA.
WHAT?
I THOUGHT WE HAD MOVED PAST THIS.
PAST WHAT?
PAST YOU KEEPING YOUR OWN COUNSEL.
YELENA. I CANNOT SHARE WITH YOU MY EVERY THOUGHT.
SO WE HAVE *NOT* MOVED PAST THIS.
YELENA. WE'RE *SPIES.* WE KEEP SECRETS. I'M DOING MY BEST. LET IT GO.
I TOLD YOU I CANNOT DO THIS WITH YOU IF YOU CONTINUE TO TREAT ME AS YOUR *EMPLOYEE*, NATALIA. IT IS PARTNERS OR I MUST MOVE ON.
→SIGH←
I'M GOING TO SEE A SOURCE. HE'S NOT PARTICULARLY OPEN TO NEW PEOPLE. OKAY?
WAS THAT REALLY SO DIFFICULT?
YES.
I HEARD THAT!
OF COURSE YOU DID.

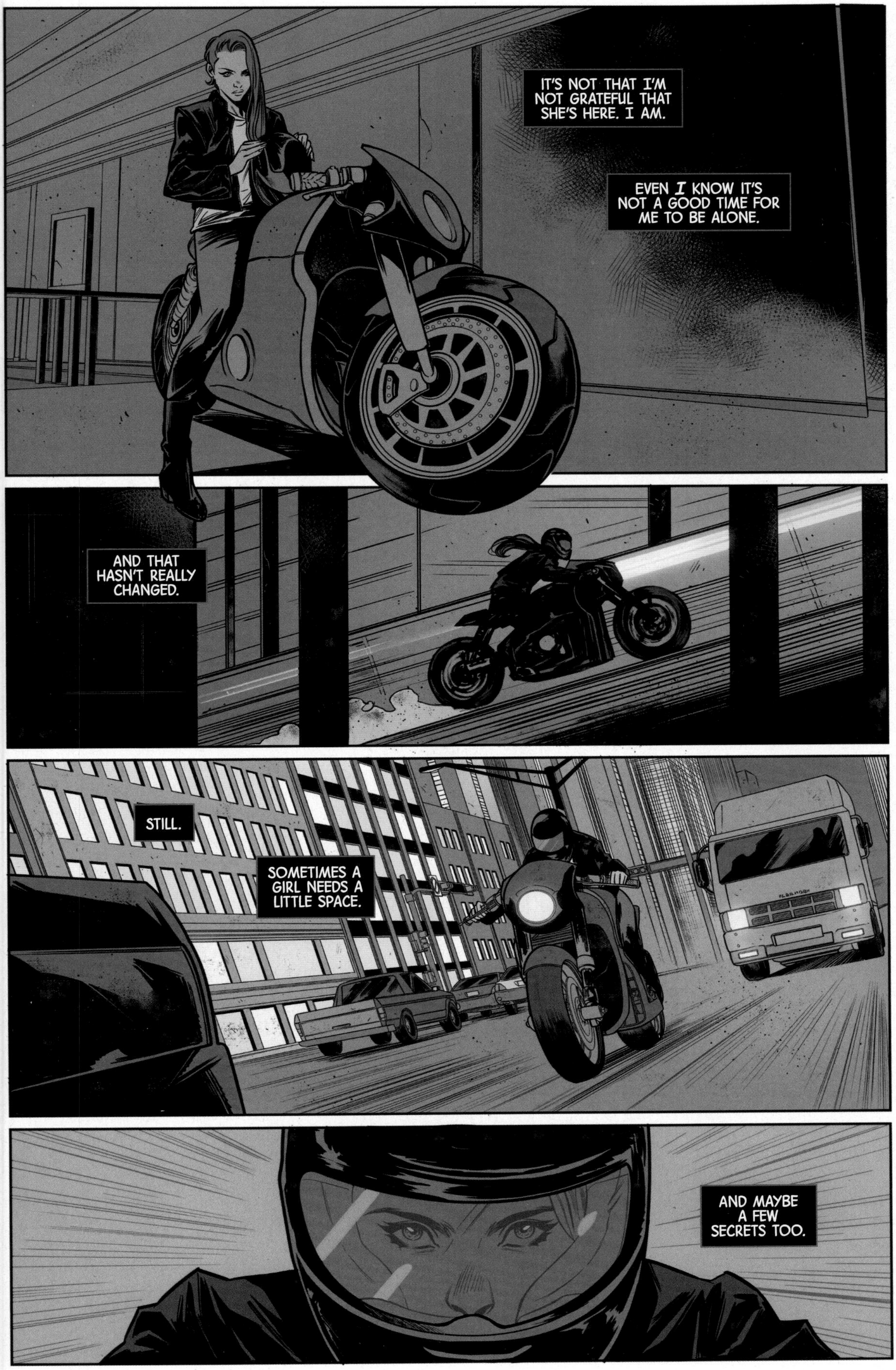
IT'S NOT THAT I'M NOT GRATEFUL THAT SHE'S HERE. I AM.
EVEN I KNOW IT'S NOT A GOOD TIME FOR ME TO BE ALONE.
AND THAT HASN'T REALLY CHANGED.
STILL.
SOMETIMES A GIRL NEEDS A LITTLE SPACE.
AND MAYBE A FEW SECRETS TOO.

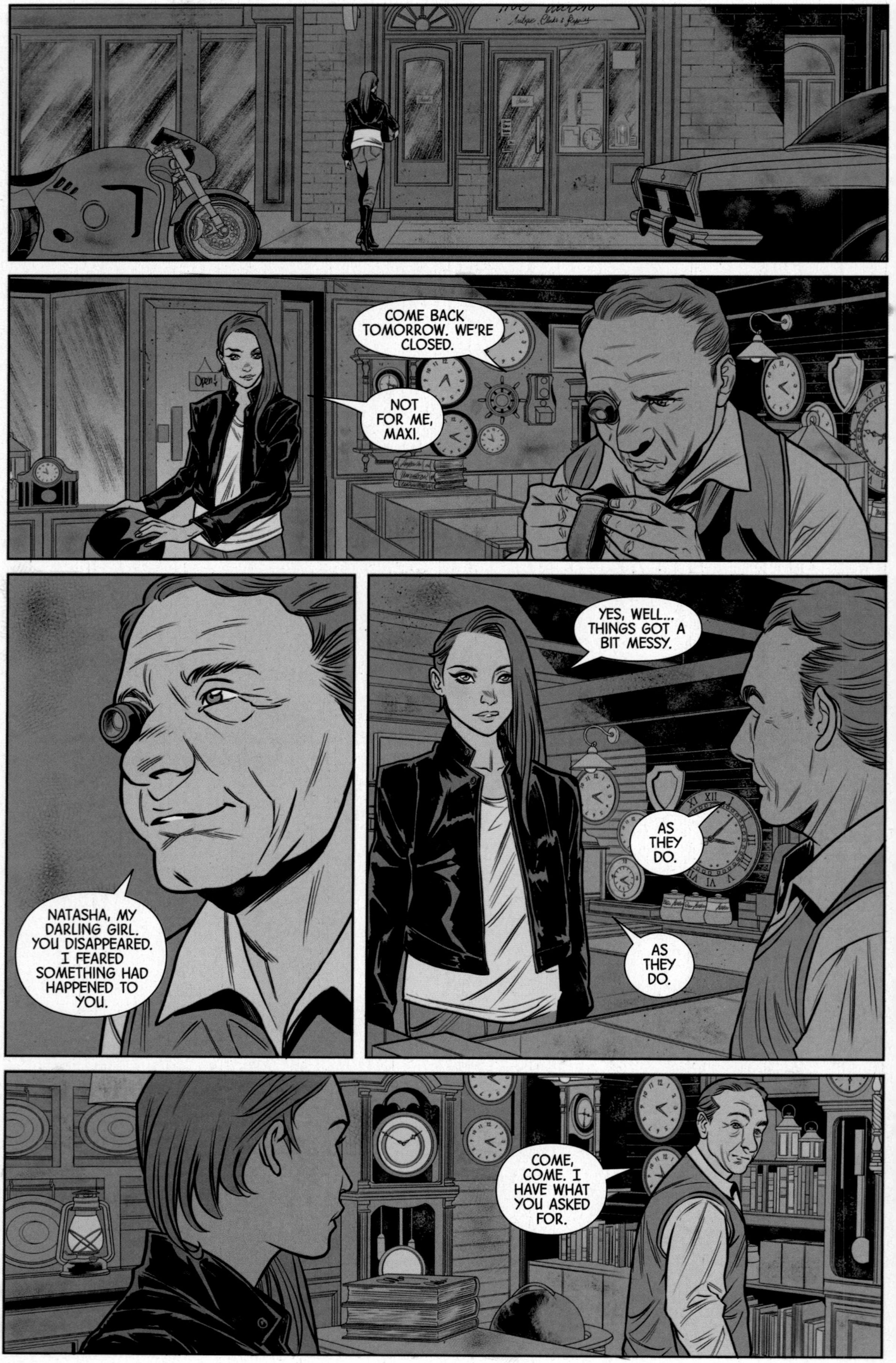
COME BACK TOMORROW. WE'RE CLOSED.
NOT FOR ME, MAXI.
NATASHA, MY DARLING GIRL. YOU DISAPPEARED. I FEARED SOMETHING HAD HAPPENED TO YOU.
YES, WELL... THINGS GOT A BIT MESSY.
AS THEY DO.
AS THEY DO.
COME, COME. I HAVE WHAT YOU ASKED FOR.

WAS SORTA HOPING AFTER ALL THIS TIME AWAY, YOU'D BRING ME SOMETHING A BIT MORE CHALLENGING.

BUT THE *BASICS* ARE ALWAYS FUN.

YOU'VE DONE SOME UPGRADES SINCE I WAS HERE LAST.

YES, WELL, HAVE TO KEEP UP WITH THE TIMES. BUT I STILL MOSTLY PREFER THE OLD WAYS, IF I'M HONEST.

I DON'T DISAGREE.

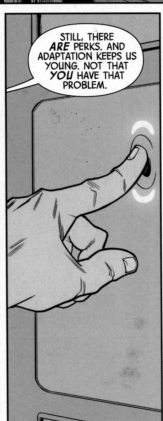

STILL, THERE *ARE* PERKS. AND ADAPTATION KEEPS US YOUNG. NOT THAT *YOU* HAVE THAT PROBLEM.

THERE YOU GO. EVERYTHING A YOUNG LADY NEEDS TO START ALL OVER. GO ANYWHERE. BE ANYONE. SKY'S THE LIMIT.

THANKS, MAXI.

ON THE SUBJECT OF MORE CHALLENGING...

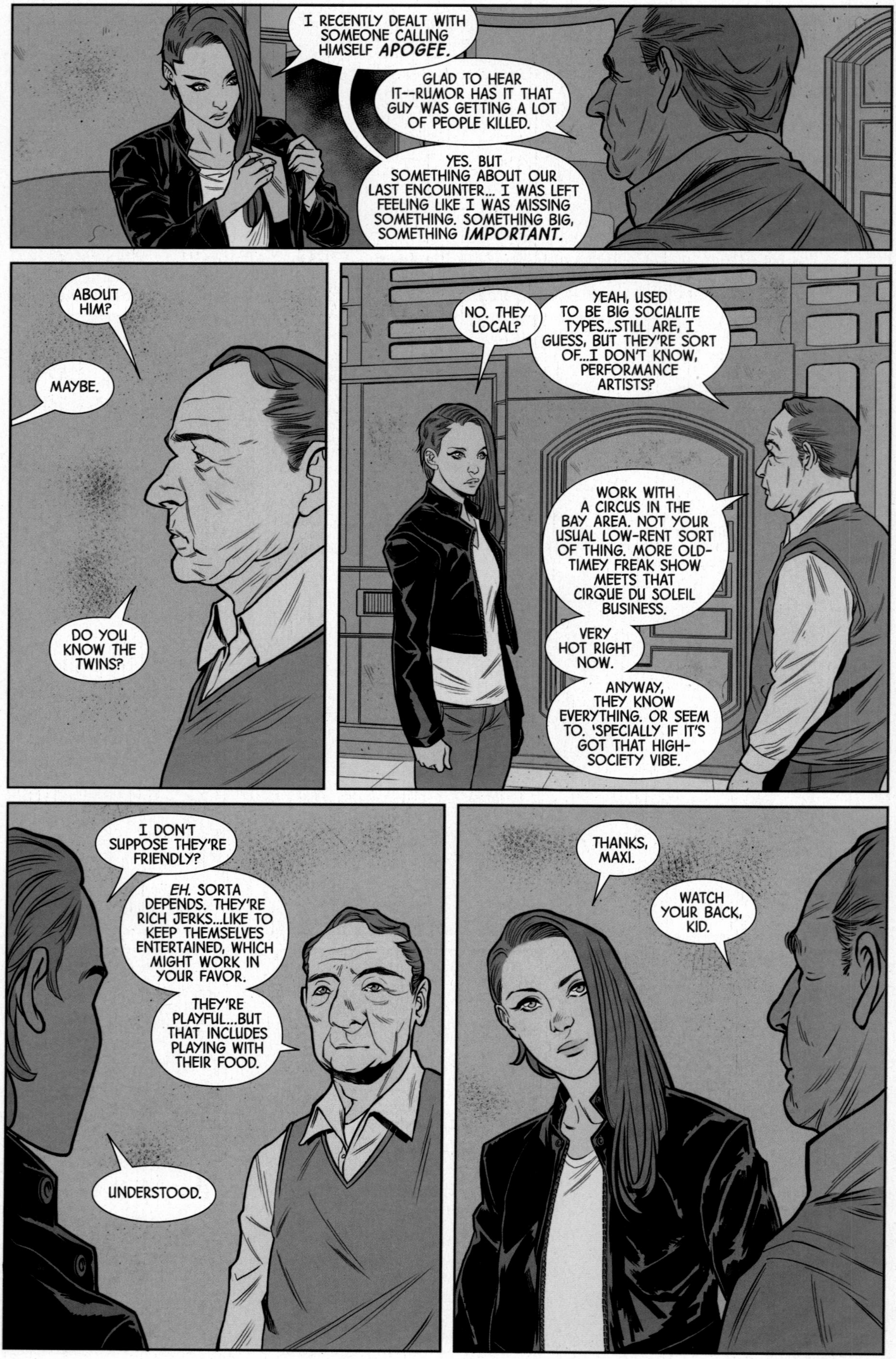
I RECENTLY DEALT WITH SOMEONE CALLING HIMSELF *APOGEE.*
GLAD TO HEAR IT--RUMOR HAS IT THAT GUY WAS GETTING A LOT OF PEOPLE KILLED.
YES. BUT SOMETHING ABOUT OUR LAST ENCOUNTER... I WAS LEFT FEELING LIKE I WAS MISSING SOMETHING. SOMETHING BIG, SOMETHING *IMPORTANT.*
ABOUT HIM?
MAYBE.
DO YOU KNOW THE TWINS?
NO. THEY LOCAL?
YEAH, USED TO BE BIG SOCIALITE TYPES...STILL ARE, I GUESS, BUT THEY'RE SORT OF...I DON'T KNOW, PERFORMANCE ARTISTS?
WORK WITH A CIRCUS IN THE BAY AREA. NOT YOUR USUAL LOW-RENT SORT OF THING. MORE OLD-TIMEY FREAK SHOW MEETS THAT CIRQUE DU SOLEIL BUSINESS.
VERY HOT RIGHT NOW.
ANYWAY, THEY KNOW EVERYTHING. OR SEEM TO. 'SPECIALLY IF IT'S GOT THAT HIGH-SOCIETY VIBE.
I DON'T SUPPOSE THEY'RE FRIENDLY?
EH. SORTA DEPENDS. THEY'RE RICH JERKS...LIKE TO KEEP THEMSELVES ENTERTAINED, WHICH MIGHT WORK IN YOUR FAVOR.
THEY'RE PLAYFUL...BUT THAT INCLUDES PLAYING WITH THEIR FOOD.
UNDERSTOOD.
THANKS, MAXI.
WATCH YOUR BACK, KID.

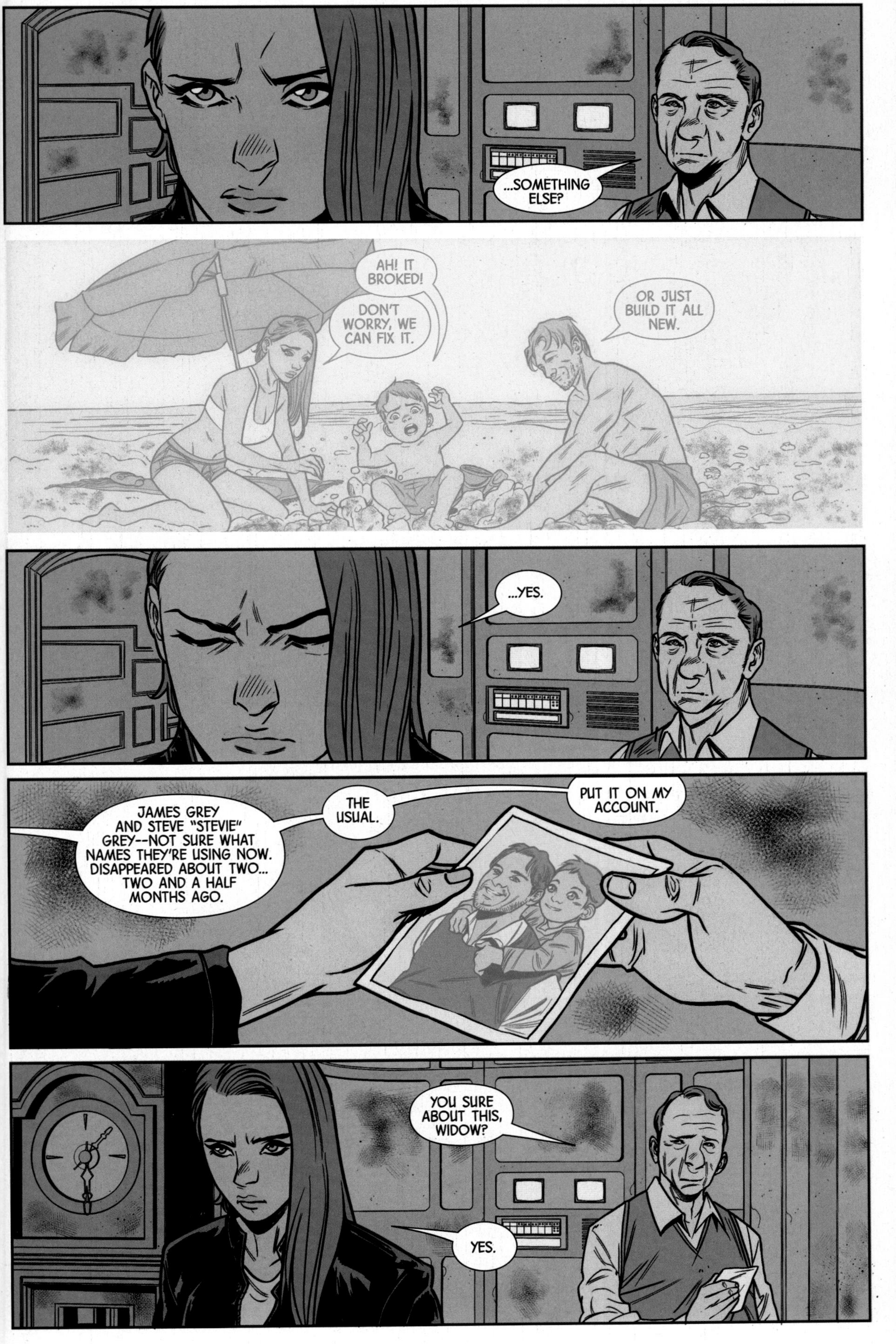
...SOMETHING ELSE?
AH! IT BROKED!
DON'T WORRY, WE CAN FIX IT.
OR JUST BUILD IT ALL NEW.
...YES.
JAMES GREY AND STEVE "STEVIE" GREY--NOT SURE WHAT NAMES THEY'RE USING NOW. DISAPPEARED ABOUT TWO... TWO AND A HALF MONTHS AGO.
THE USUAL.
PUT IT ON MY ACCOUNT.
YOU SURE ABOUT THIS, WIDOW?
YES.

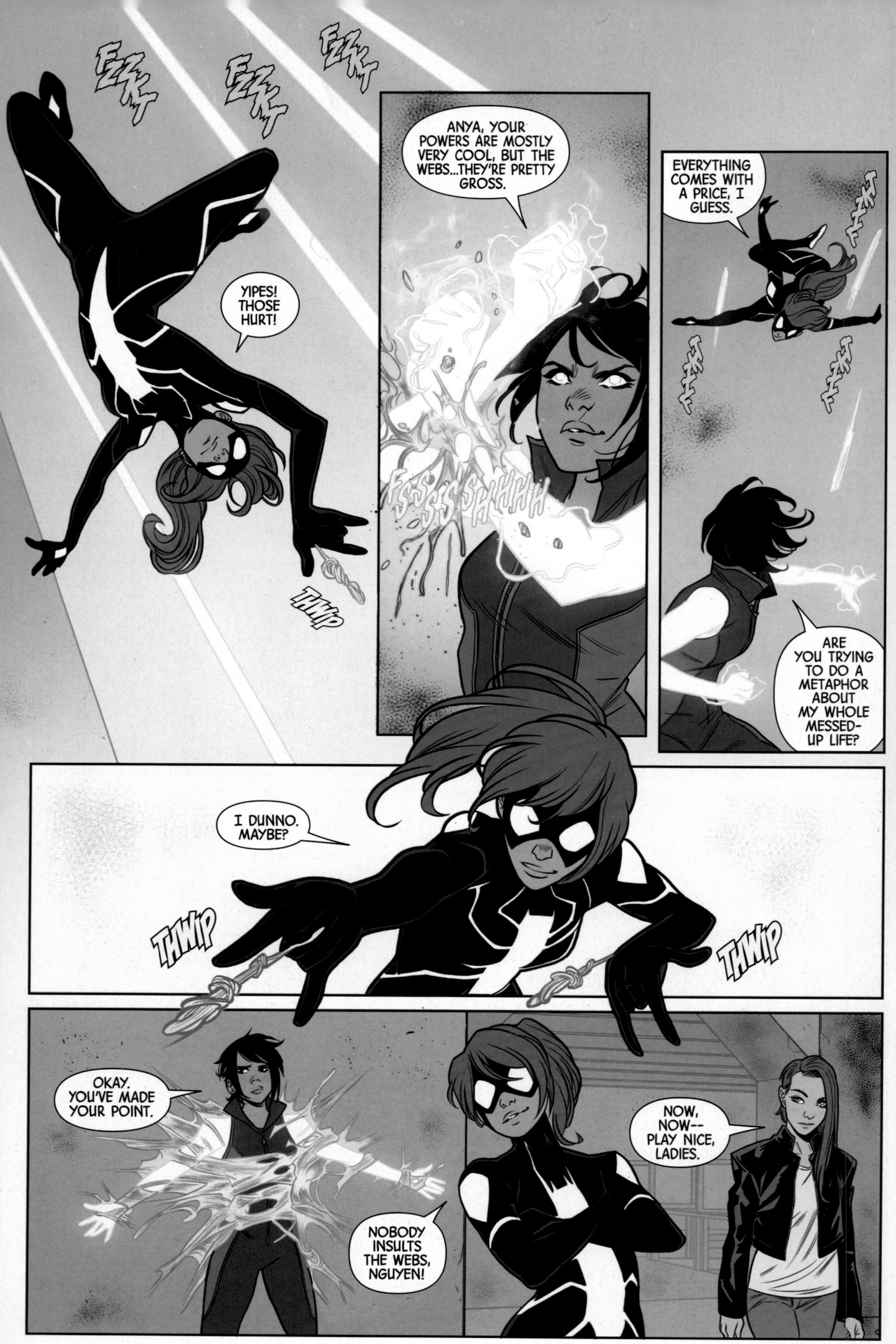

FZZKT
FZZKT
FZZKT
YIPES! THOSE HURT!
THWIP
ANYA, YOUR POWERS ARE MOSTLY VERY COOL, BUT THE WEBS...THEY'RE PRETTY GROSS.
FSSSSSSHHHHH
EVERYTHING COMES WITH A PRICE, I GUESS.
ARE YOU TRYING TO DO A METAPHOR ABOUT MY WHOLE MESSED-UP LIFE?
I DUNNO. MAYBE?
THWIP
THWIP
OKAY. YOU'VE MADE YOUR POINT.
NOBODY INSULTS THE WEBS, NGUYEN!
NOW, NOW-- PLAY NICE, LADIES.

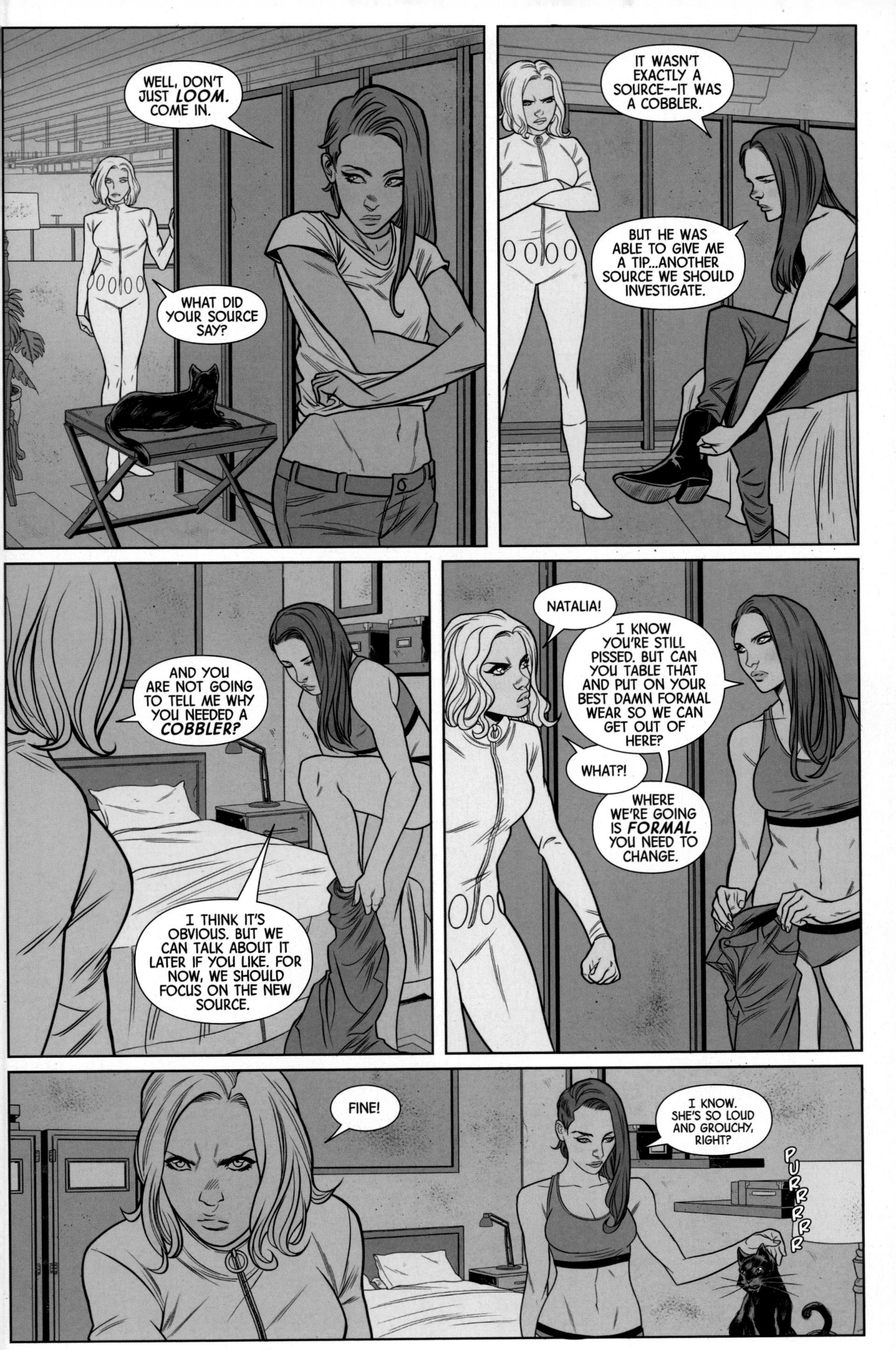
WELL, DON'T JUST *LOOM.* COME IN.
WHAT DID YOUR SOURCE SAY?
IT WASN'T EXACTLY A SOURCE--IT WAS A COBBLER.
BUT HE WAS ABLE TO GIVE ME A TIP...ANOTHER SOURCE WE SHOULD INVESTIGATE.
AND YOU ARE NOT GOING TO TELL ME WHY YOU NEEDED A *COBBLER?*
I THINK IT'S OBVIOUS. BUT WE CAN TALK ABOUT IT LATER IF YOU LIKE. FOR NOW, WE SHOULD FOCUS ON THE NEW SOURCE.
NATALIA!
I KNOW YOU'RE STILL PISSED. BUT CAN YOU TABLE THAT AND PUT ON YOUR BEST DAMN FORMAL WEAR SO WE CAN GET OUT OF HERE?
WHAT?!
WHERE WE'RE GOING IS *FORMAL.* YOU NEED TO CHANGE.
FINE!
I KNOW. SHE'S SO LOUD AND GROUCHY, RIGHT?
PURRRR

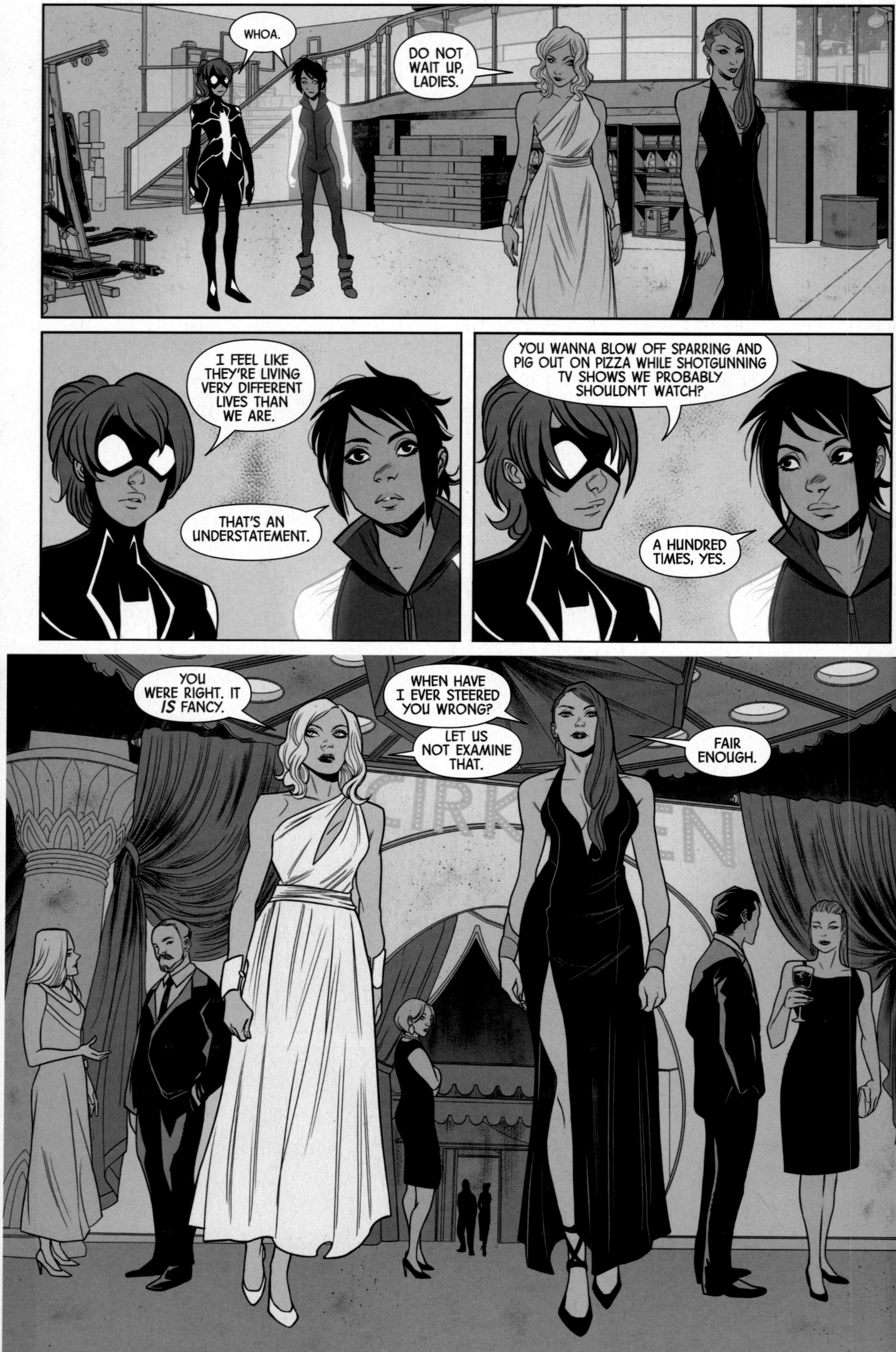
WHOA.
DO NOT WAIT UP, LADIES.
I FEEL LIKE THEY'RE LIVING VERY DIFFERENT LIVES THAN WE ARE.
THAT'S AN UNDERSTATEMENT.
YOU WANNA BLOW OFF SPARRING AND PIG OUT ON PIZZA WHILE SHOTGUNNING TV SHOWS WE PROBABLY SHOULDN'T WATCH?
A HUNDRED TIMES, YES.
YOU WERE RIGHT. IT *IS* FANCY.
WHEN HAVE I EVER STEERED YOU WRONG?
LET US NOT EXAMINE THAT.
FAIR ENOUGH.
CIRK EN

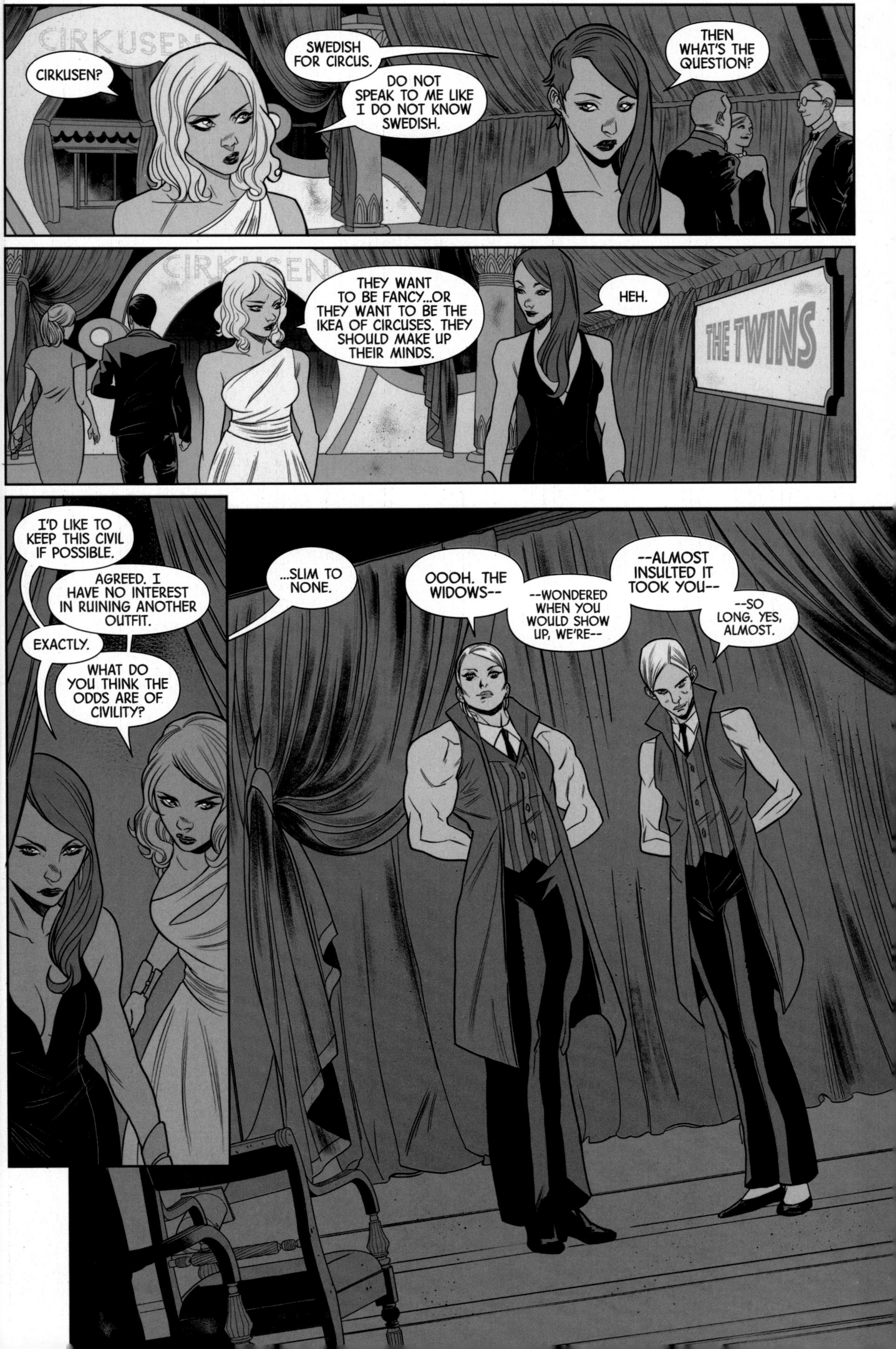
CIRKUSEN
CIRKUSEN?
SWEDISH FOR CIRCUS.
DO NOT SPEAK TO ME LIKE I DO NOT KNOW SWEDISH.
THEN WHAT'S THE QUESTION?
CIRKUSEN
THEY WANT TO BE FANCY...OR THEY WANT TO BE THE IKEA OF CIRCUSES. THEY SHOULD MAKE UP THEIR MINDS.
HEH.
THE TWINS
I'D LIKE TO KEEP THIS CIVIL IF POSSIBLE.
AGREED. I HAVE NO INTEREST IN RUINING ANOTHER OUTFIT.
EXACTLY.
WHAT DO YOU THINK THE ODDS ARE OF CIVILITY?
...SLIM TO NONE.
OOOH. THE WIDOWS--
--WONDERED WHEN YOU WOULD SHOW UP, WE'RE--
--ALMOST INSULTED IT TOOK YOU--
--SO LONG. YES, ALMOST.

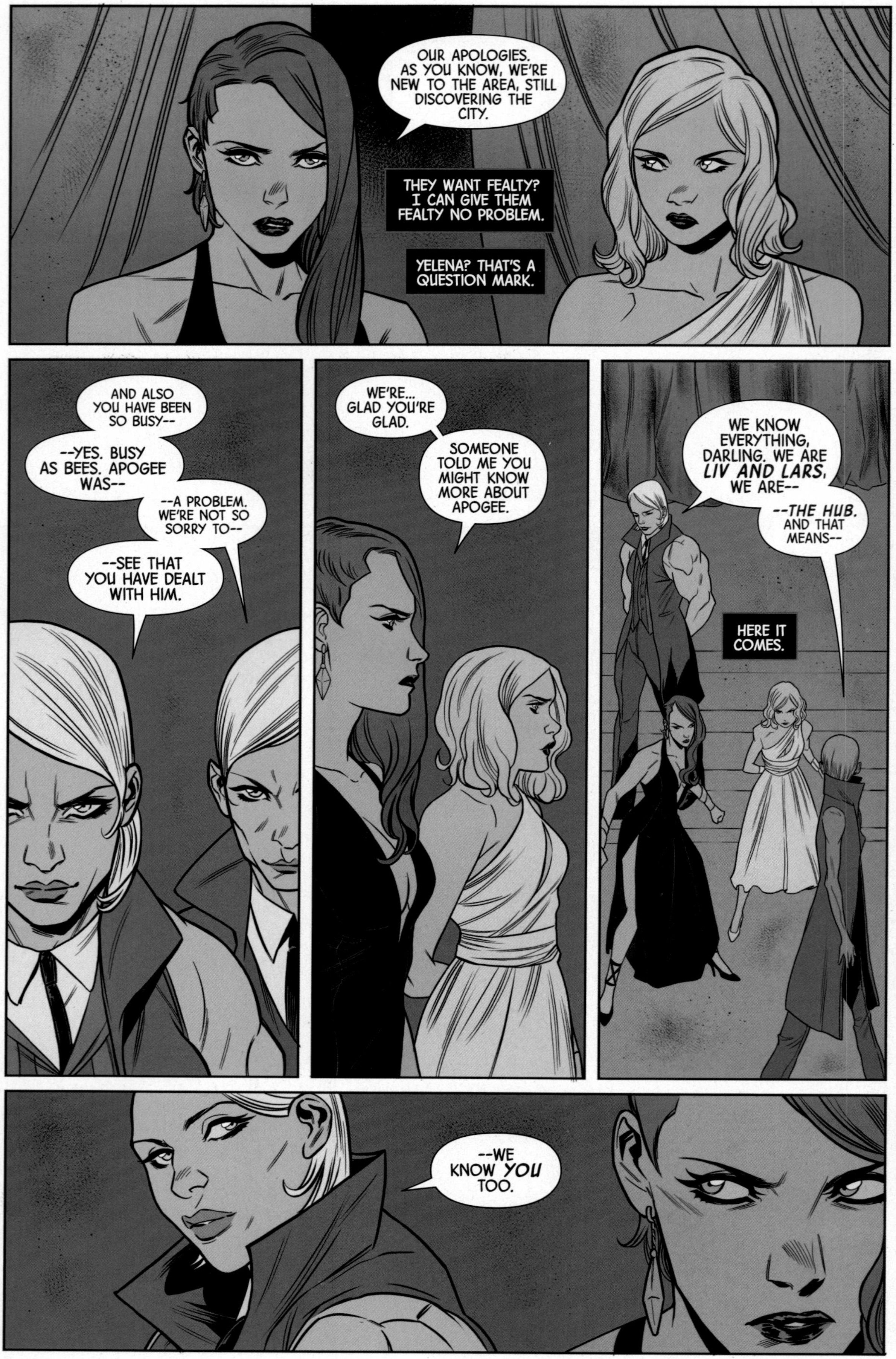
OUR APOLOGIES. AS YOU KNOW, WE'RE NEW TO THE AREA, STILL DISCOVERING THE CITY.
THEY WANT FEALTY? I CAN GIVE THEM FEALTY NO PROBLEM.
YELENA? THAT'S A QUESTION MARK.
AND ALSO YOU HAVE BEEN SO BUSY--
--YES. BUSY AS BEES. APOGEE WAS--
--A PROBLEM. WE'RE NOT SO SORRY TO--
--SEE THAT YOU HAVE DEALT WITH HIM.
WE'RE... GLAD YOU'RE GLAD.
SOMEONE TOLD ME YOU MIGHT KNOW MORE ABOUT APOGEE.
WE KNOW EVERYTHING, DARLING. WE ARE LIV AND LARS, WE ARE--
--THE HUB. AND THAT MEANS--
HERE IT COMES.
--WE KNOW YOU TOO.

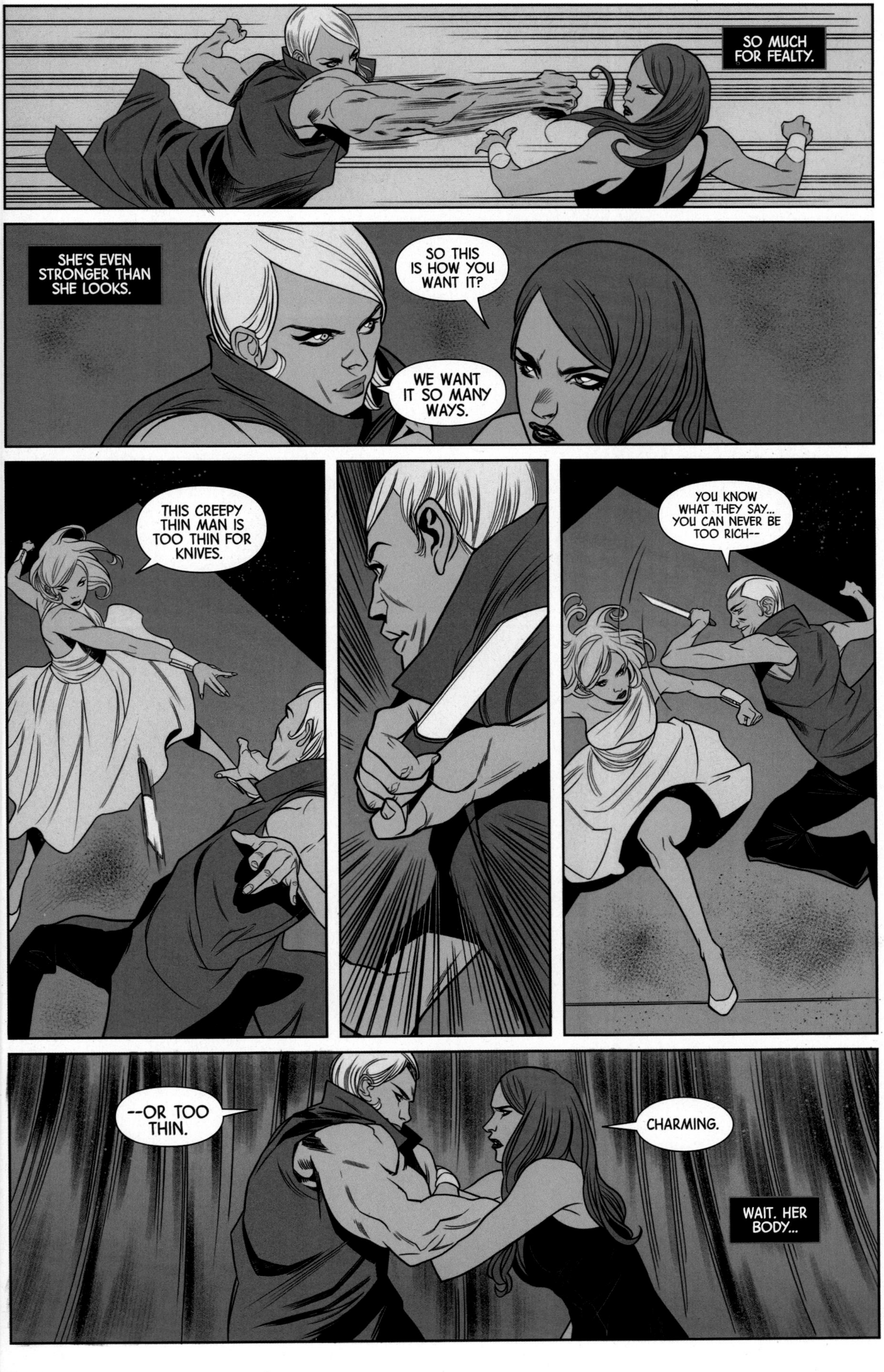
SO MUCH FOR FEALTY.
SHE'S EVEN STRONGER THAN SHE LOOKS.
SO THIS IS HOW YOU WANT IT?
WE WANT IT SO MANY WAYS.
THIS CREEPY THIN MAN IS TOO THIN FOR KNIVES.
YOU KNOW WHAT THEY SAY... YOU CAN NEVER BE TOO RICH--
--OR TOO THIN.
CHARMING.
WAIT. HER BODY...

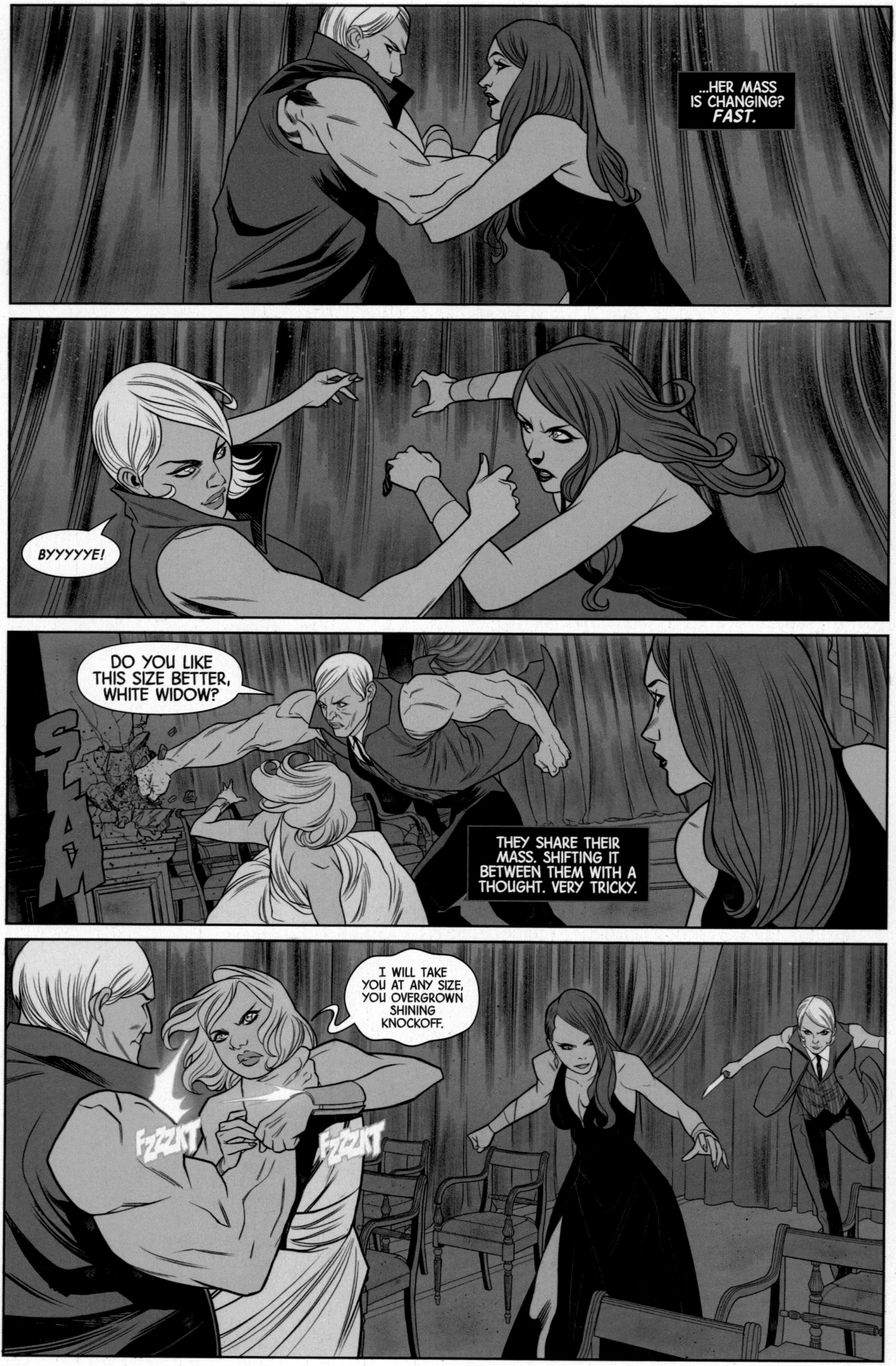
...HER MASS IS CHANGING? FAST.
BYYYYYE!
DO YOU LIKE THIS SIZE BETTER, WHITE WIDOW?
SLAM
THEY SHARE THEIR MASS. SHIFTING IT BETWEEN THEM WITH A THOUGHT. VERY TRICKY.
I WILL TAKE YOU AT ANY SIZE, YOU OVERGROWN SHINING KNOCKOFF.
FZZZKT
FZZZKT

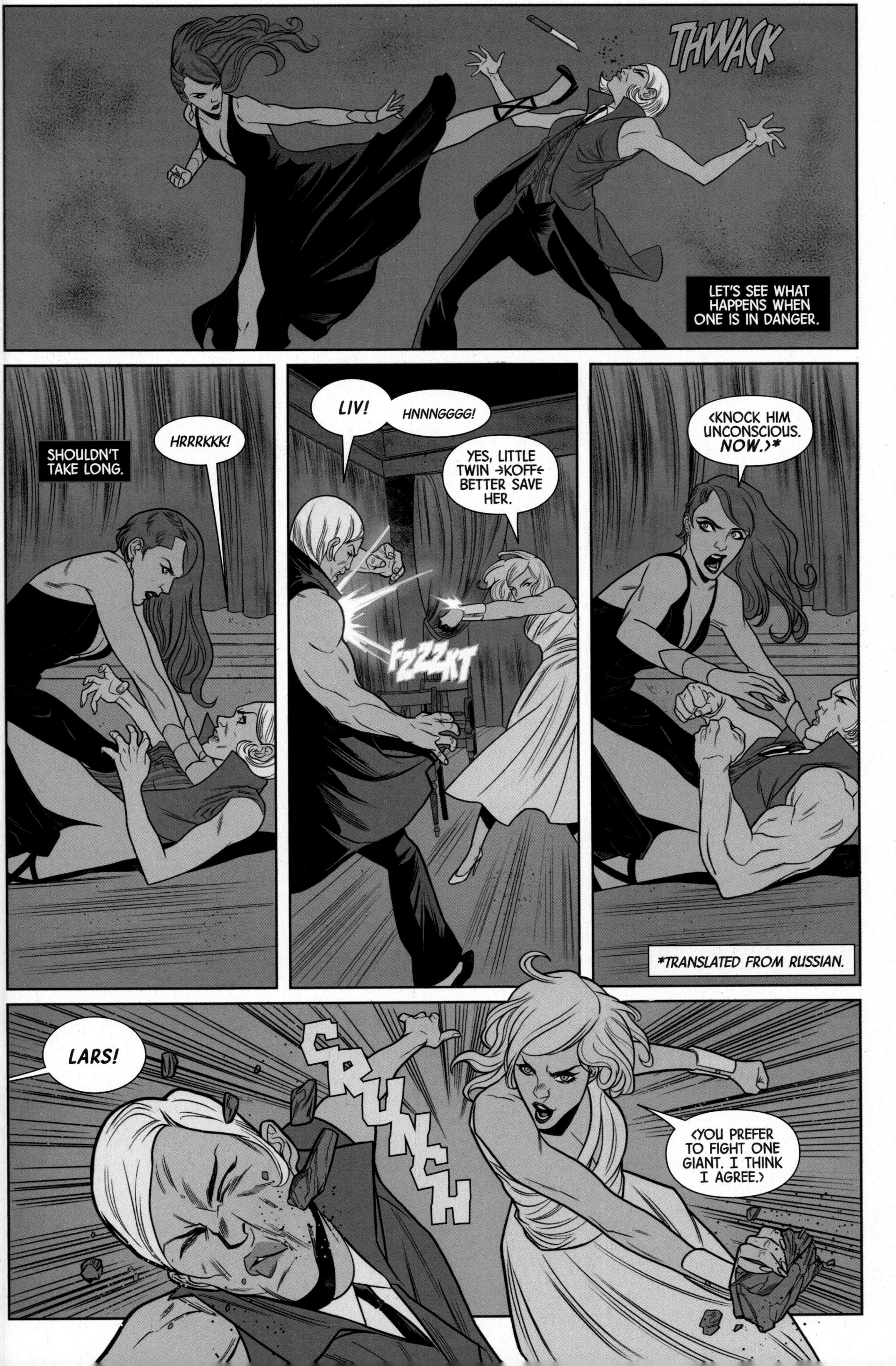
THWACK
LET'S SEE WHAT HAPPENS WHEN ONE IS IN DANGER.
SHOULDN'T TAKE LONG.
HRRRKKK!
LIV!
HNNNGGGG!
YES, LITTLE TWIN →KOFF← BETTER SAVE HER.
FZZZKT
<KNOCK HIM UNCONSCIOUS. NOW.>*
*TRANSLATED FROM RUSSIAN.
LARS!
CRUNCH
<YOU PREFER TO FIGHT ONE GIANT. I THINK I AGREE.>

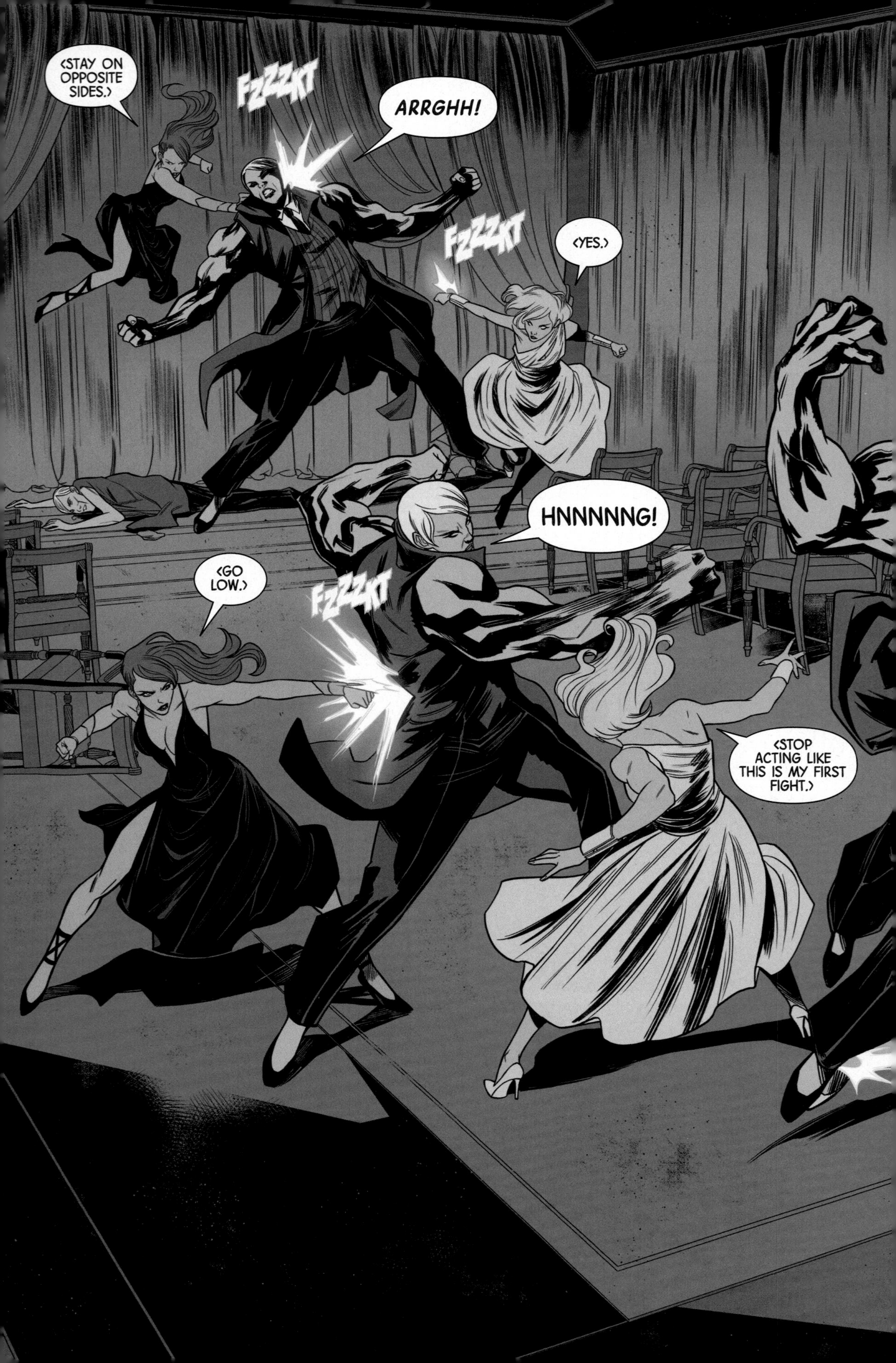

<STAY ON OPPOSITE SIDES.>
FZZZKT
ARRGHH!
FZZZKT
<YES.>
HNNNNNG!
<GO LOW.>
FZZZKT
<STOP ACTING LIKE THIS IS MY FIRST FIGHT.>

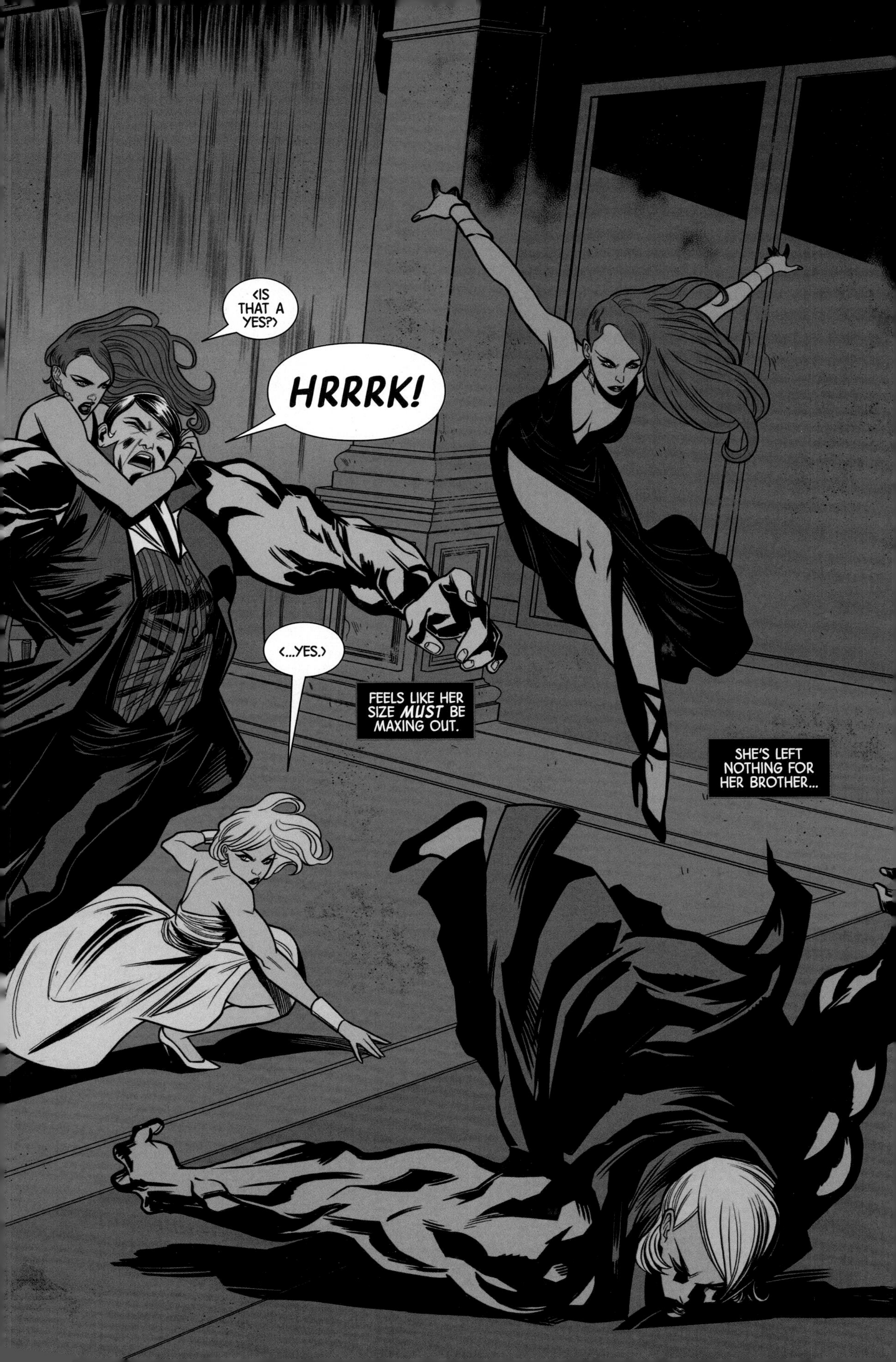

<IS THAT A YES?>
HRRRK!
<...YES.>
FEELS LIKE HER SIZE *MUST* BE MAXING OUT.
SHE'S LEFT NOTHING FOR HER BROTHER...

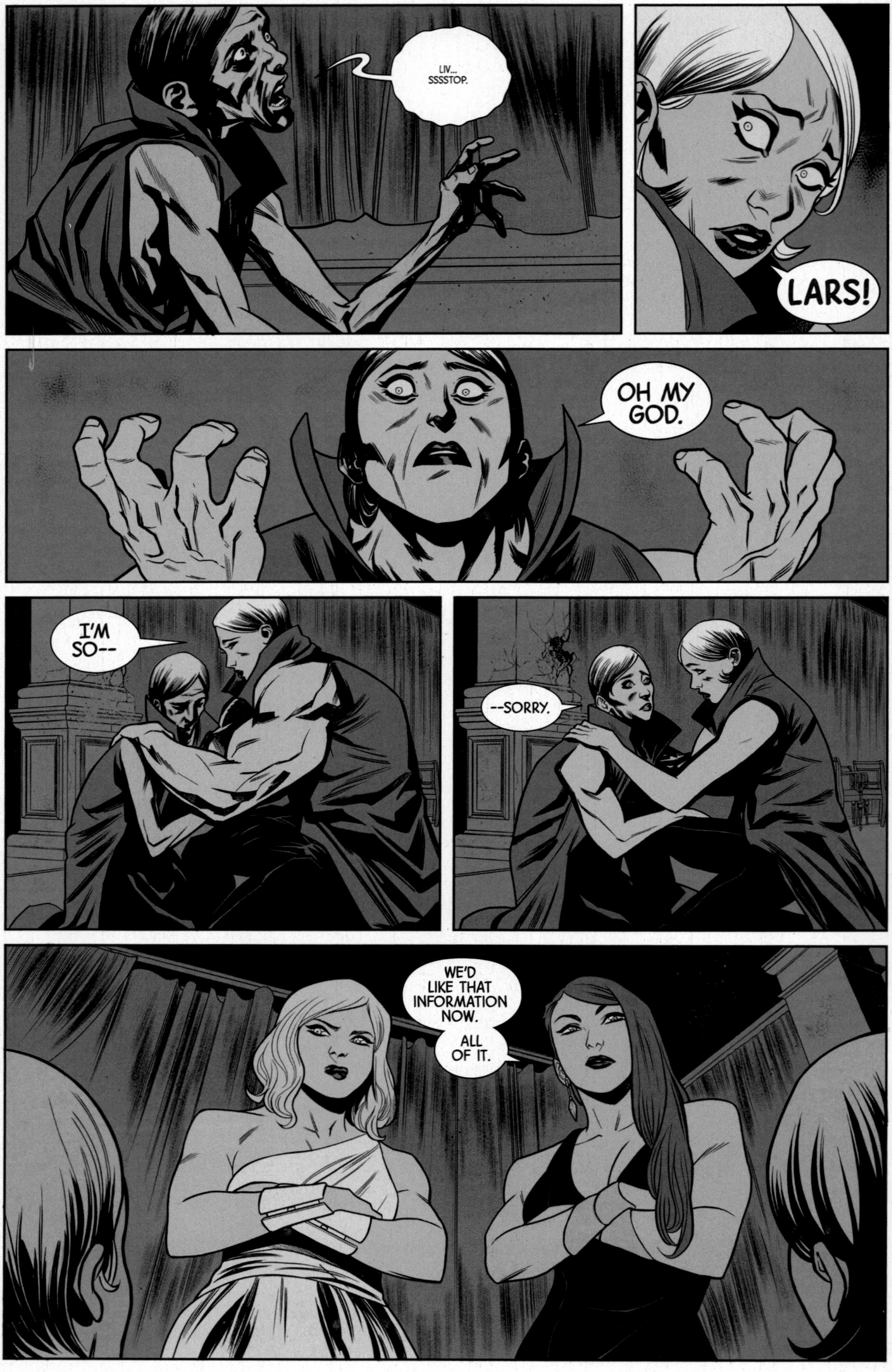

LIV... SSSSTOP.
LARS!
OH MY GOD.
I'M SO--
--SORRY.
WE'D LIKE THAT INFORMATION NOW.
ALL OF IT.

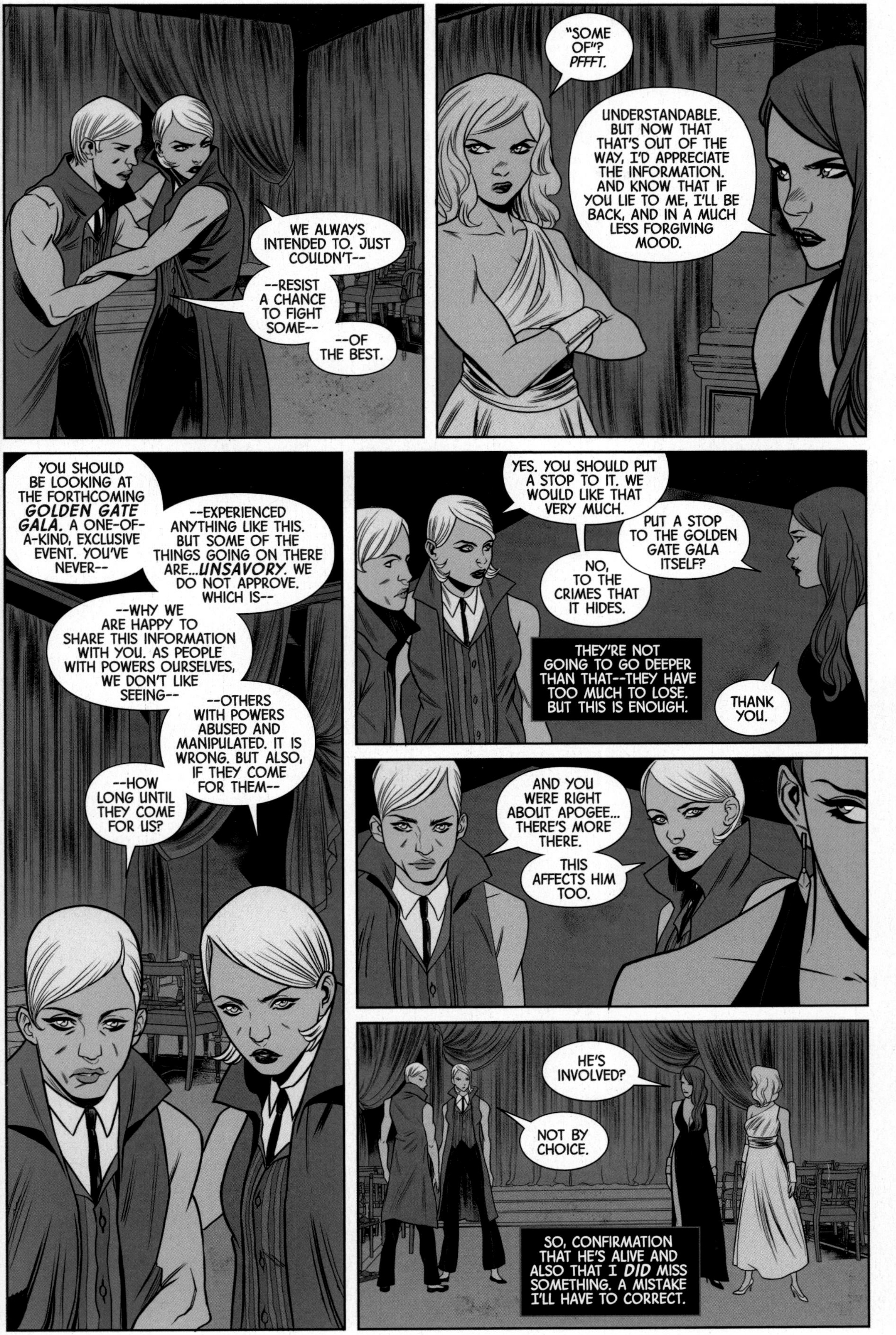

WE ALWAYS INTENDED TO. JUST COULDN'T--
--RESIST A CHANCE TO FIGHT SOME--
--OF THE BEST.
"SOME OF"? PFFFT.
UNDERSTANDABLE. BUT NOW THAT THAT'S OUT OF THE WAY, I'D APPRECIATE THE INFORMATION. AND KNOW THAT IF YOU LIE TO ME, I'LL BE BACK, AND IN A MUCH LESS FORGIVING MOOD.
YOU SHOULD BE LOOKING AT THE FORTHCOMING GOLDEN GATE GALA. A ONE-OF-A-KIND, EXCLUSIVE EVENT. YOU'VE NEVER--
--EXPERIENCED ANYTHING LIKE THIS. BUT SOME OF THE THINGS GOING ON THERE ARE...UNSAVORY. WE DO NOT APPROVE. WHICH IS--
--WHY WE ARE HAPPY TO SHARE THIS INFORMATION WITH YOU. AS PEOPLE WITH POWERS OURSELVES, WE DON'T LIKE SEEING--
--OTHERS WITH POWERS ABUSED AND MANIPULATED. IT IS WRONG. BUT ALSO, IF THEY COME FOR THEM--
--HOW LONG UNTIL THEY COME FOR US?
YES. YOU SHOULD PUT A STOP TO IT. WE WOULD LIKE THAT VERY MUCH.
PUT A STOP TO THE GOLDEN GATE GALA ITSELF?
NO, TO THE CRIMES THAT IT HIDES.
THEY'RE NOT GOING TO GO DEEPER THAN THAT--THEY HAVE TOO MUCH TO LOSE. BUT THIS IS ENOUGH.
THANK YOU.
AND YOU WERE RIGHT ABOUT APOGEE... THERE'S MORE THERE.
THIS AFFECTS HIM TOO.
HE'S INVOLVED?
NOT BY CHOICE.
SO, CONFIRMATION THAT HE'S ALIVE AND ALSO THAT I DID MISS SOMETHING. A MISTAKE I'LL HAVE TO CORRECT.

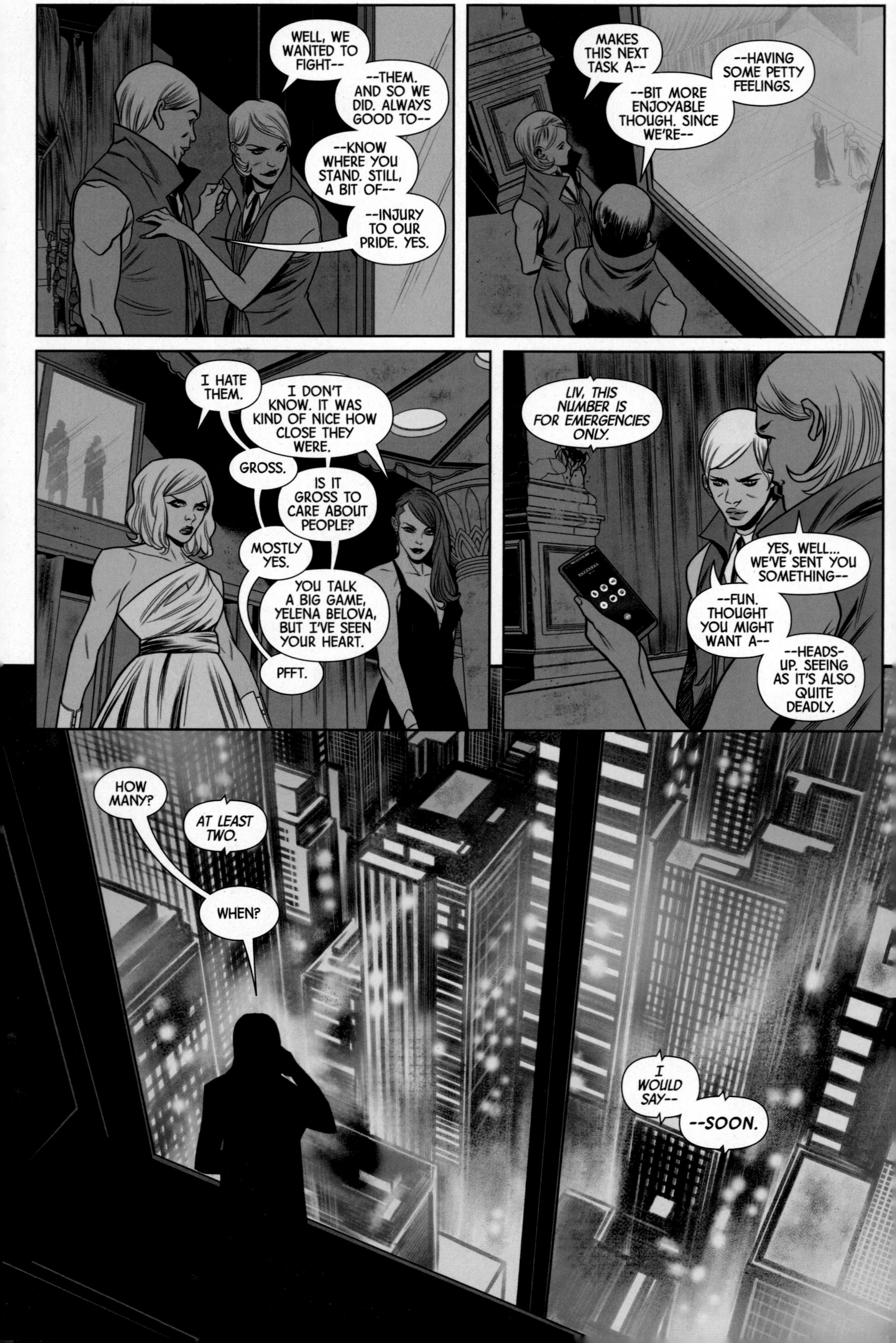
WELL, WE WANTED TO FIGHT--
--THEM. AND SO WE DID. ALWAYS GOOD TO--
--KNOW WHERE YOU STAND. STILL, A BIT OF--
--INJURY TO OUR PRIDE. YES.
MAKES THIS NEXT TASK A--
--BIT MORE ENJOYABLE THOUGH. SINCE WE'RE--
--HAVING SOME PETTY FEELINGS.
I HATE THEM.
I DON'T KNOW. IT WAS KIND OF NICE HOW CLOSE THEY WERE.
GROSS.
IS IT GROSS TO CARE ABOUT PEOPLE?
MOSTLY YES.
YOU TALK A BIG GAME, YELENA BELOVA, BUT I'VE SEEN YOUR HEART.
PFFT.
LIV, THIS NUMBER IS FOR EMERGENCIES ONLY.
YES, WELL... WE'VE SENT YOU SOMETHING--
--FUN. THOUGHT YOU MIGHT WANT A--
--HEADS-UP. SEEING AS IT'S ALSO QUITE DEADLY.
HOW MANY?
AT LEAST TWO.
WHEN?
I WOULD SAY--
--SOON.

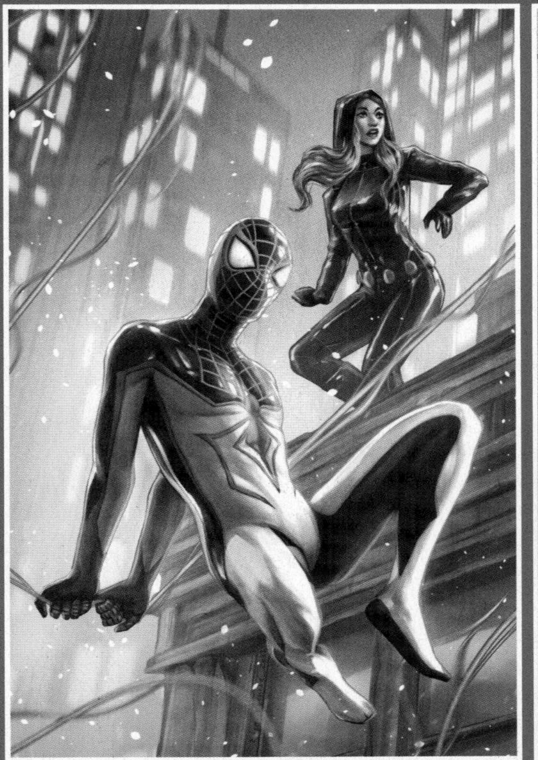

#11 MILES MORALES: SPIDER-MAN 10TH ANNIVERSARY VARIANT BY
EJIWA "EDGE" EBENEBE

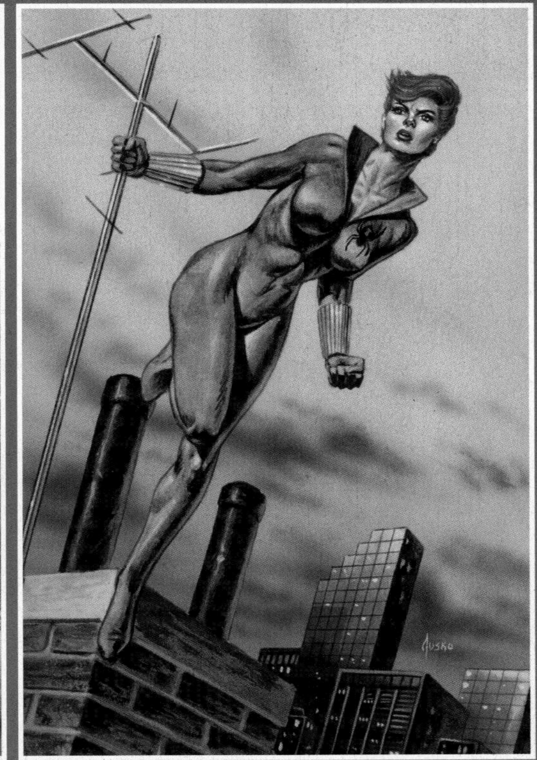

#12 MARVEL MASTERPIECES VARIANT BY
JOE JUSKO

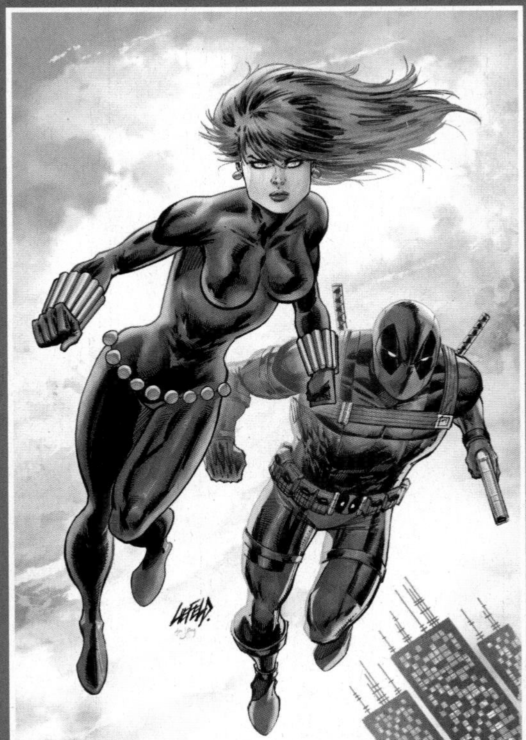

#13 DEADPOOL 30TH ANNIVERSARY VARIANT BY
ROB LIEFELD

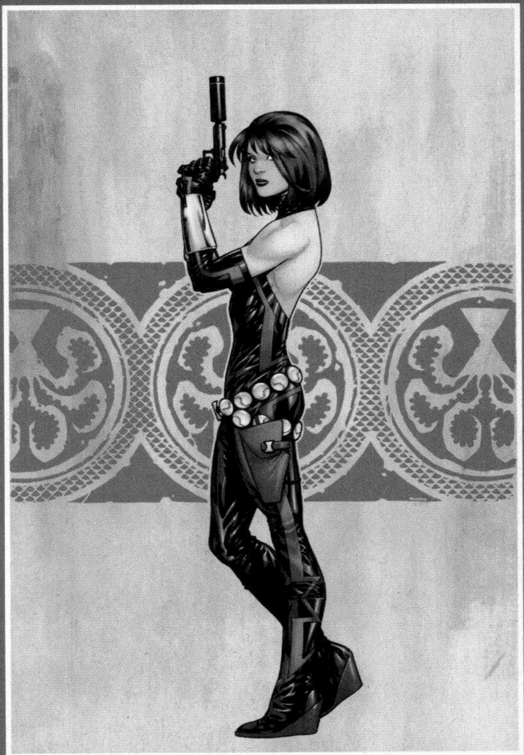

#13 DEVIL'S REIGN VARIANT BY
MIKE McKONE & CHRIS SOTOMAYOR

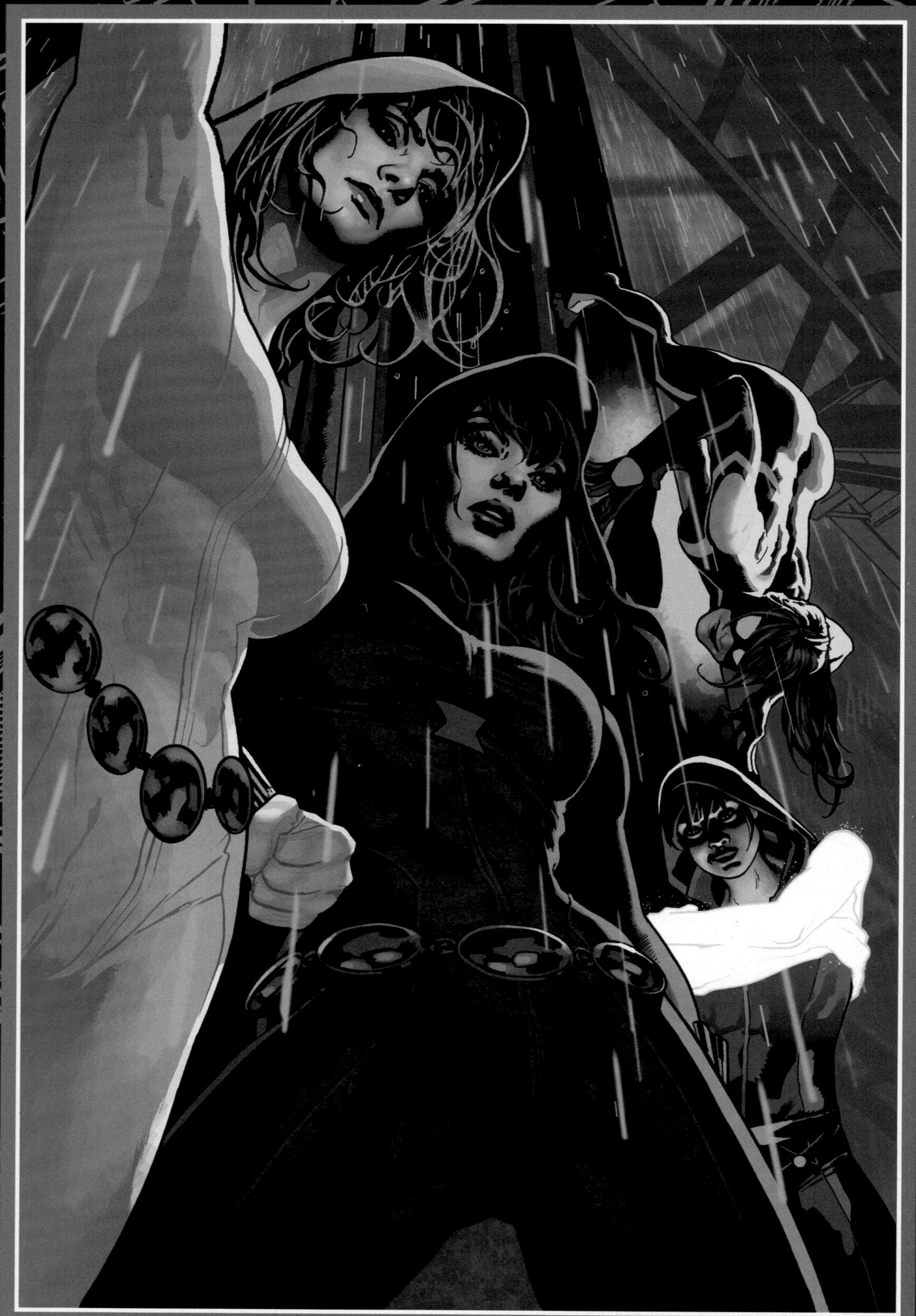

TWELVE

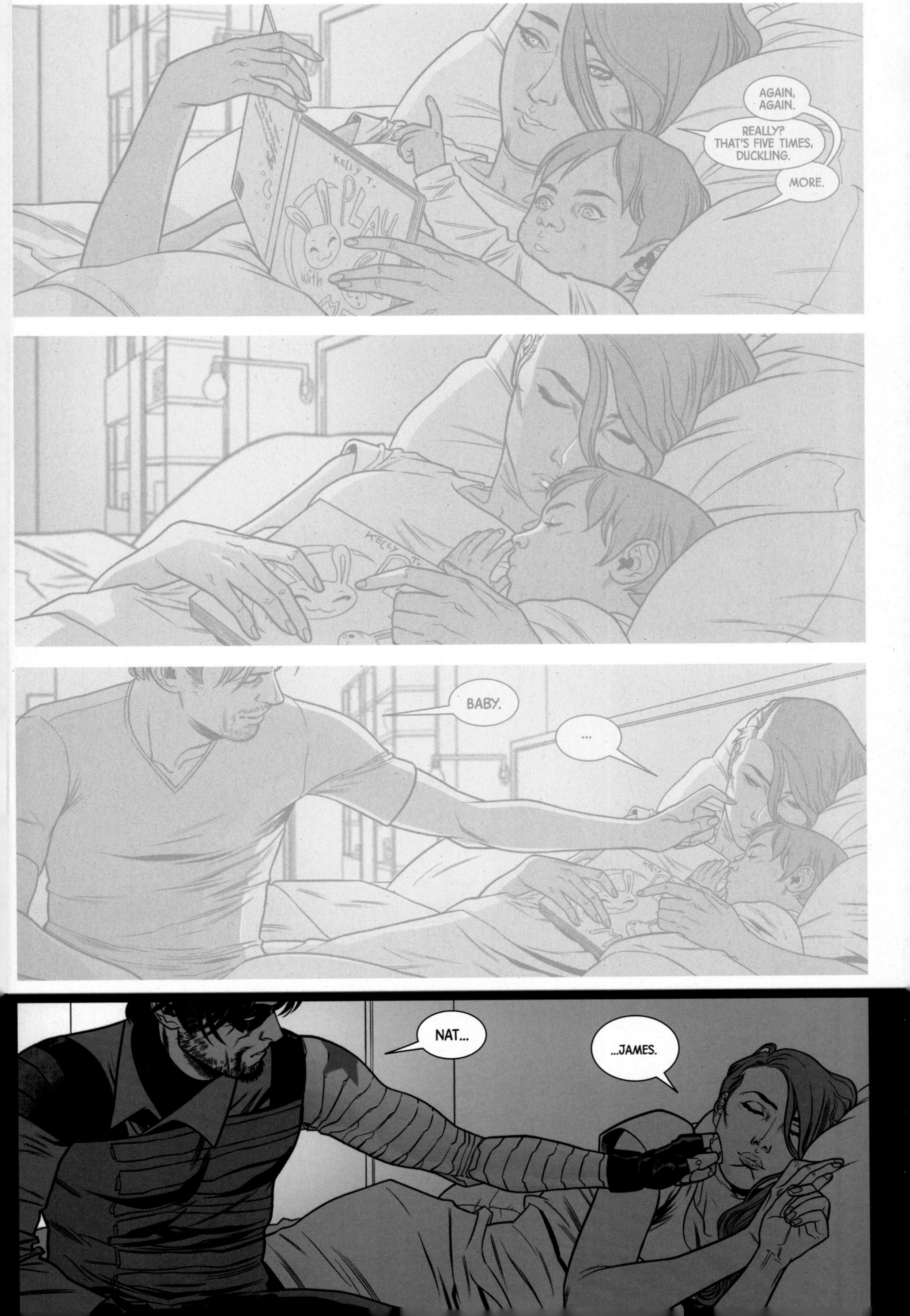
AGAIN, AGAIN.
REALLY? THAT'S FIVE TIMES, DUCKLING.
MORE.
BABY.
...
NAT...
...JAMES.

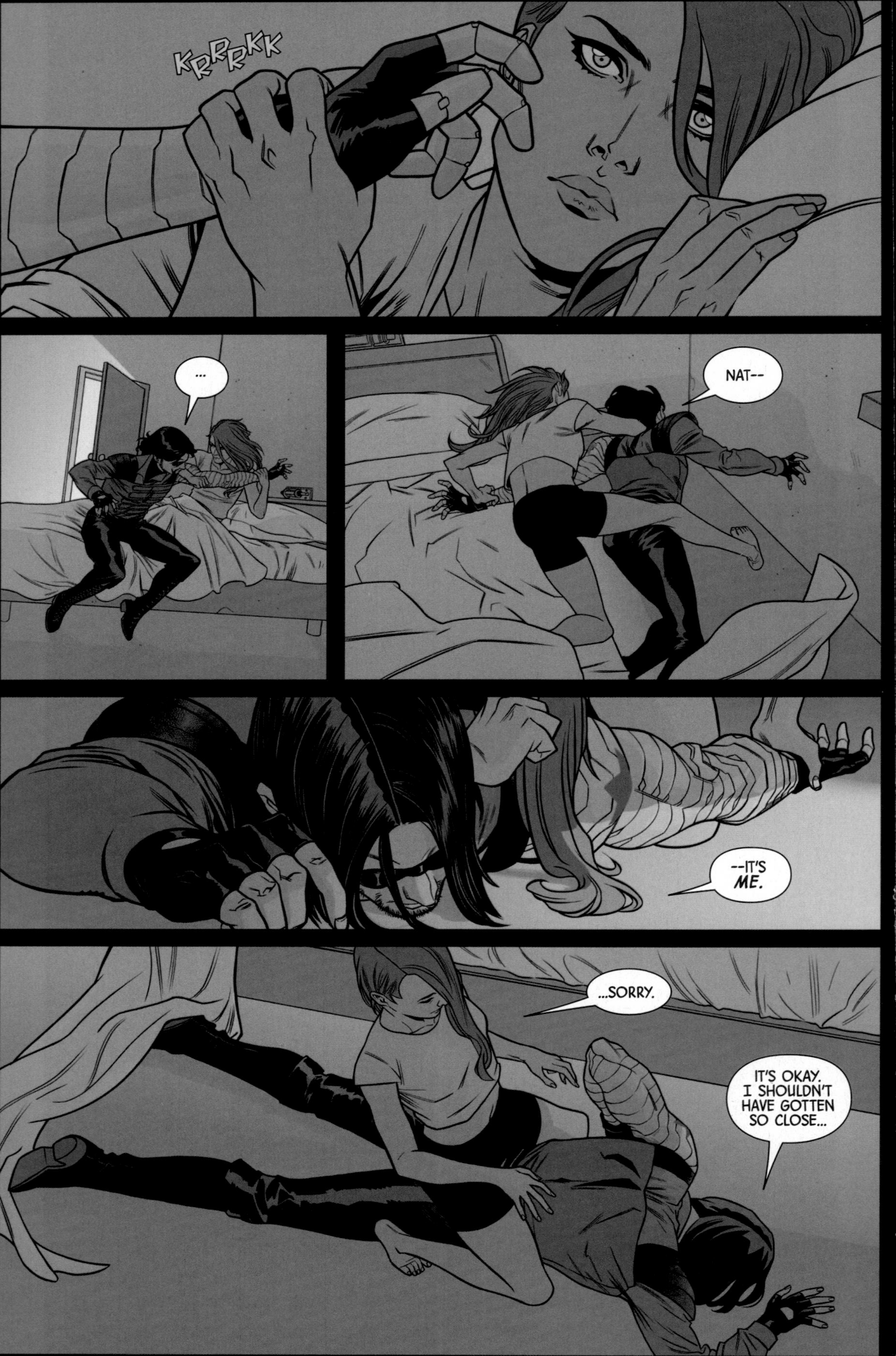
KRRRKK
...
NAT--
--IT'S ME.
...SORRY.
IT'S OKAY. I SHOULDN'T HAVE GOTTEN SO CLOSE...

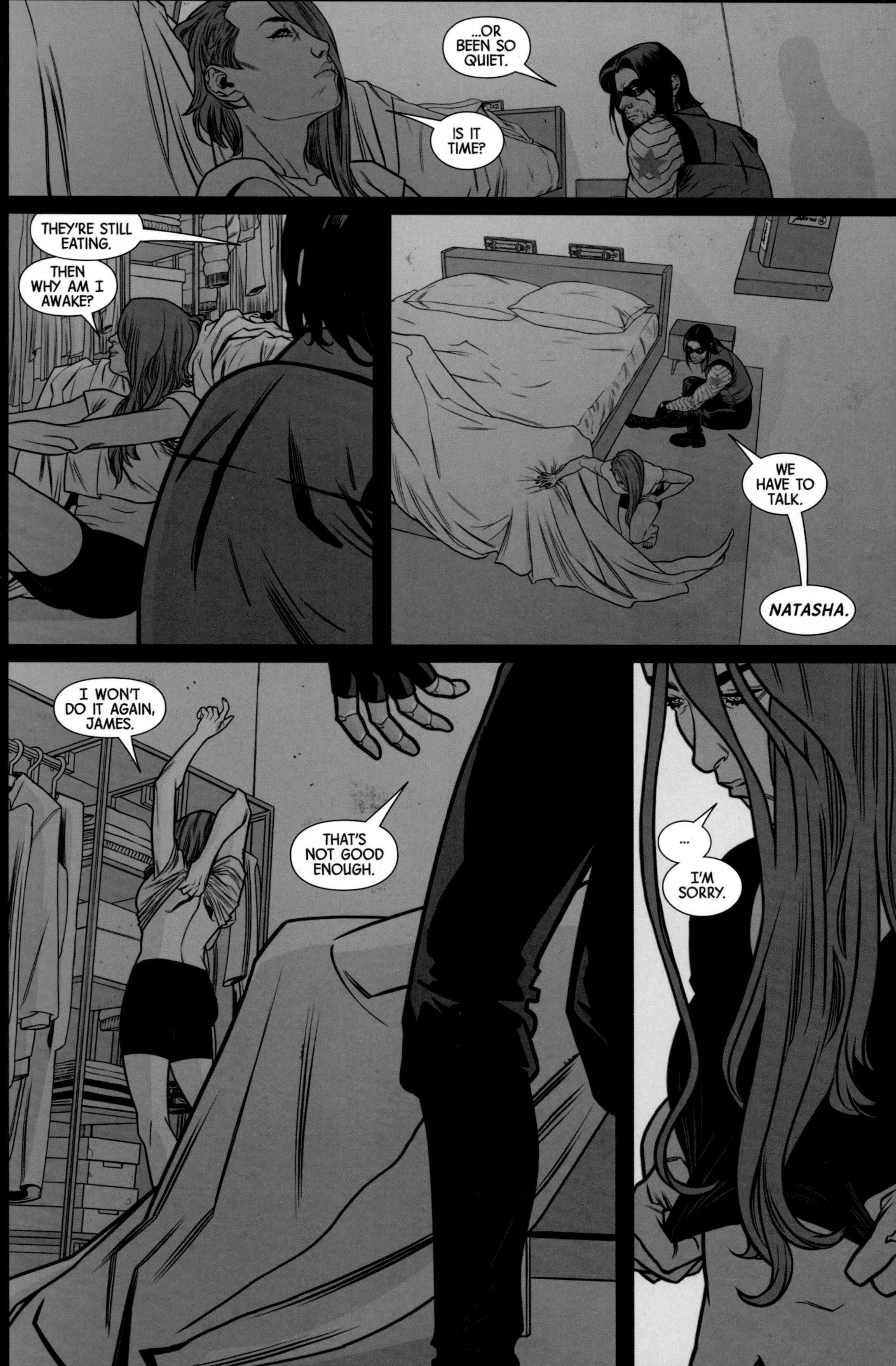

...OR BEEN SO QUIET.
IS IT TIME?
THEY'RE STILL EATING.
THEN WHY AM I AWAKE?
WE HAVE TO TALK.
NATASHA.
I WON'T DO IT AGAIN, JAMES.
THAT'S NOT GOOD ENOUGH.
...
I'M SORRY.

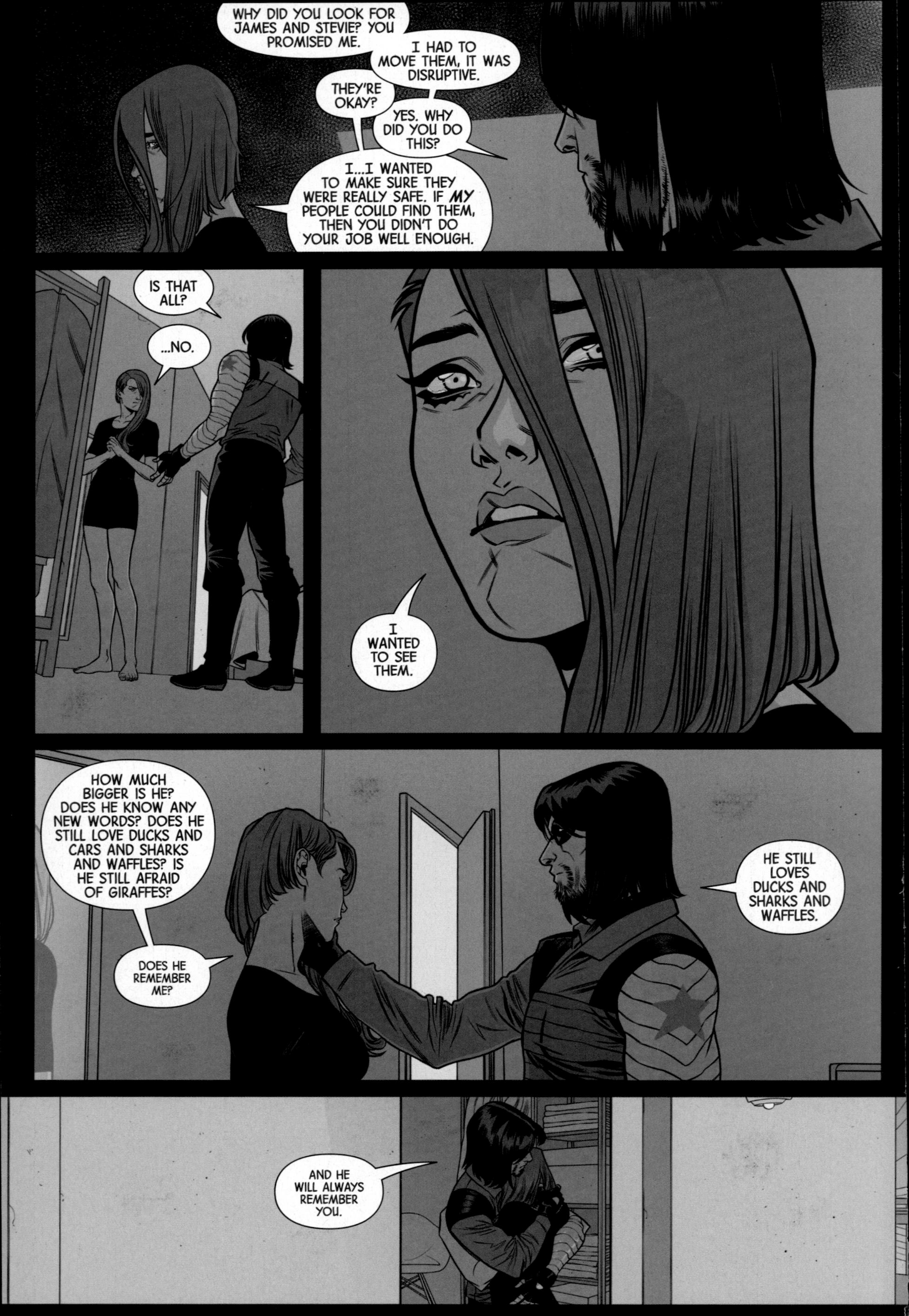
WHY DID YOU LOOK FOR JAMES AND STEVIE? YOU PROMISED ME.
I HAD TO MOVE THEM, IT WAS DISRUPTIVE.
THEY'RE OKAY?
YES. WHY DID YOU DO THIS?
I...I WANTED TO MAKE SURE THEY WERE REALLY SAFE. IF *MY* PEOPLE COULD FIND THEM, THEN YOU DIDN'T DO YOUR JOB WELL ENOUGH.
IS THAT ALL?
...NO.
I WANTED TO SEE THEM.
HOW MUCH BIGGER IS HE? DOES HE KNOW ANY NEW WORDS? DOES HE STILL LOVE DUCKS AND CARS AND SHARKS AND WAFFLES? IS HE STILL AFRAID OF GIRAFFES?
DOES HE REMEMBER ME?
HE STILL LOVES DUCKS AND SHARKS AND WAFFLES.
AND HE WILL ALWAYS REMEMBER YOU.

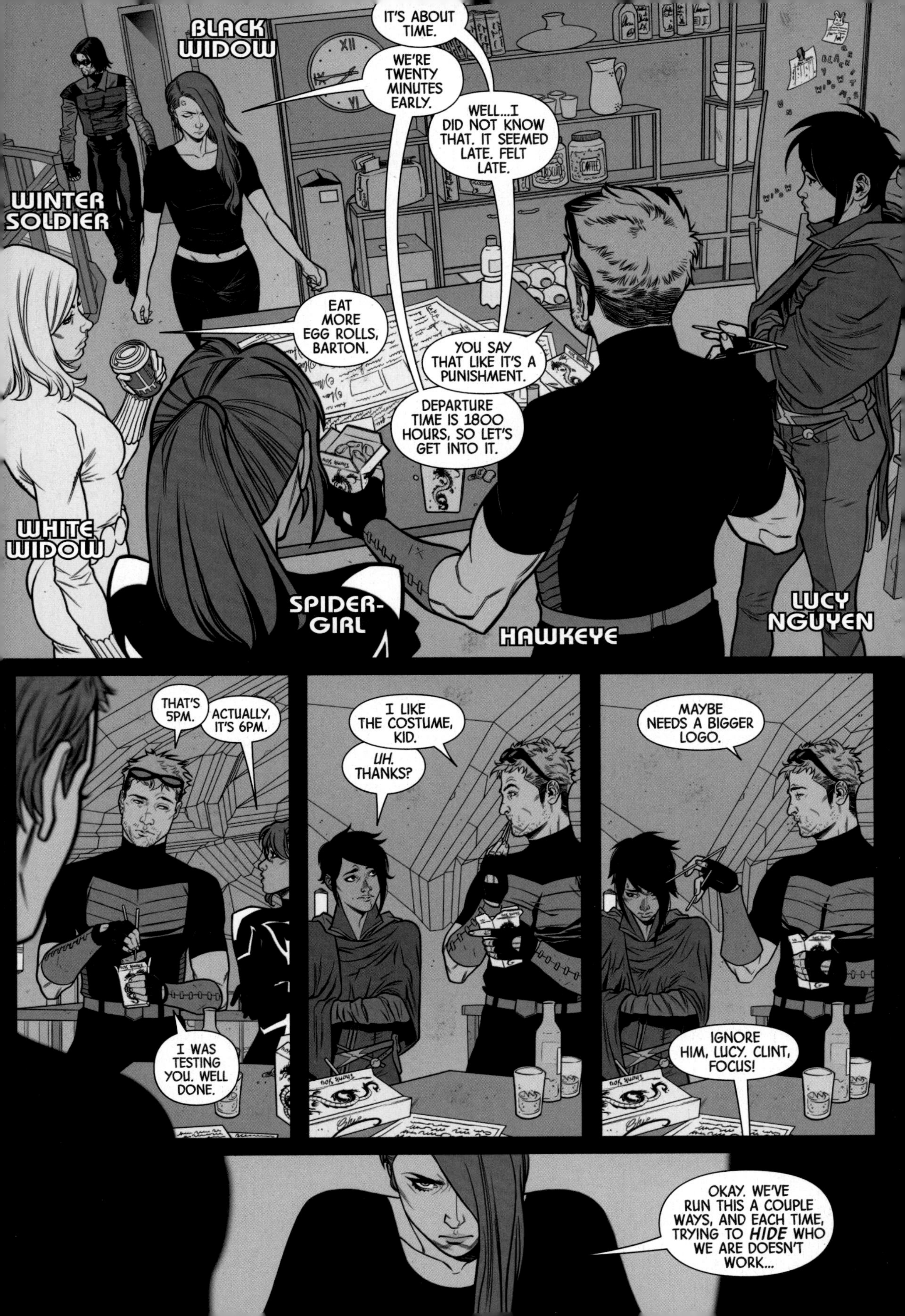
BLACK WIDOW
WINTER SOLDIER
WHITE WIDOW
SPIDER-GIRL
HAWKEYE
LUCY NGUYEN
IT'S ABOUT TIME.
WE'RE TWENTY MINUTES EARLY.
WELL...I DID NOT KNOW THAT. IT SEEMED LATE. FELT LATE.
EAT MORE EGG ROLLS, BARTON.
YOU SAY THAT LIKE IT'S A PUNISHMENT.
DEPARTURE TIME IS 1800 HOURS, SO LET'S GET INTO IT.
THAT'S 5PM.
ACTUALLY, IT'S 6PM.
I WAS TESTING YOU. WELL DONE.
I LIKE THE COSTUME, KID.
UH. THANKS?
MAYBE NEEDS A BIGGER LOGO.
IGNORE HIM, LUCY. CLINT, FOCUS!
OKAY. WE'VE RUN THIS A COUPLE WAYS, AND EACH TIME, TRYING TO HIDE WHO WE ARE DOESN'T WORK...

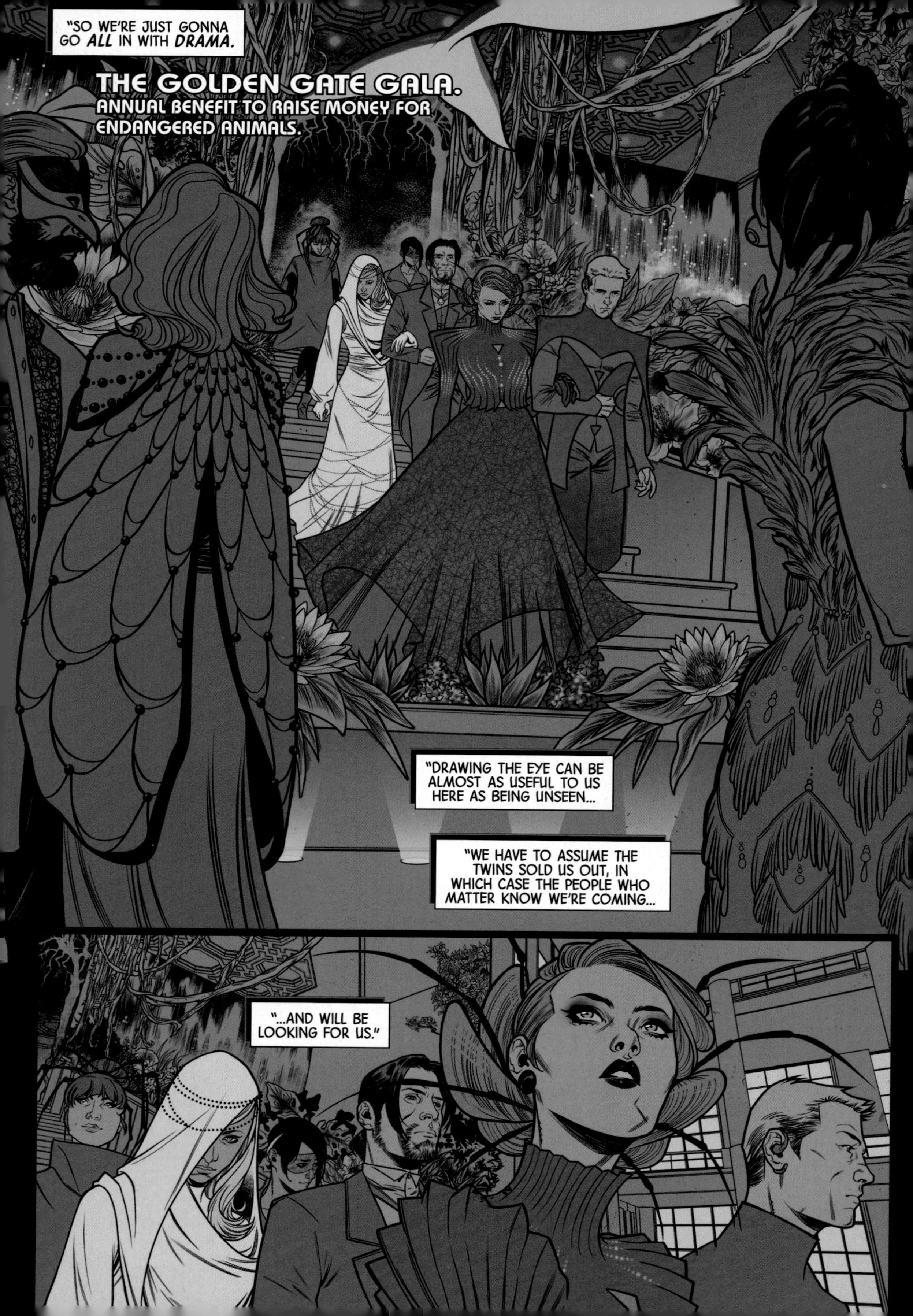
"SO WE'RE JUST GONNA GO *ALL* IN WITH *DRAMA*.
THE GOLDEN GATE GALA.
ANNUAL BENEFIT TO RAISE MONEY FOR ENDANGERED ANIMALS.
"DRAWING THE EYE CAN BE ALMOST AS USEFUL TO US HERE AS BEING UNSEEN...
"WE HAVE TO ASSUME THE TWINS SOLD US OUT, IN WHICH CASE THE PEOPLE WHO MATTER KNOW WE'RE COMING...
"...AND WILL BE LOOKING FOR US."

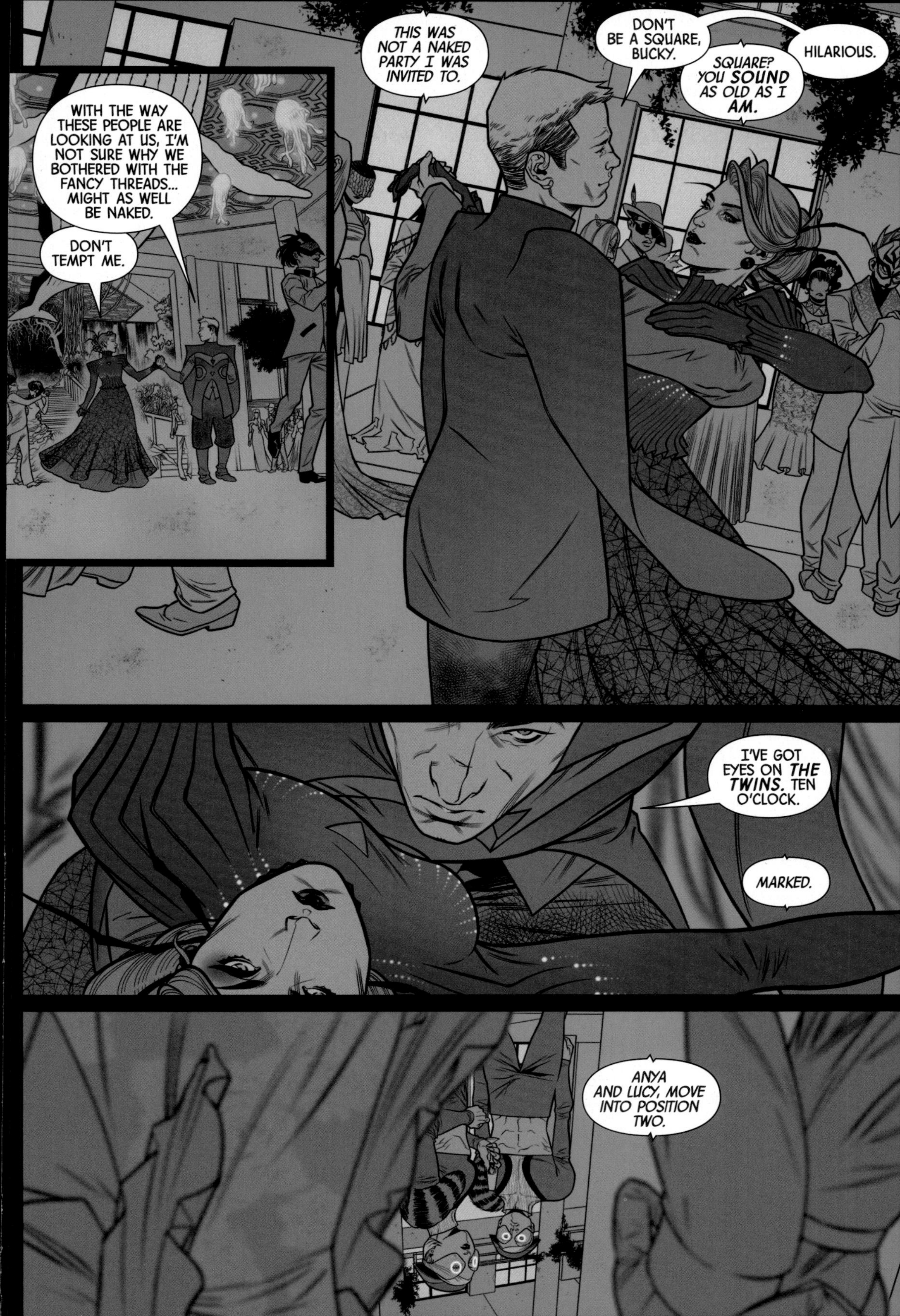

WITH THE WAY THESE PEOPLE ARE LOOKING AT US, I'M NOT SURE WHY WE BOTHERED WITH THE FANCY THREADS... MIGHT AS WELL BE NAKED.
DON'T TEMPT ME.
THIS WAS NOT A NAKED PARTY I WAS INVITED TO.
DON'T BE A SQUARE, BUCKY.
SQUARE? YOU SOUND AS OLD AS I AM.
HILARIOUS.
I'VE GOT EYES ON THE TWINS. TEN O'CLOCK.
MARKED.
ANYA AND LUCY, MOVE INTO POSITION TWO.

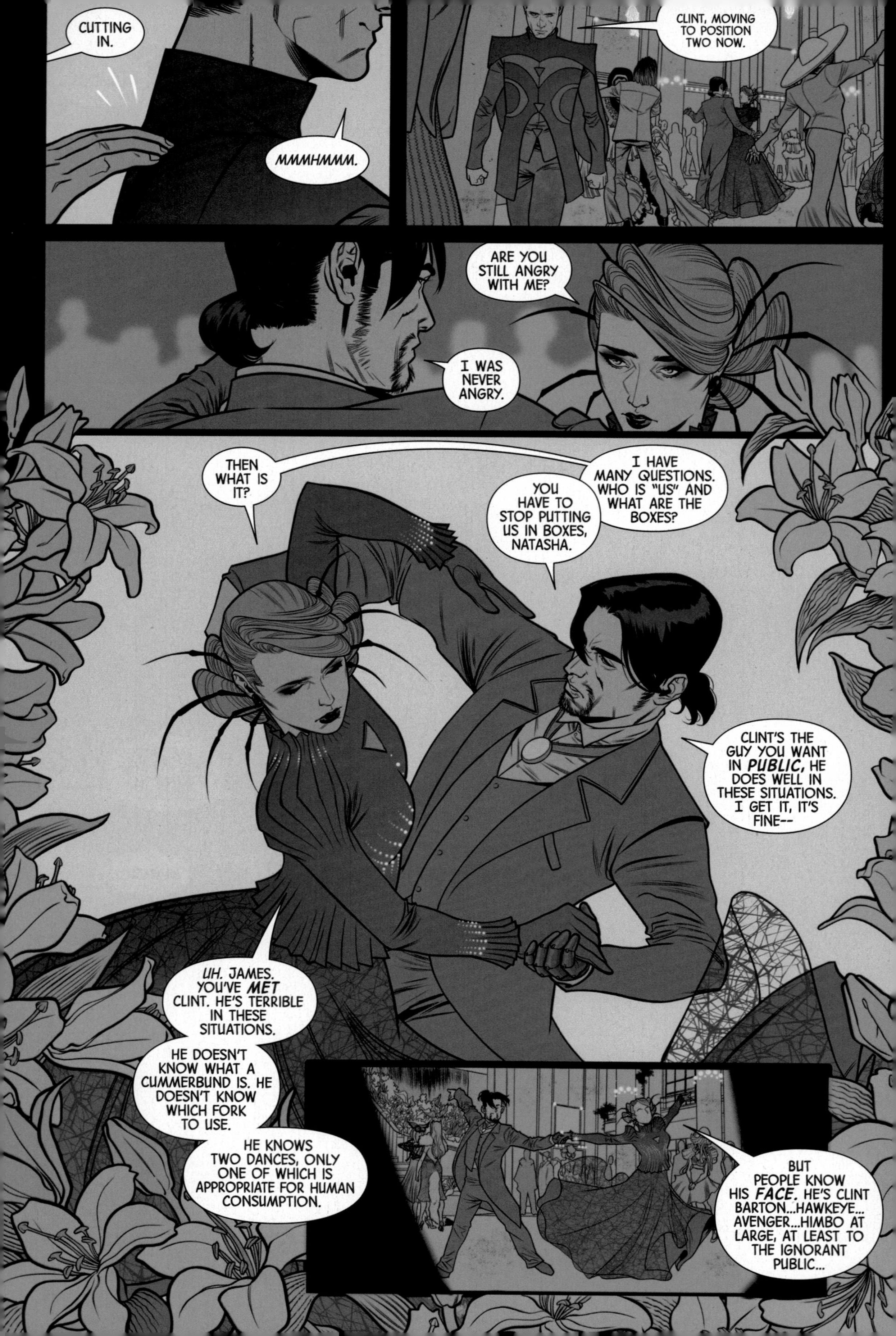
CUTTING IN.
MMMHMMM.
CLINT, MOVING TO POSITION TWO NOW.
ARE YOU STILL ANGRY WITH ME?
I WAS NEVER ANGRY.
THEN WHAT IS IT?
I HAVE MANY QUESTIONS. WHO IS "US" AND WHAT ARE THE BOXES?
YOU HAVE TO STOP PUTTING US IN BOXES, NATASHA.
CLINT'S THE GUY YOU WANT IN PUBLIC, HE DOES WELL IN THESE SITUATIONS. I GET IT, IT'S FINE--
UH. JAMES. YOU'VE MET CLINT. HE'S TERRIBLE IN THESE SITUATIONS.
HE DOESN'T KNOW WHAT A CUMMERBUND IS. HE DOESN'T KNOW WHICH FORK TO USE.
HE KNOWS TWO DANCES, ONLY ONE OF WHICH IS APPROPRIATE FOR HUMAN CONSUMPTION.
BUT PEOPLE KNOW HIS FACE. HE'S CLINT BARTON...HAWKEYE... AVENGER...HIMBO AT LARGE, AT LEAST TO THE IGNORANT PUBLIC...

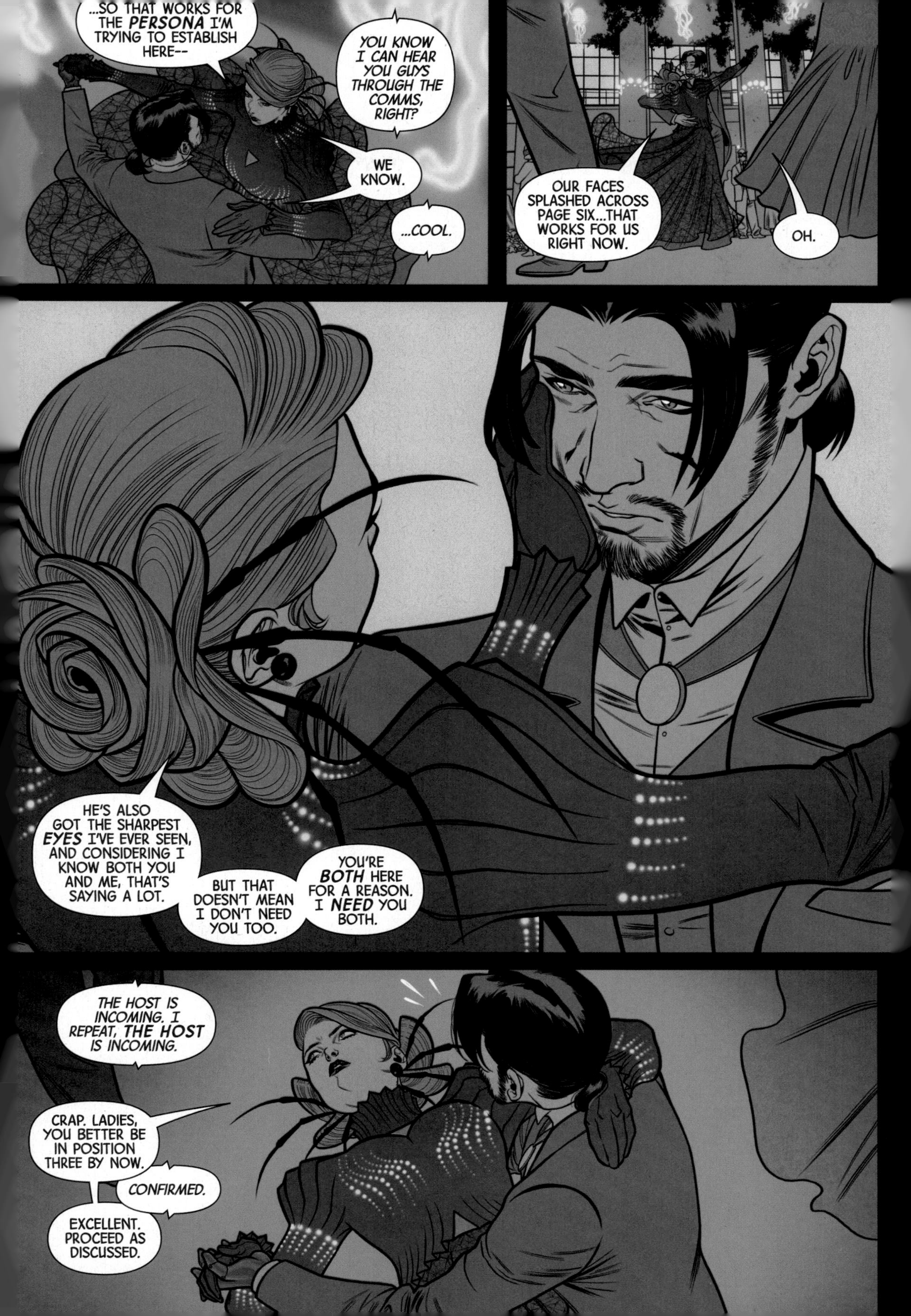
...SO THAT WORKS FOR THE *PERSONA* I'M TRYING TO ESTABLISH HERE--
YOU KNOW I CAN HEAR YOU GUYS THROUGH THE COMMS, RIGHT?
WE KNOW.
...COOL.
OUR FACES SPLASHED ACROSS PAGE SIX...THAT WORKS FOR US RIGHT NOW.
OH.
HE'S ALSO GOT THE SHARPEST *EYES* I'VE EVER SEEN, AND CONSIDERING I KNOW BOTH YOU AND ME, THAT'S SAYING A LOT.
BUT THAT DOESN'T MEAN I DON'T NEED YOU TOO.
YOU'RE *BOTH* HERE FOR A REASON. I *NEED* YOU BOTH.
THE HOST IS INCOMING. I REPEAT, THE HOST IS INCOMING.
CRAP. LADIES, YOU BETTER BE IN POSITION THREE BY NOW.
CONFIRMED.
EXCELLENT. PROCEED AS DISCUSSED.

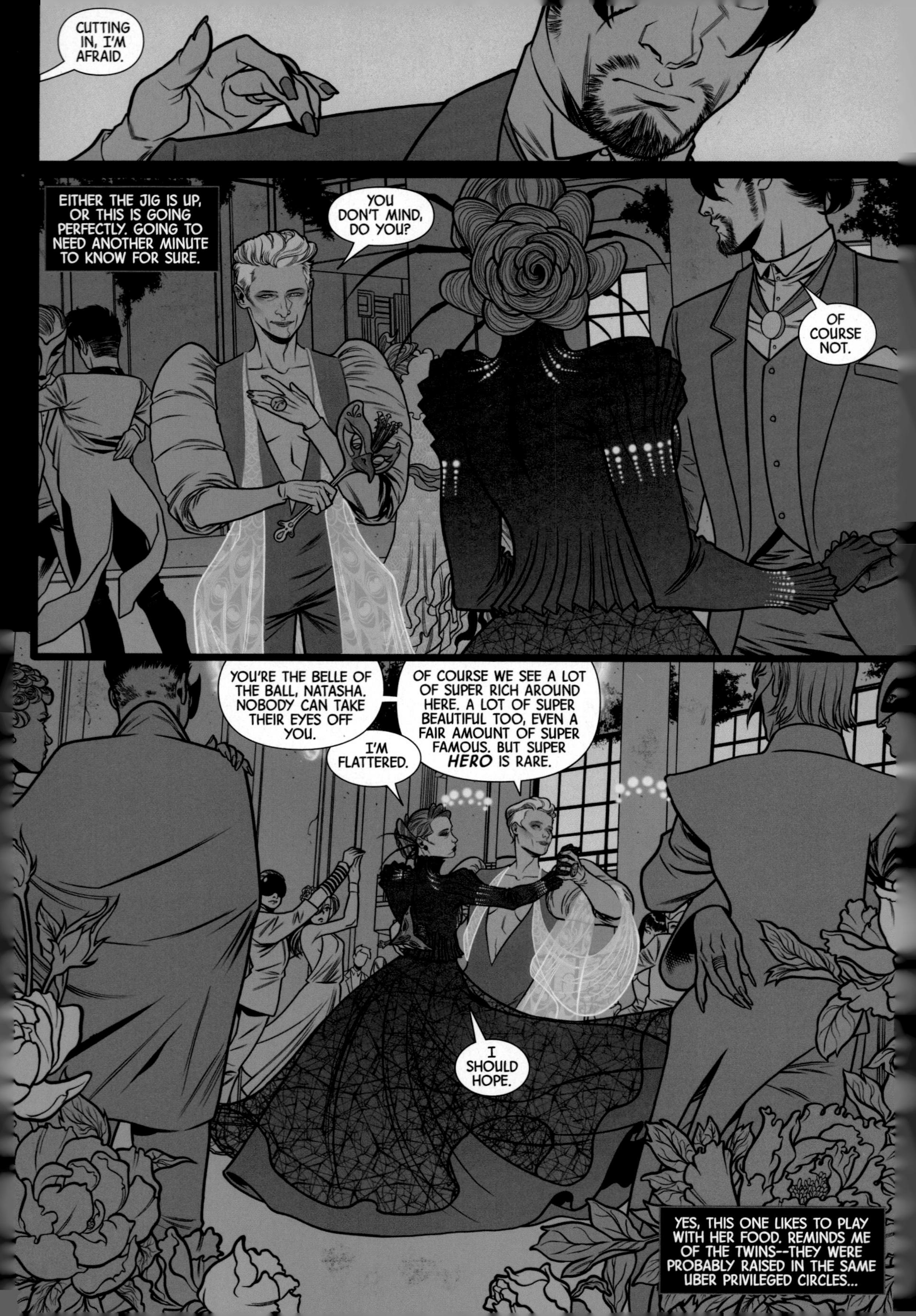

CUTTING IN, I'M AFRAID.
EITHER THE JIG IS UP, OR THIS IS GOING PERFECTLY. GOING TO NEED ANOTHER MINUTE TO KNOW FOR SURE.
YOU DON'T MIND, DO YOU?
OF COURSE NOT.
YOU'RE THE BELLE OF THE BALL, NATASHA. NOBODY CAN TAKE THEIR EYES OFF YOU.
OF COURSE WE SEE A LOT OF SUPER RICH AROUND HERE. A LOT OF SUPER BEAUTIFUL TOO, EVEN A FAIR AMOUNT OF SUPER FAMOUS. BUT SUPER HERO IS RARE.
I'M FLATTERED.
I SHOULD HOPE.
YES, THIS ONE LIKES TO PLAY WITH HER FOOD. REMINDS ME OF THE TWINS--THEY WERE PROBABLY RAISED IN THE SAME UBER PRIVILEGED CIRCLES...

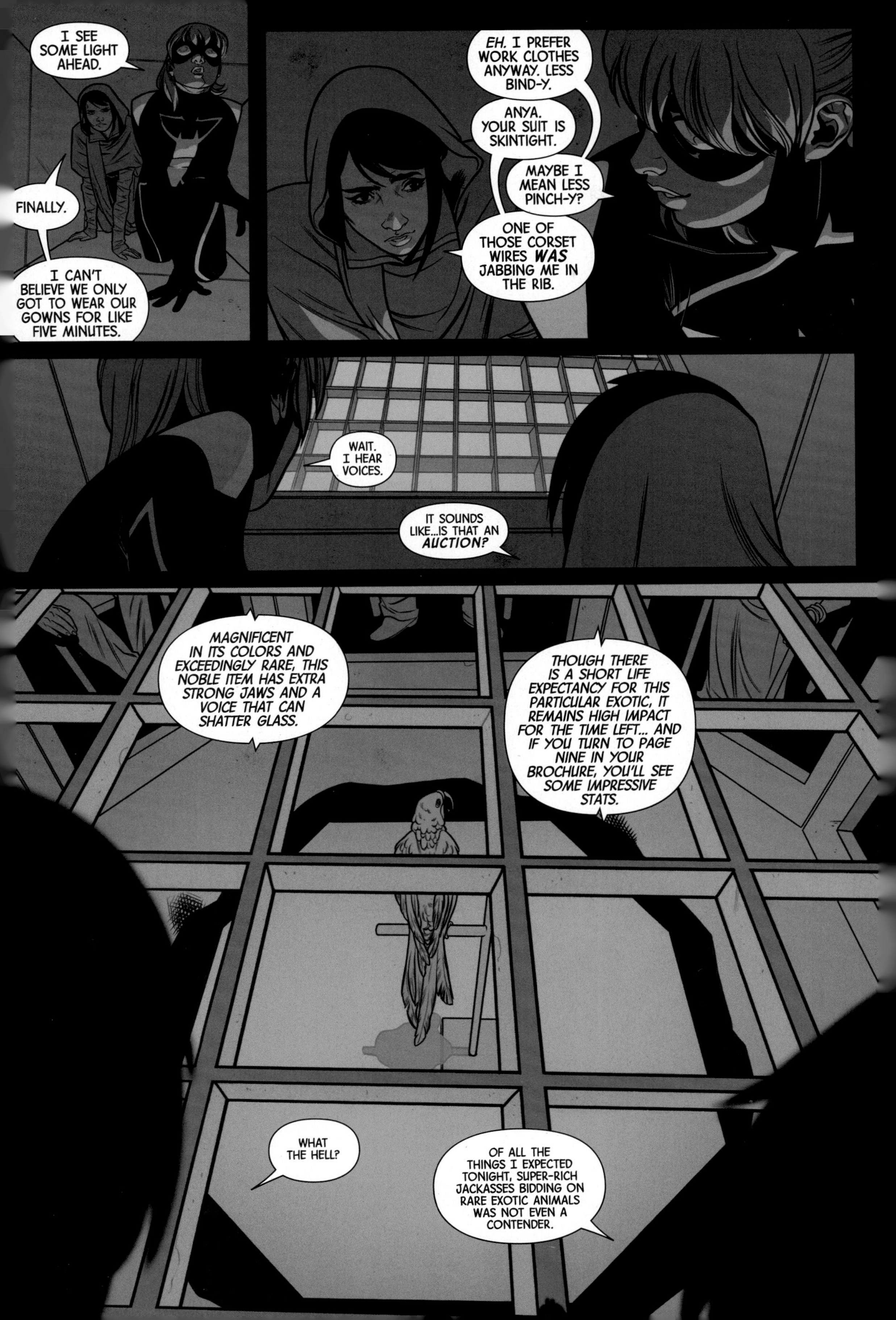
I SEE SOME LIGHT AHEAD.
FINALLY.
I CAN'T BELIEVE WE ONLY GOT TO WEAR OUR GOWNS FOR LIKE FIVE MINUTES.
EH. I PREFER WORK CLOTHES ANYWAY. LESS BIND-Y.
ANYA. YOUR SUIT IS SKINTIGHT.
MAYBE I MEAN LESS PINCH-Y?
ONE OF THOSE CORSET WIRES WAS JABBING ME IN THE RIB.
WAIT. I HEAR VOICES.
IT SOUNDS LIKE...IS THAT AN AUCTION?
MAGNIFICENT IN ITS COLORS AND EXCEEDINGLY RARE, THIS NOBLE ITEM HAS EXTRA STRONG JAWS AND A VOICE THAT CAN SHATTER GLASS.
THOUGH THERE IS A SHORT LIFE EXPECTANCY FOR THIS PARTICULAR EXOTIC, IT REMAINS HIGH IMPACT FOR THE TIME LEFT... AND IF YOU TURN TO PAGE NINE IN YOUR BROCHURE, YOU'LL SEE SOME IMPRESSIVE STATS.
WHAT THE HELL?
OF ALL THE THINGS I EXPECTED TONIGHT, SUPER-RICH JACKASSES BIDDING ON RARE EXOTIC ANIMALS WAS NOT EVEN A CONTENDER.

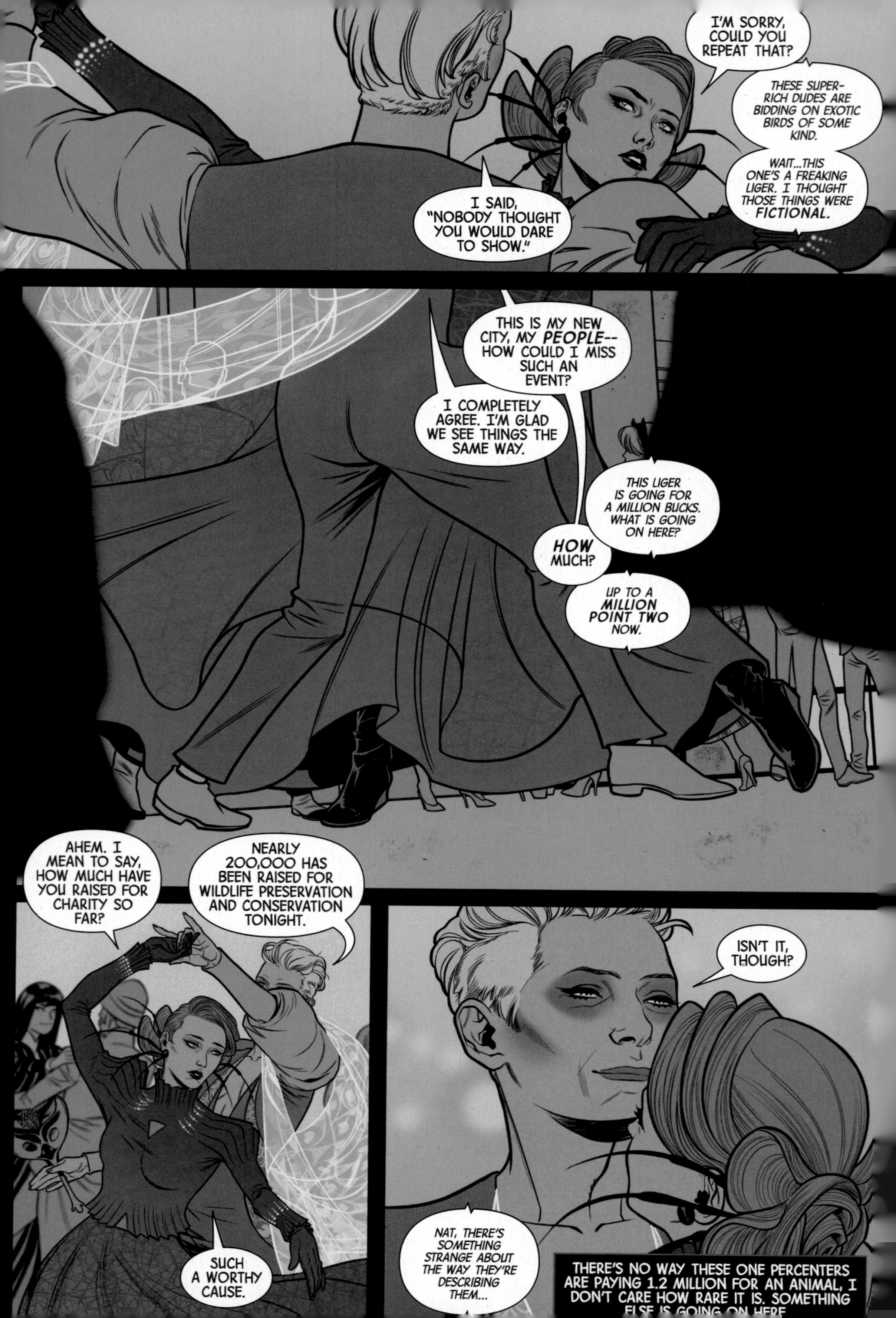
I'M SORRY, COULD YOU REPEAT THAT?
THESE SUPER-RICH DUDES ARE BIDDING ON EXOTIC BIRDS OF SOME KIND.
WAIT...THIS ONE'S A FREAKING LIGER. I THOUGHT THOSE THINGS WERE FICTIONAL.
I SAID, "NOBODY THOUGHT YOU WOULD DARE TO SHOW."
THIS IS MY NEW CITY, MY PEOPLE-- HOW COULD I MISS SUCH AN EVENT?
I COMPLETELY AGREE. I'M GLAD WE SEE THINGS THE SAME WAY.
THIS LIGER IS GOING FOR A MILLION BUCKS. WHAT IS GOING ON HERE?
HOW MUCH?
UP TO A MILLION POINT TWO NOW.
AHEM. I MEAN TO SAY, HOW MUCH HAVE YOU RAISED FOR CHARITY SO FAR?
NEARLY 200,000 HAS BEEN RAISED FOR WILDLIFE PRESERVATION AND CONSERVATION TONIGHT.
SUCH A WORTHY CAUSE.
ISN'T IT, THOUGH?
NAT, THERE'S SOMETHING STRANGE ABOUT THE WAY THEY'RE DESCRIBING THEM...
THERE'S NO WAY THESE ONE PERCENTERS ARE PAYING 1.2 MILLION FOR AN ANIMAL, I DON'T CARE HOW RARE IT IS. SOMETHING

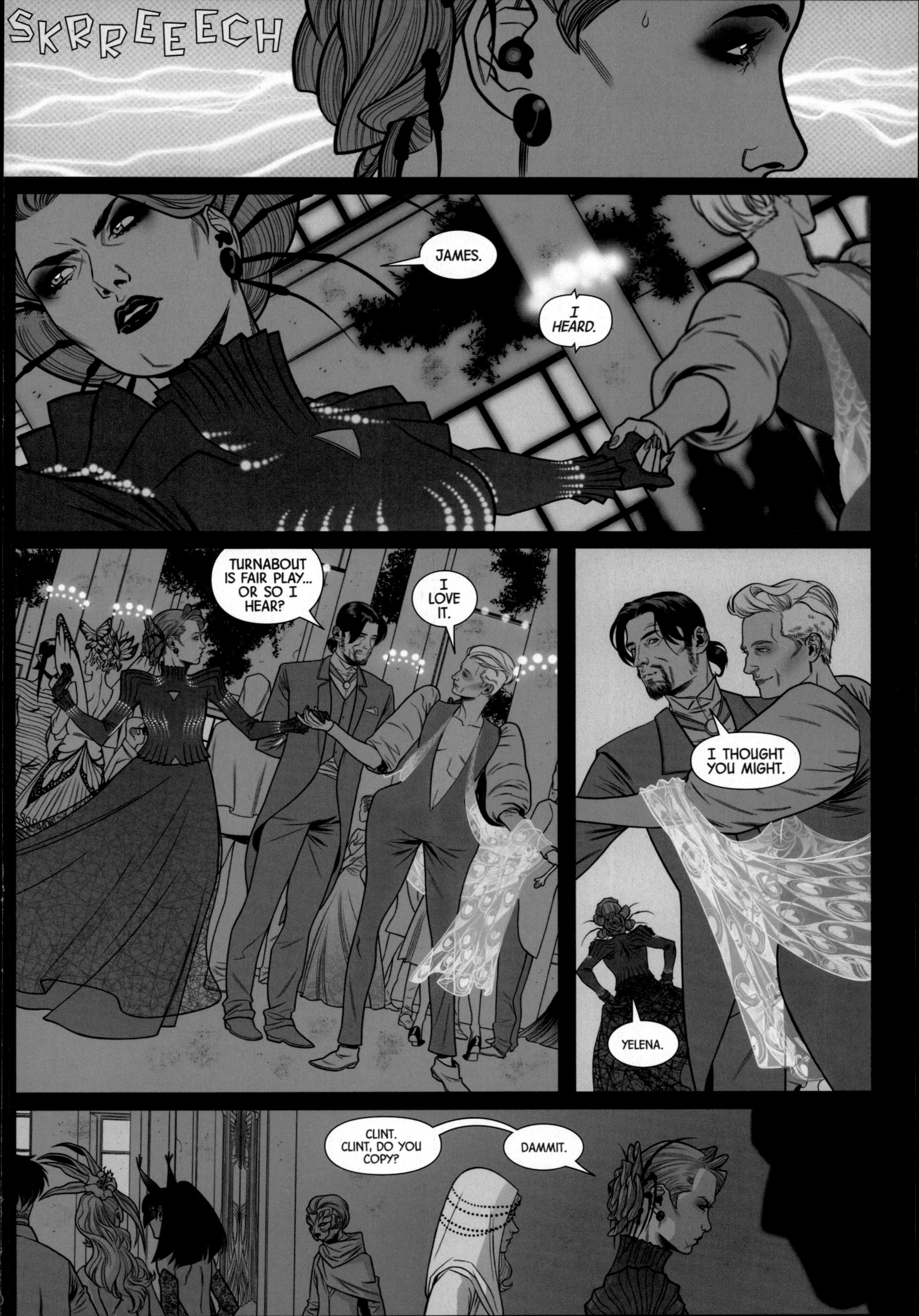
SKRREEECH
JAMES.
I HEARD.
TURNABOUT IS FAIR PLAY... OR SO I HEAR?
I LOVE IT.
I THOUGHT YOU MIGHT.
YELENA.
CLINT. CLINT, DO YOU COPY?
DAMMIT.

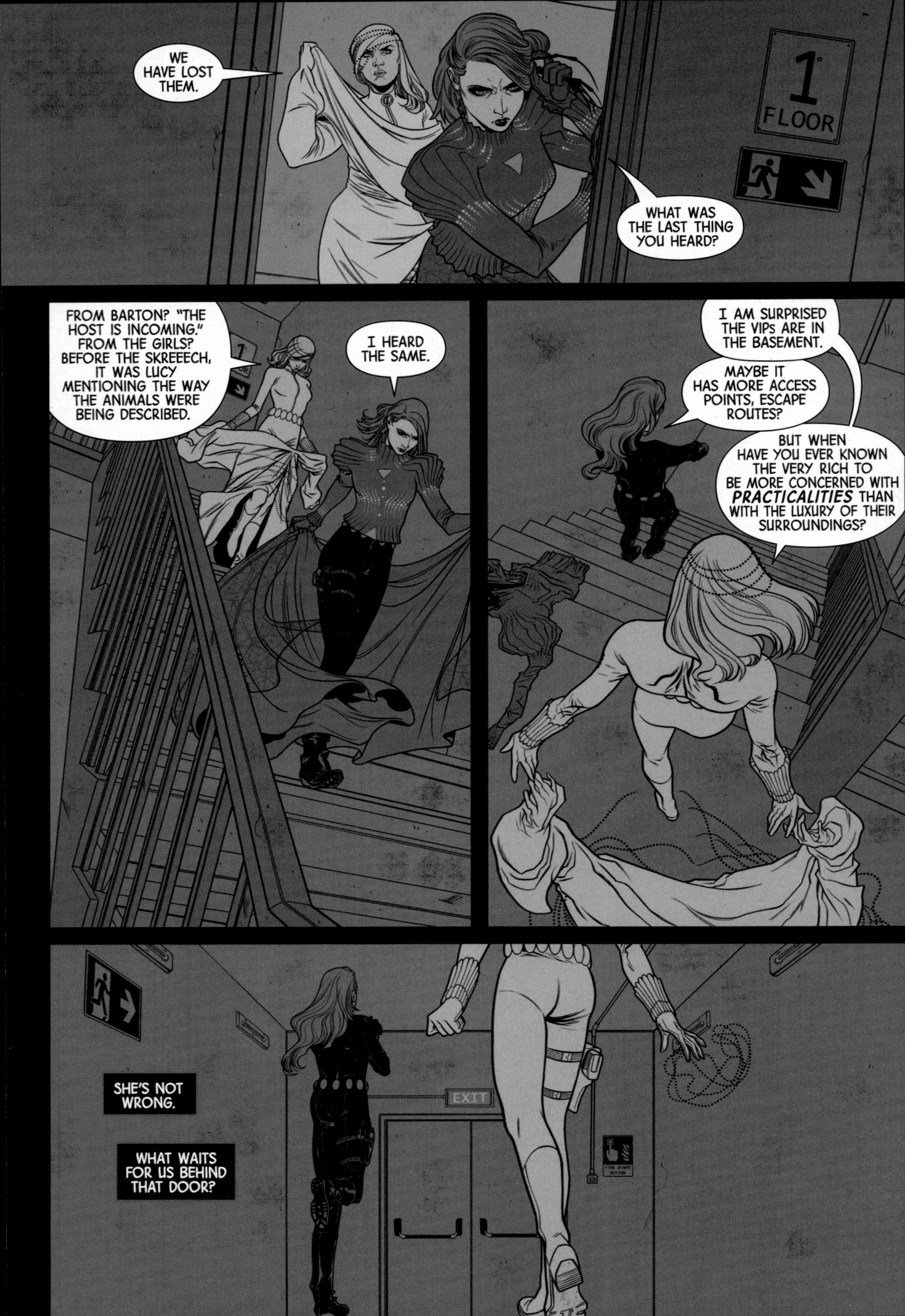

1° FLOOR
WE HAVE LOST THEM.
WHAT WAS THE LAST THING YOU HEARD?
FROM BARTON? "THE HOST IS INCOMING." FROM THE GIRLS? BEFORE THE SKREEECH, IT WAS LUCY MENTIONING THE WAY THE ANIMALS WERE BEING DESCRIBED.
I HEARD THE SAME.
I AM SURPRISED THE VIPs ARE IN THE BASEMENT.
MAYBE IT HAS MORE ACCESS POINTS, ESCAPE ROUTES?
BUT WHEN HAVE YOU EVER KNOWN THE VERY RICH TO BE MORE CONCERNED WITH *PRACTICALITIES* THAN WITH THE LUXURY OF THEIR SURROUNDINGS?
EXIT
SHE'S NOT WRONG.
WHAT WAITS FOR US BEHIND THAT DOOR?

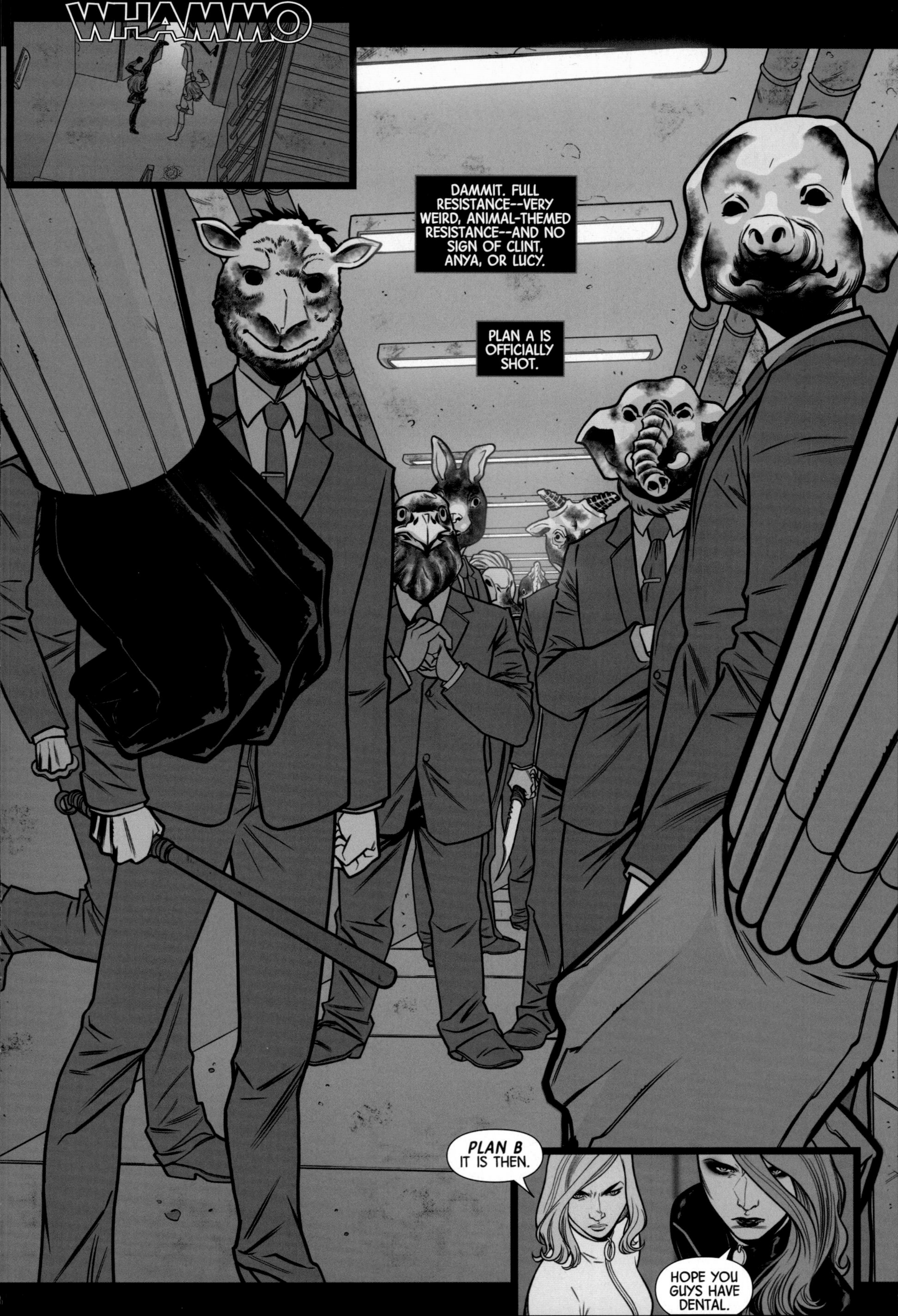
WHAMMO
DAMMIT. FULL RESISTANCE--VERY WEIRD, ANIMAL-THEMED RESISTANCE--AND NO SIGN OF CLINT, ANYA, OR LUCY.
PLAN A IS OFFICIALLY SHOT.
PLAN B IT IS THEN.
HOPE YOU GUYS HAVE DENTAL.

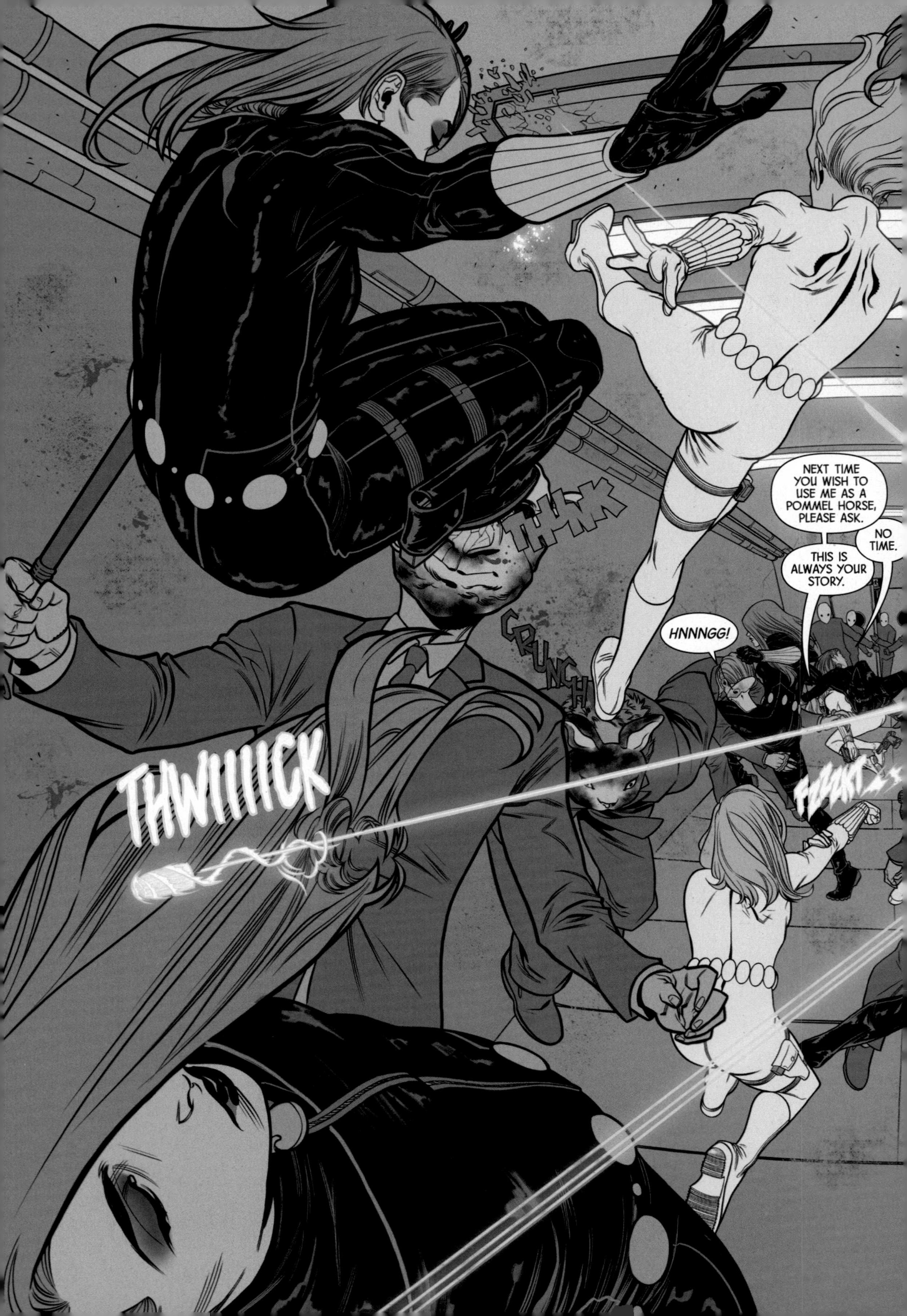
NEXT TIME YOU WISH TO USE ME AS A POMMEL HORSE, PLEASE ASK.
NO TIME.
THIS IS ALWAYS YOUR STORY.
THUNK
CRUNCH
HNNNGG!
THWIIIICK
FZZZKT

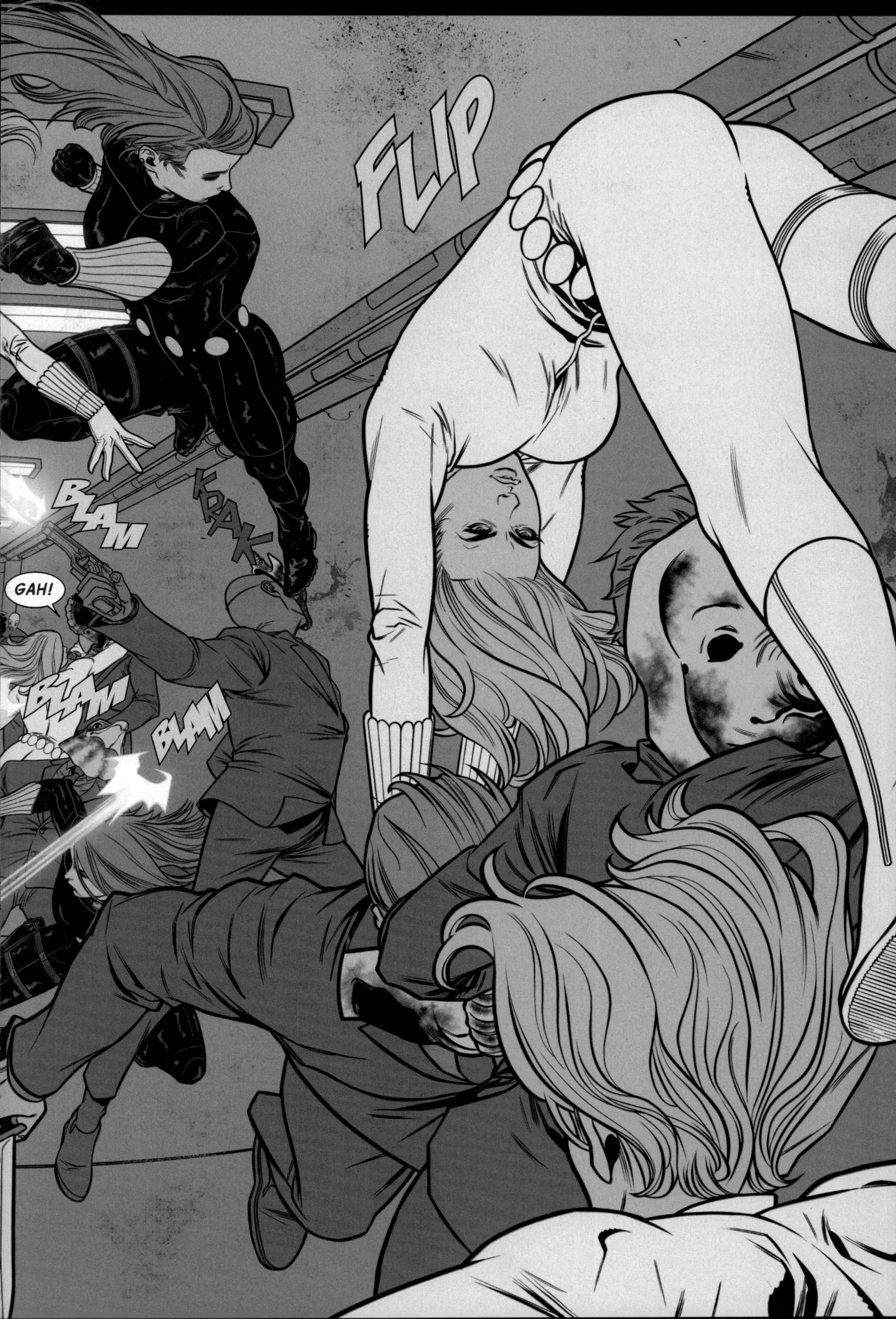
FLIP
KRAK
BLAM
GAH!
BLAM
BLAM

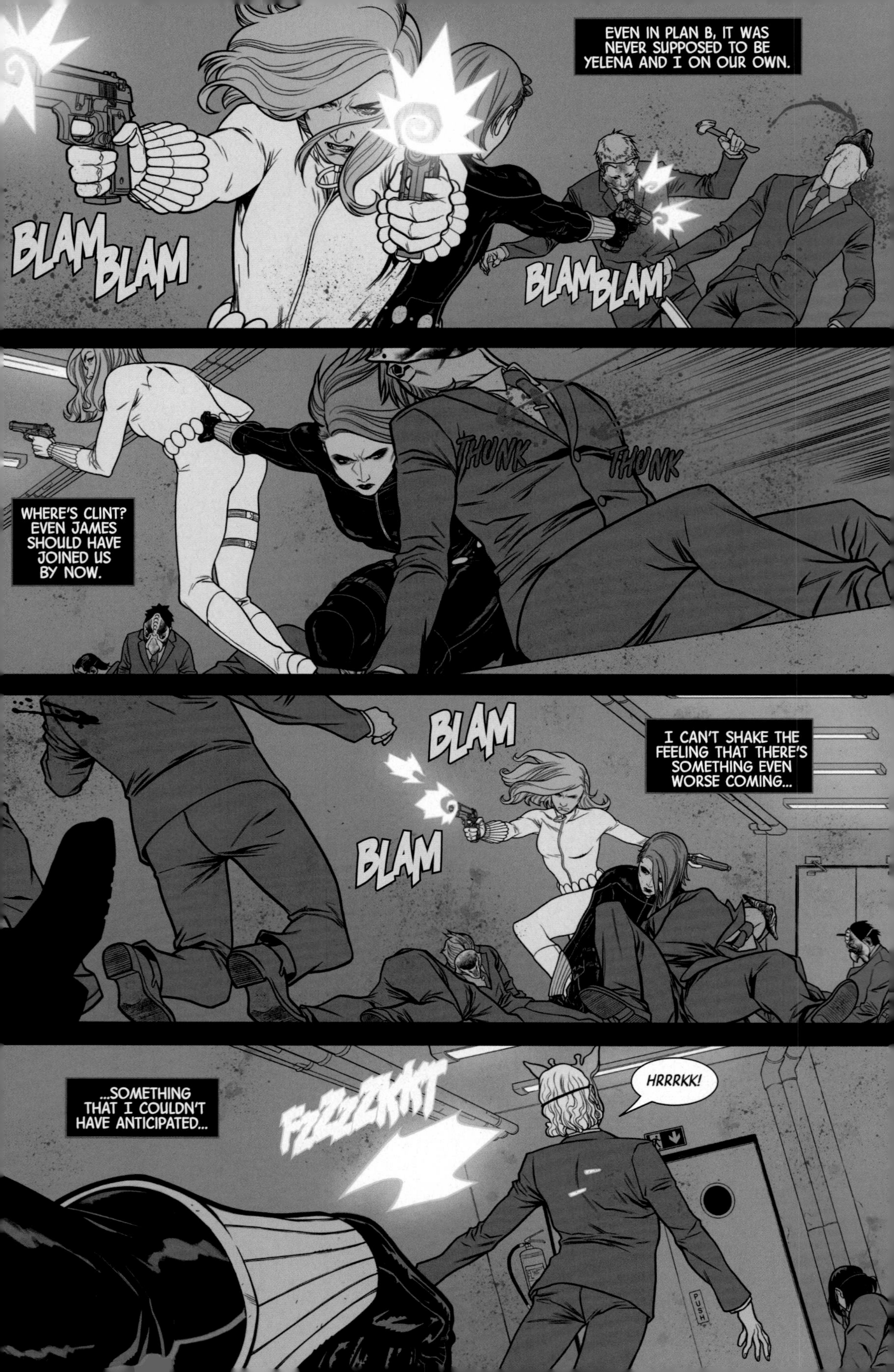
EVEN IN PLAN B, IT WAS NEVER SUPPOSED TO BE YELENA AND I ON OUR OWN.
BLAM BLAM
BLAMBLAM
WHERE'S CLINT? EVEN JAMES SHOULD HAVE JOINED US BY NOW.
THUNK
THUNK
I CAN'T SHAKE THE FEELING THAT THERE'S SOMETHING EVEN WORSE COMING...
BLAM
BLAM
...SOMETHING THAT I COULDN'T HAVE ANTICIPATED...
FZZZZKKT
HRRRKK!
PUSH

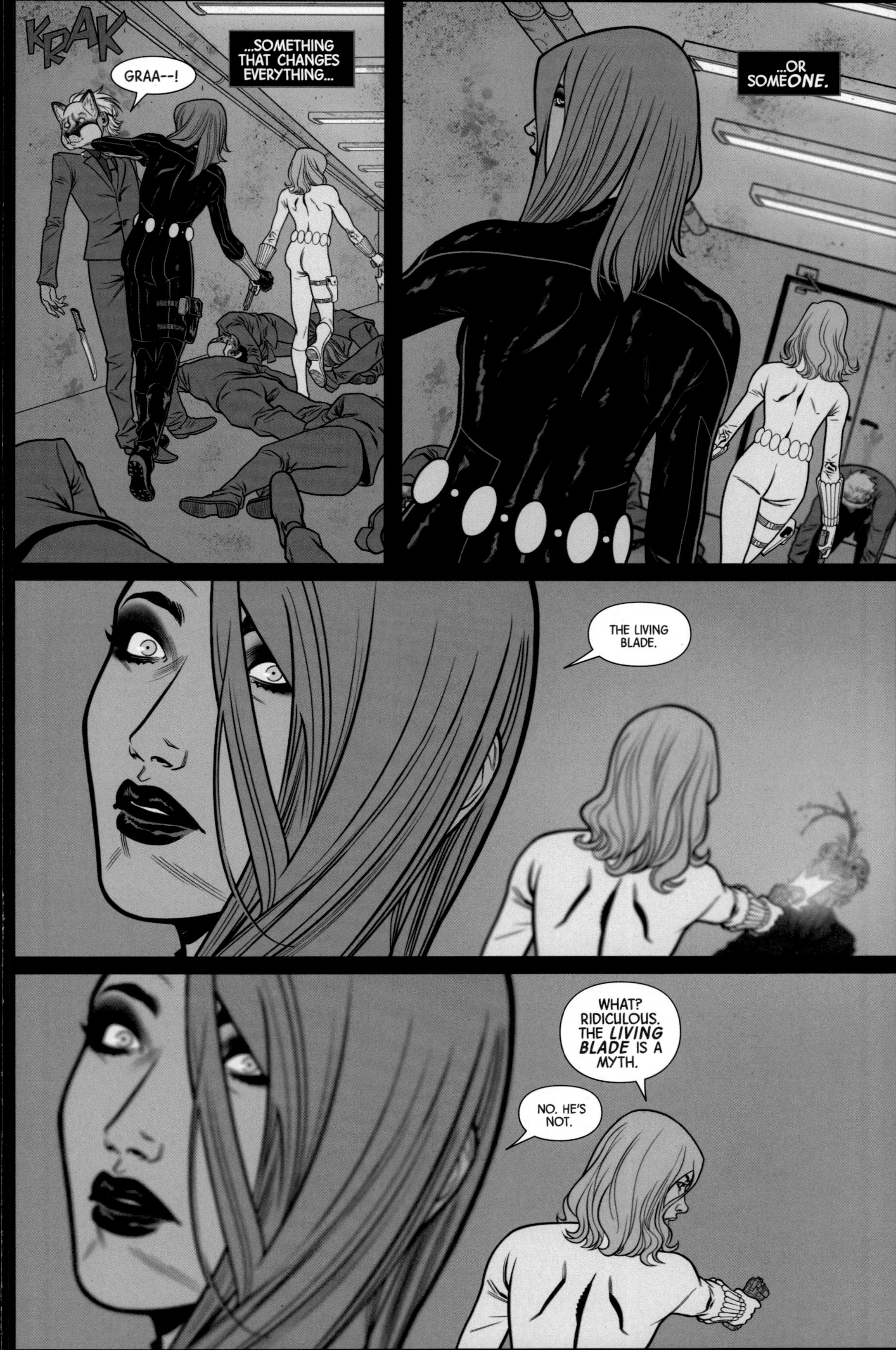
KRAK
GRAA--!
...SOMETHING THAT CHANGES EVERYTHING...
...OR SOMEONE.
THE LIVING BLADE.
WHAT? RIDICULOUS. THE LIVING BLADE IS A MYTH.
NO. HE'S NOT.

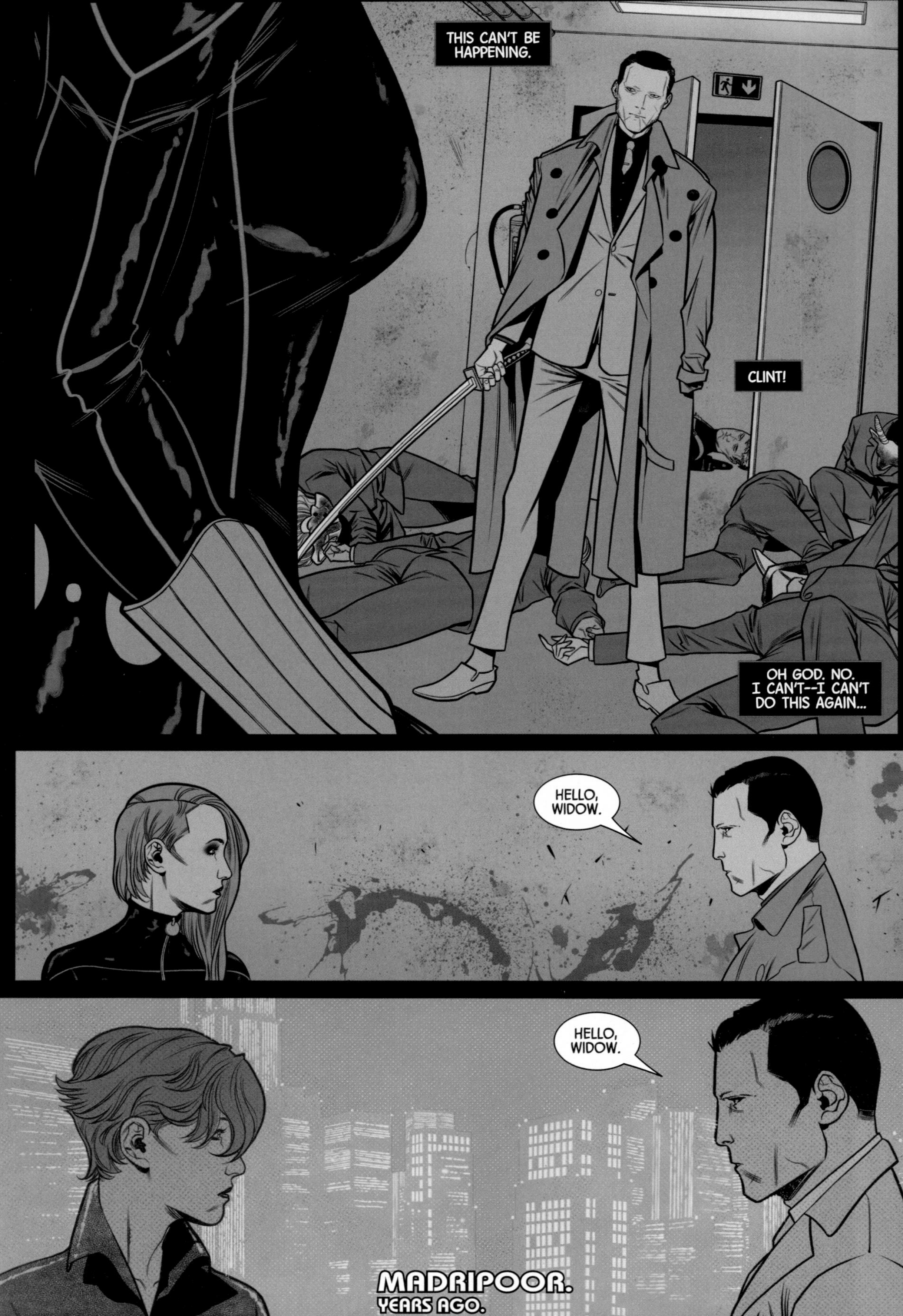
THIS CAN'T BE HAPPENING.
CLINT!
OH GOD. NO. I CAN'T--I CAN'T DO THIS AGAIN...
HELLO, WIDOW.
HELLO, WIDOW.
MADRIPOOR.
YEARS AGO.

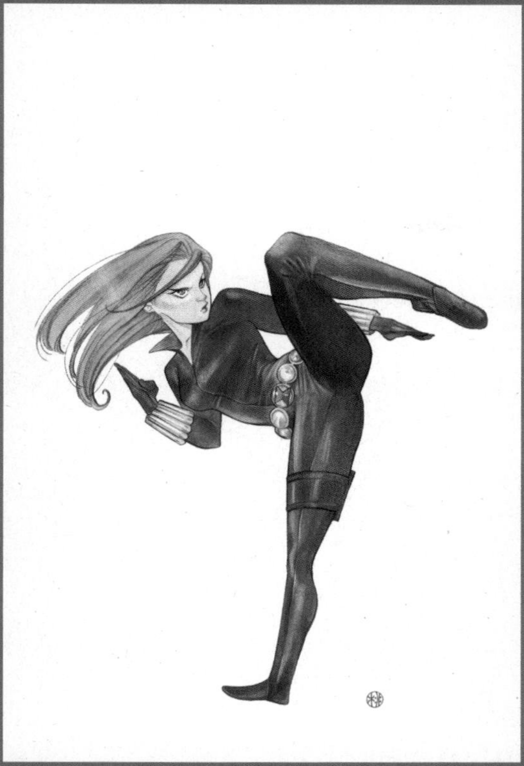

#13 VARIANT BY
PEACH MOMOKO

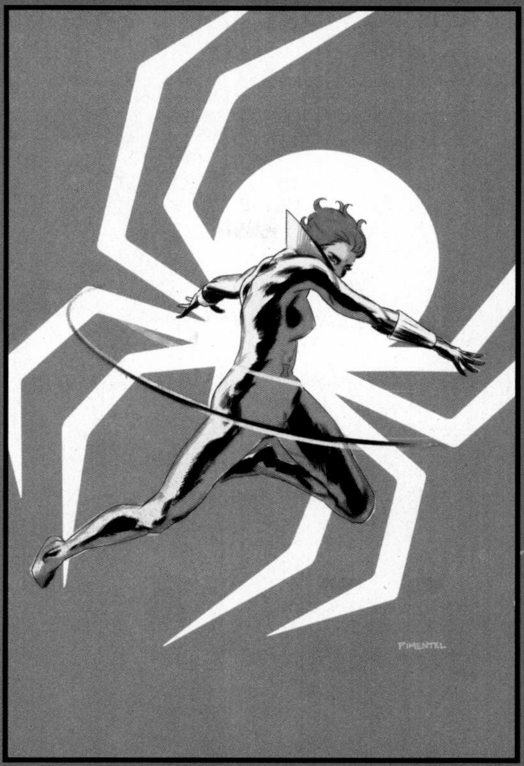
PIMENTEL

#13 DESIGN VARIANT BY
RAFAEL T. PIMENTEL

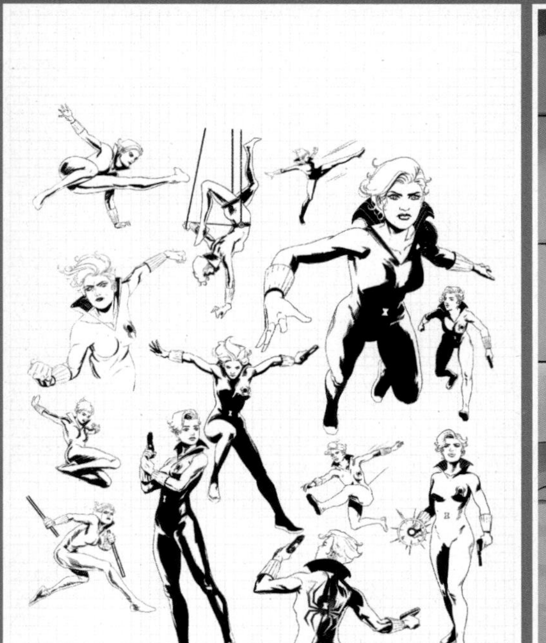
PIMENTEL

#13 VARIANT BY
RAFAEL T. PIMENTEL

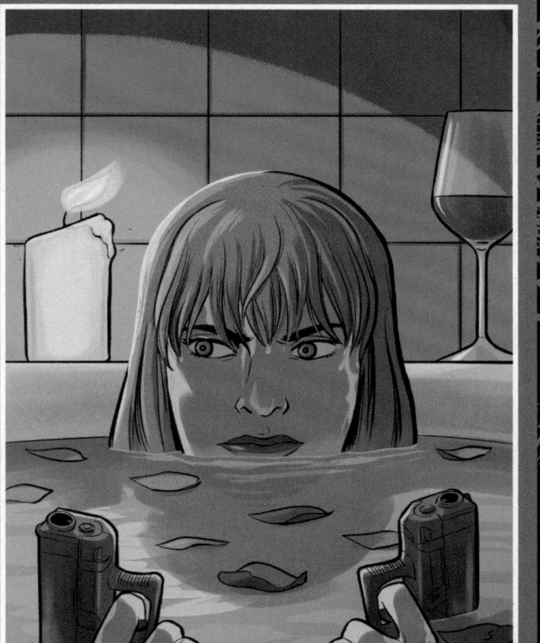

#14 VARIANT BY
NATACHA BUSTOS

BLACK
WIDOW
黑寡妇
奇迹漫画
危险
1/F & 2/F
MADRIPOOR
AH!

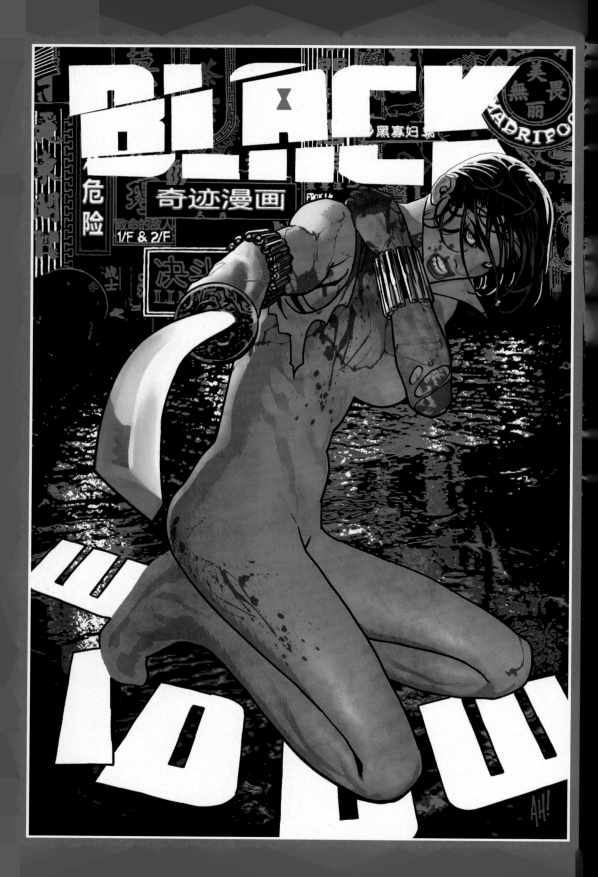

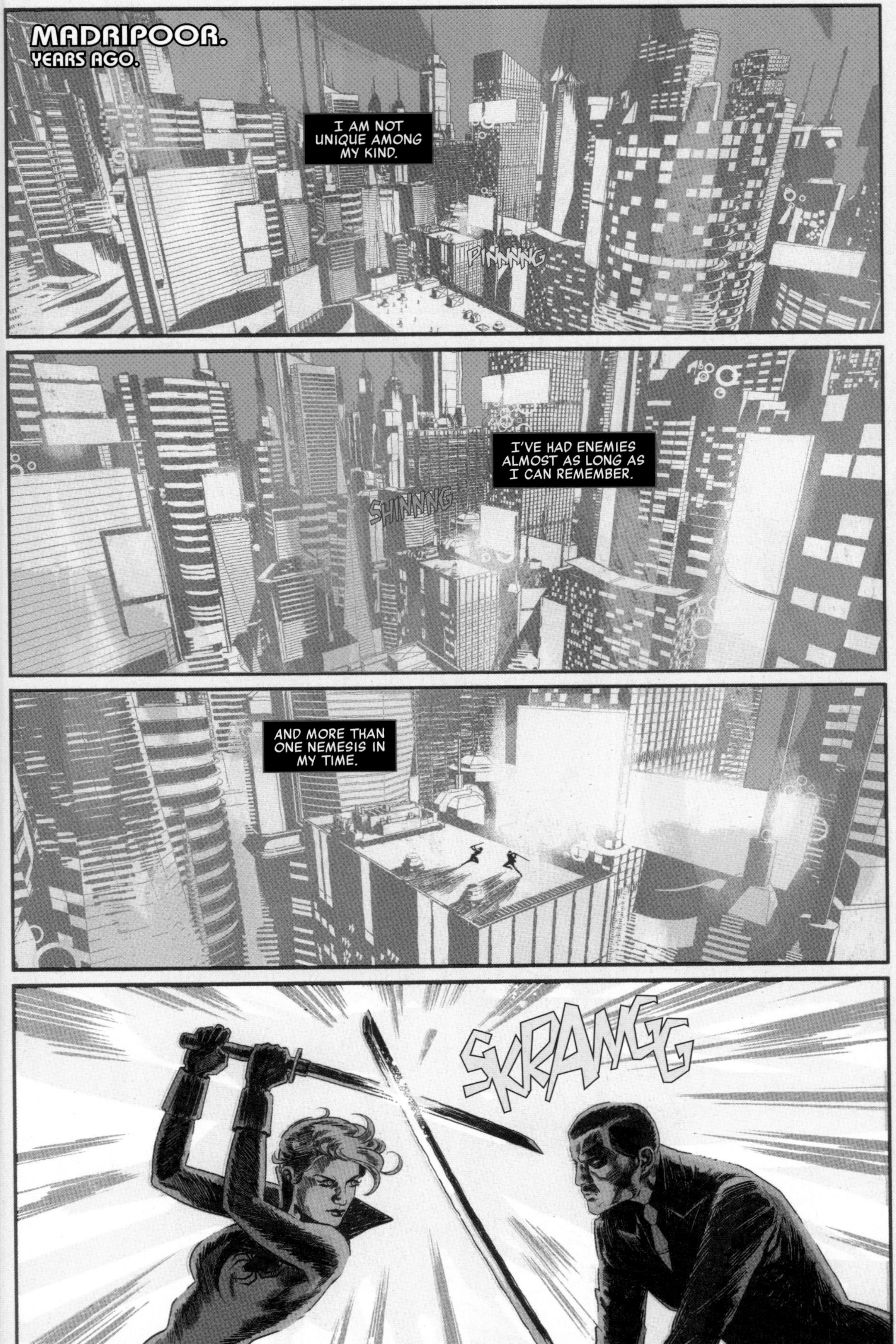
MADRIPOOR.
YEARS AGO.
I AM NOT UNIQUE AMONG MY KIND.
PINNNNG
I'VE HAD ENEMIES ALMOST AS LONG AS I CAN REMEMBER.
SHINNNG
AND MORE THAN ONE NEMESIS IN MY TIME.
SKRANGG

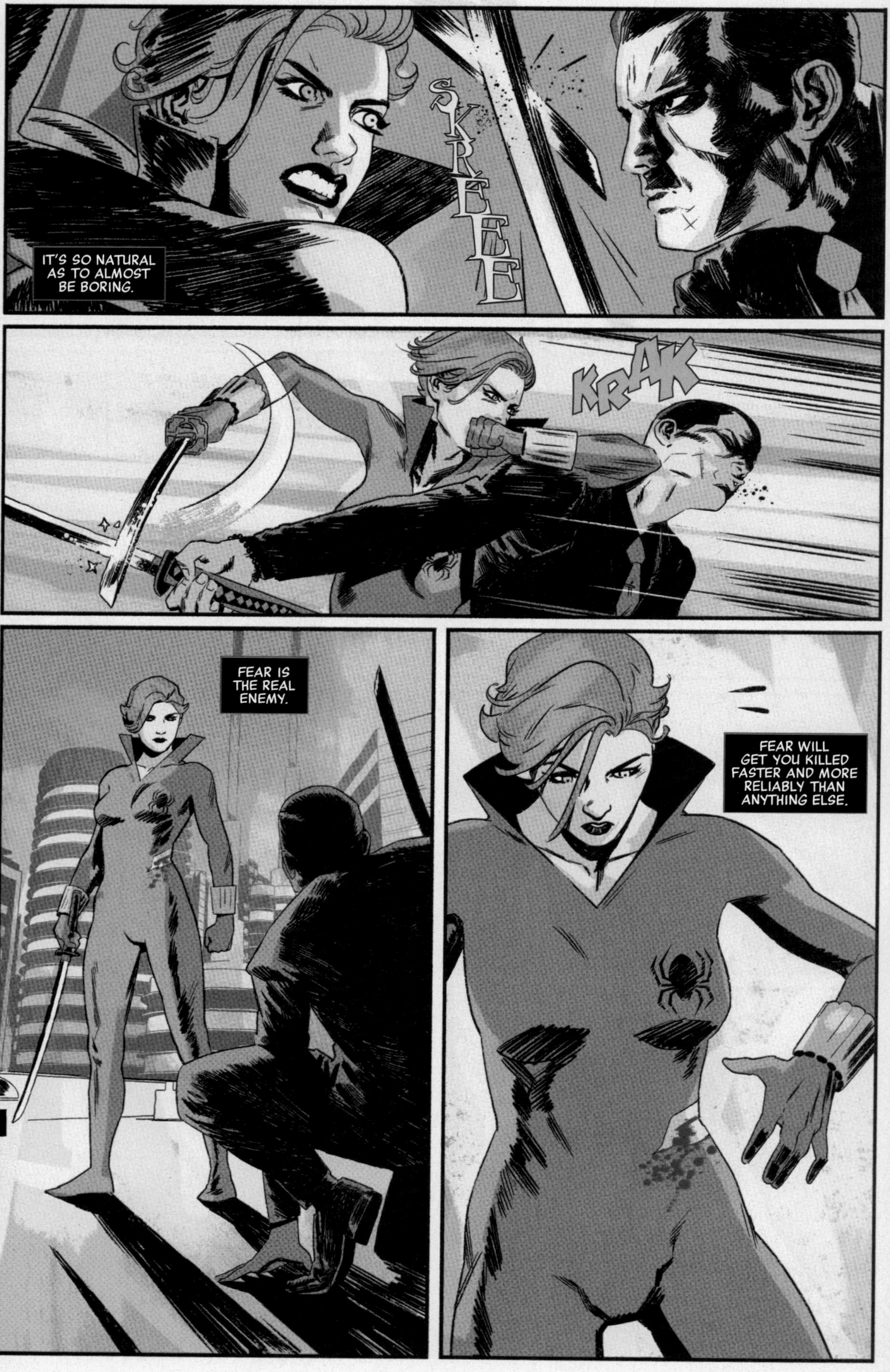
SKREEE
IT'S SO NATURAL AS TO ALMOST BE BORING.
KRAK
FEAR IS THE REAL ENEMY.
FEAR WILL GET YOU KILLED FASTER AND MORE RELIABLY THAN ANYTHING ELSE.

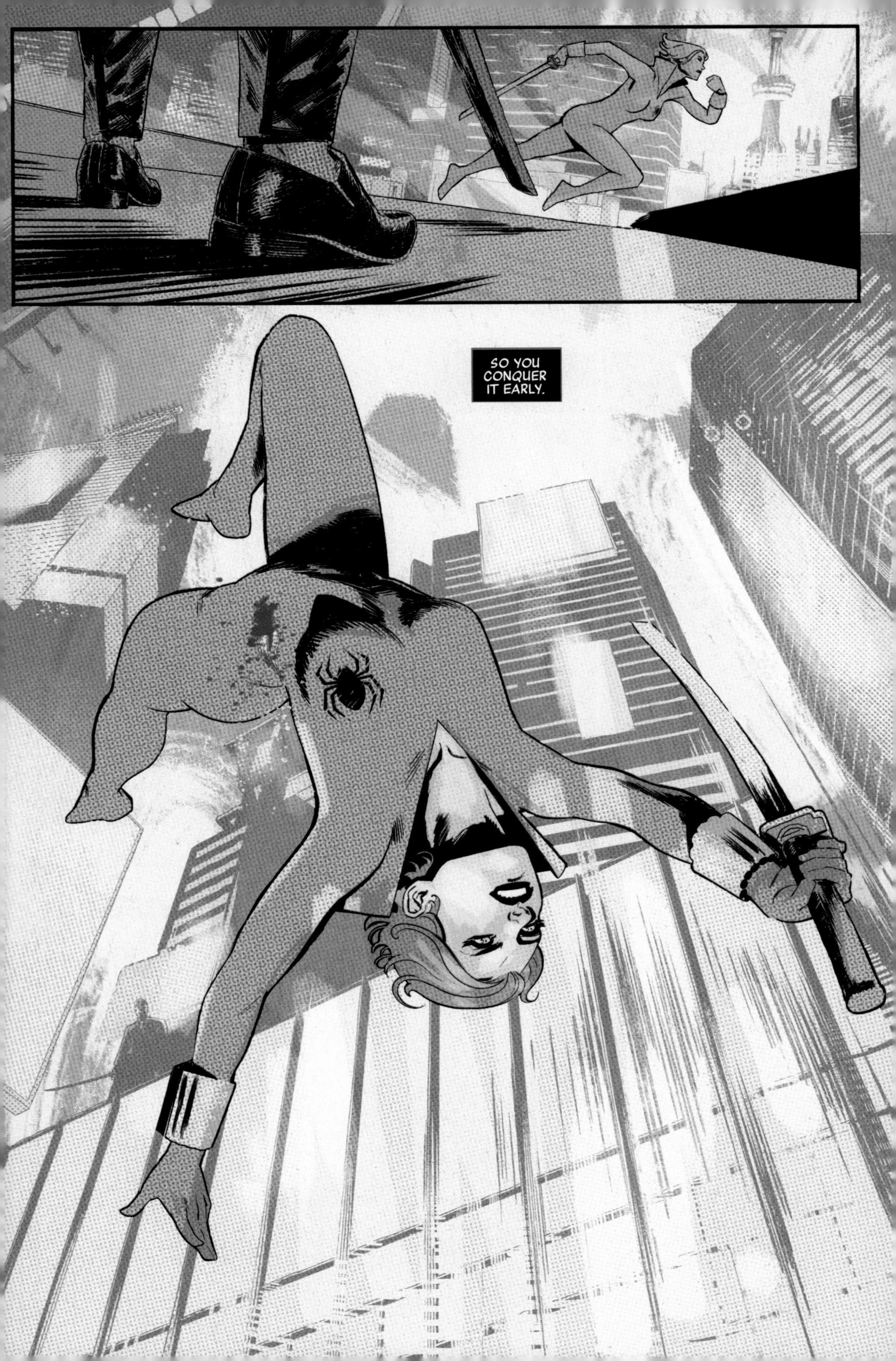
SO YOU
CONQUER
IT EARLY.

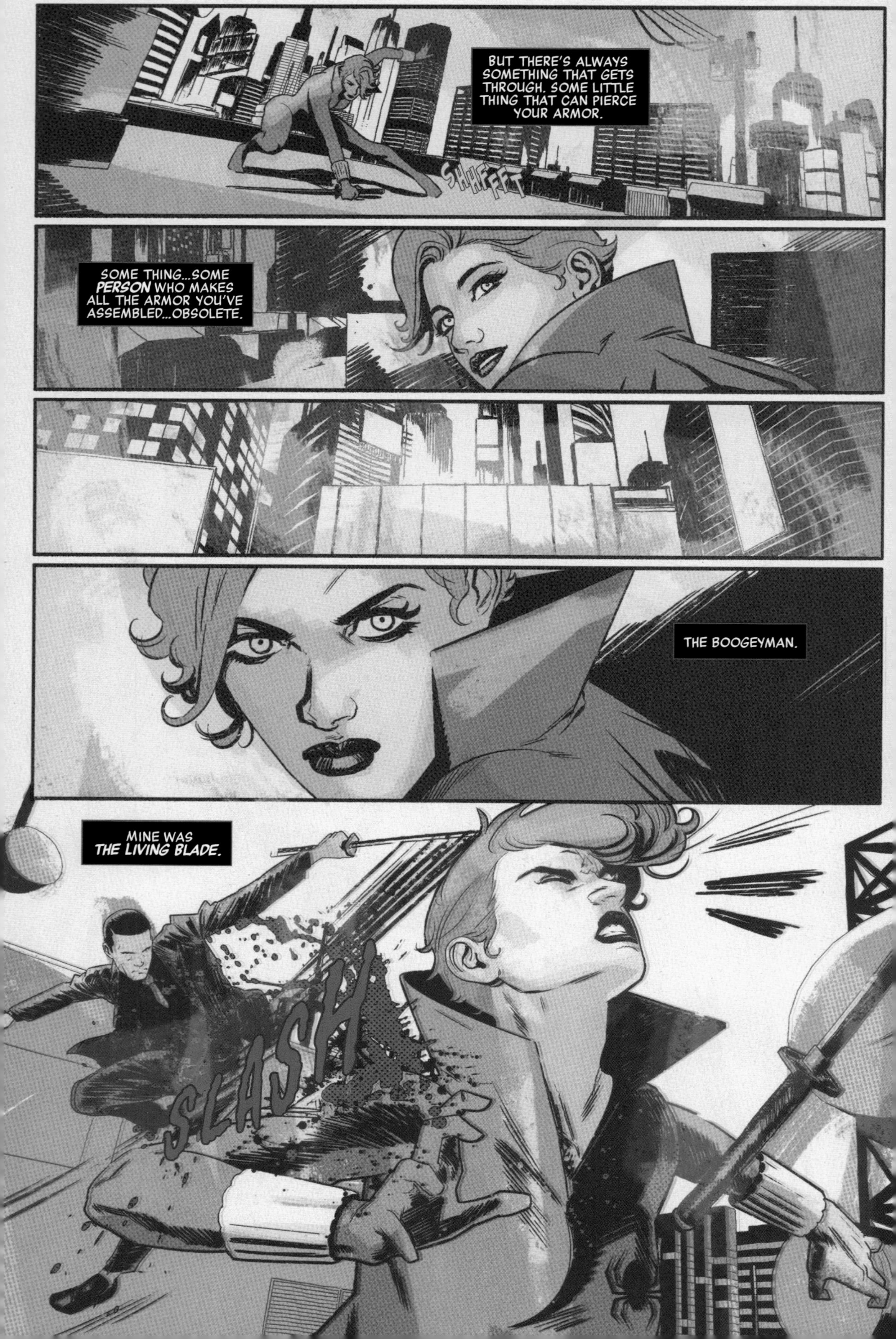
BUT THERE'S ALWAYS SOMETHING THAT GETS THROUGH. SOME LITTLE THING THAT CAN PIERCE YOUR ARMOR.
SHHFFFT
SOME THING...SOME PERSON WHO MAKES ALL THE ARMOR YOU'VE ASSEMBLED...OBSOLETE.
THE BOOGEYMAN.
MINE WAS THE LIVING BLADE.
SLASH

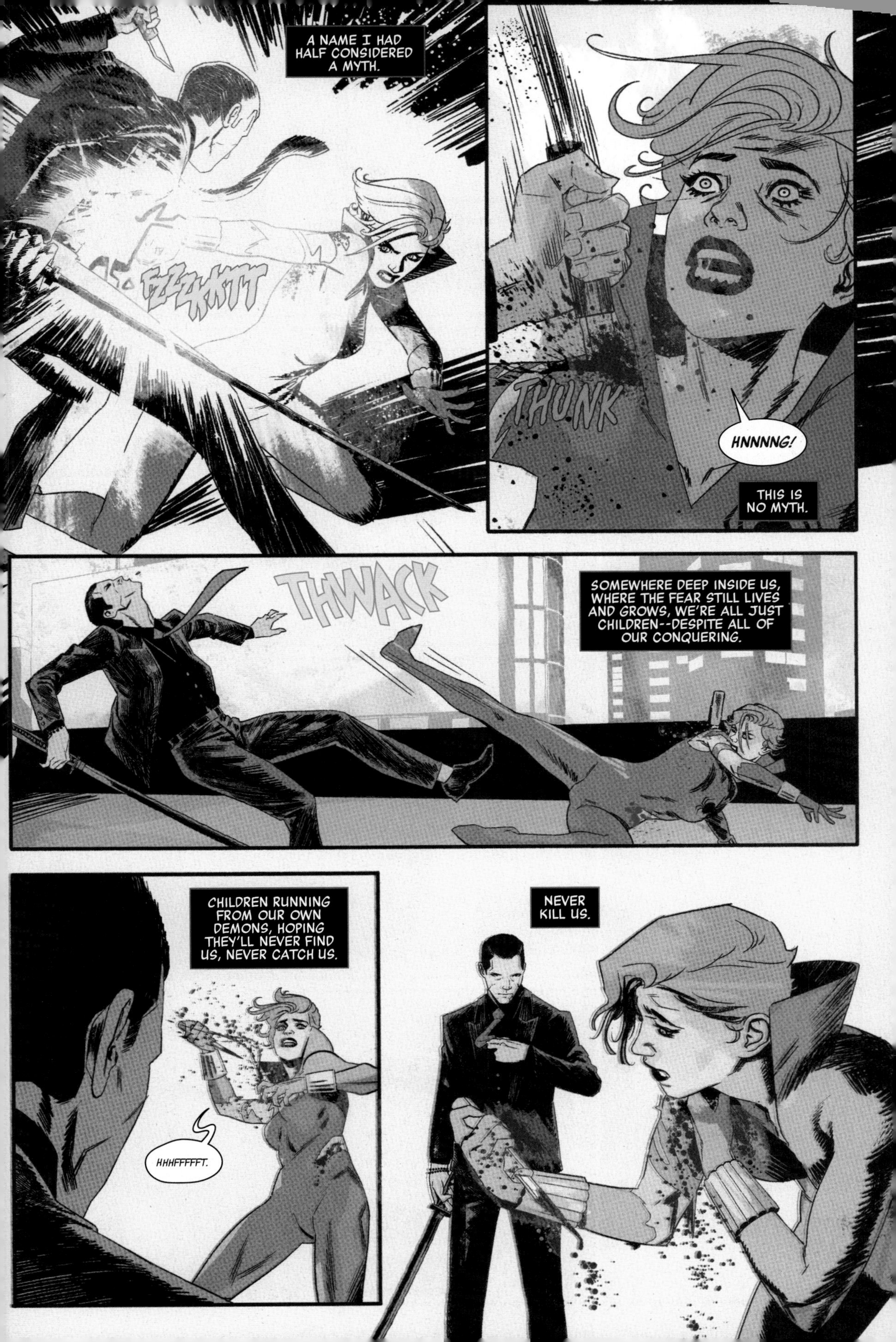
A NAME I HAD HALF CONSIDERED A MYTH.
FZZZKKTT
THUNK
HNNNNG!
THIS IS NO MYTH.
THWACK
SOMEWHERE DEEP INSIDE US, WHERE THE FEAR STILL LIVES AND GROWS, WE'RE ALL JUST CHILDREN--DESPITE ALL OF OUR CONQUERING.
CHILDREN RUNNING FROM OUR OWN DEMONS, HOPING THEY'LL NEVER FIND US, NEVER CATCH US.
HHHFFFFFT.
NEVER KILL US.

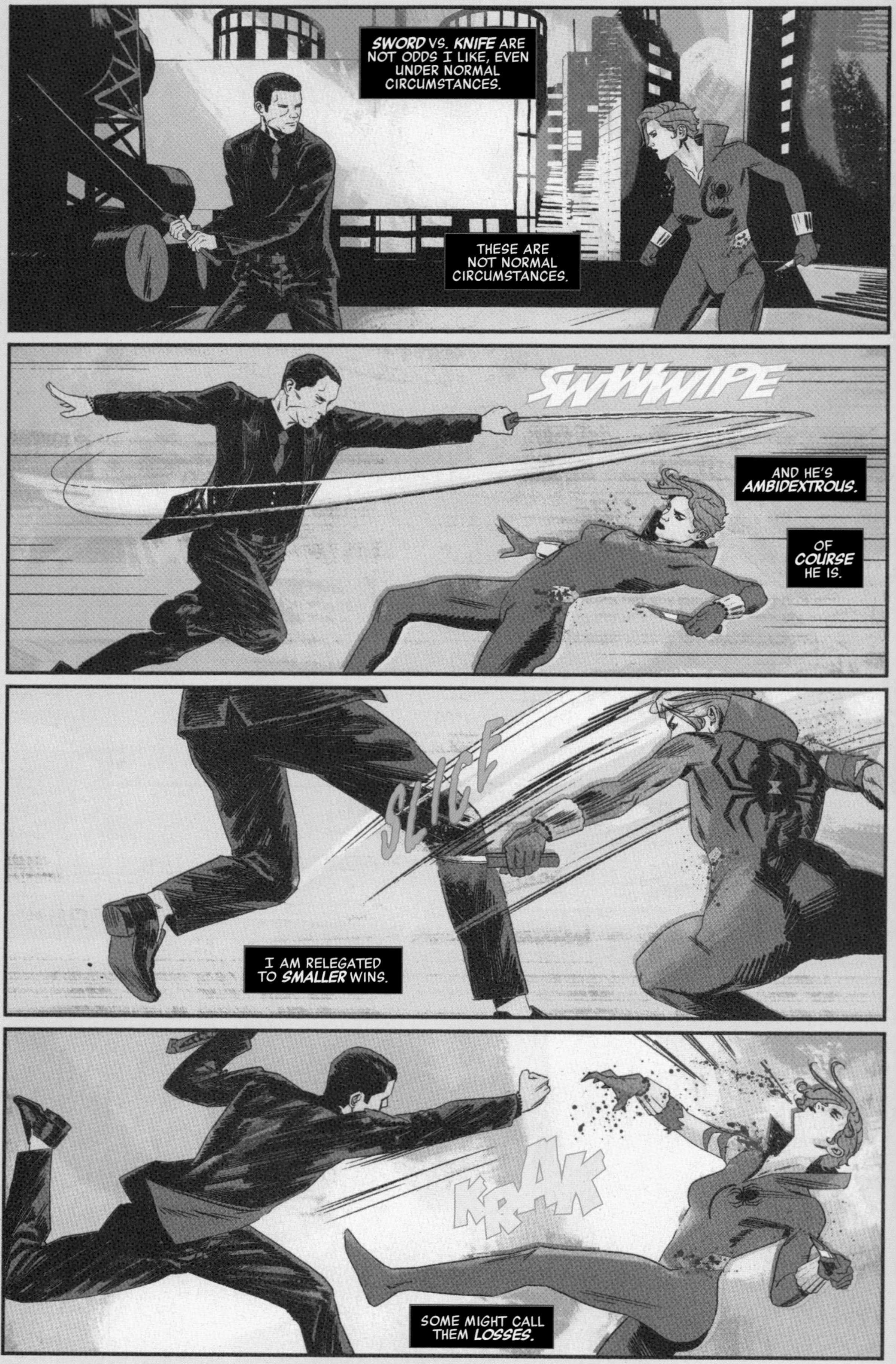
SWORD VS. KNIFE ARE NOT ODDS I LIKE, EVEN UNDER NORMAL CIRCUMSTANCES.
THESE ARE NOT NORMAL CIRCUMSTANCES.
SWWWIPE
AND HE'S AMBIDEXTROUS.
OF COURSE HE IS.
SLICE
I AM RELEGATED TO SMALLER WINS.
KRAK
SOME MIGHT CALL THEM LOSSES.

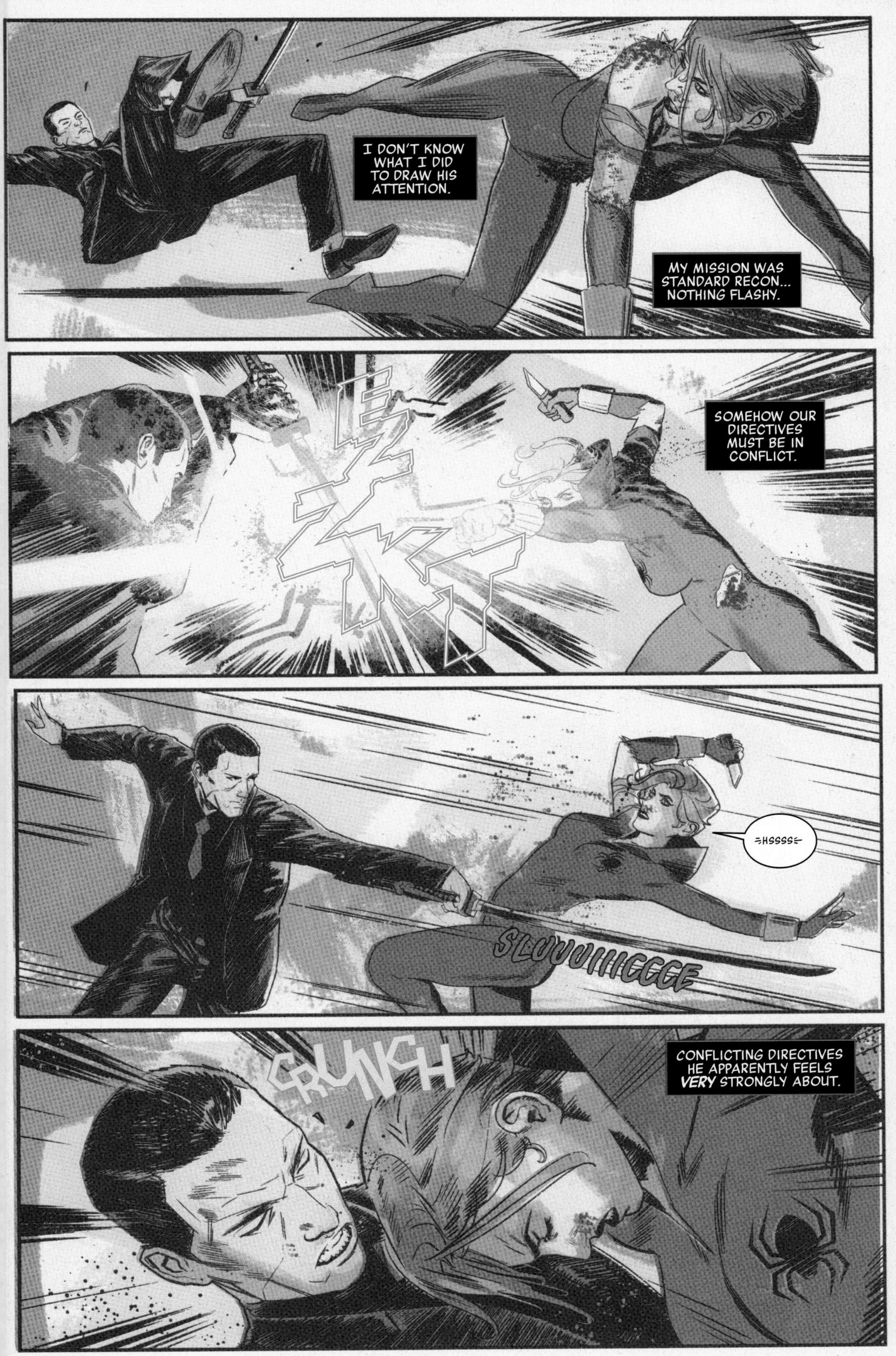
I DON'T KNOW WHAT I DID TO DRAW HIS ATTENTION.
MY MISSION WAS STANDARD RECON... NOTHING FLASHY.
SOMEHOW OUR DIRECTIVES MUST BE IN CONFLICT.
HSSSS
SLUUUIIIICCCCE
CRUNCH
CONFLICTING DIRECTIVES HE APPARENTLY FEELS VERY STRONGLY ABOUT.

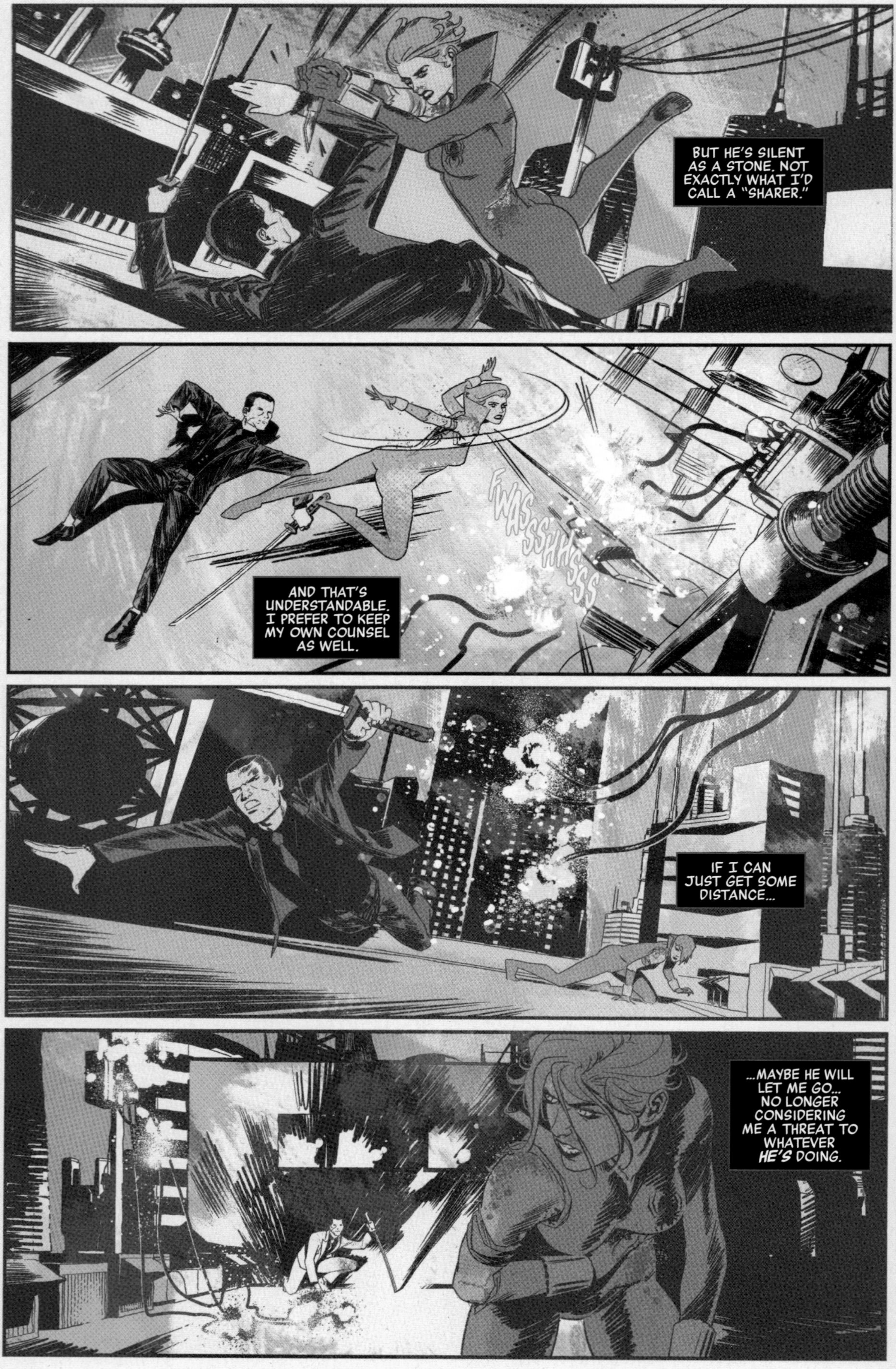
BUT HE'S SILENT AS A STONE. NOT EXACTLY WHAT I'D CALL A "SHARER."
FWASSSHHHSSS
AND THAT'S UNDERSTANDABLE. I PREFER TO KEEP MY OWN COUNSEL AS WELL.
IF I CAN JUST GET SOME DISTANCE...
...MAYBE HE WILL LET ME GO... NO LONGER CONSIDERING ME A THREAT TO WHATEVER *HE'S* DOING.

IT'S WORTH A TRY.

FWWITTTT

THUNK

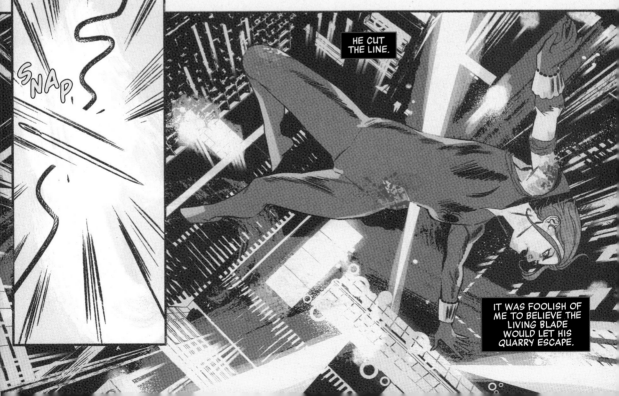

SNAP.

HE CUT THE LINE.

IT WAS FOOLISH OF ME TO BELIEVE THE LIVING BLADE WOULD LET HIS QUARRY ESCAPE.

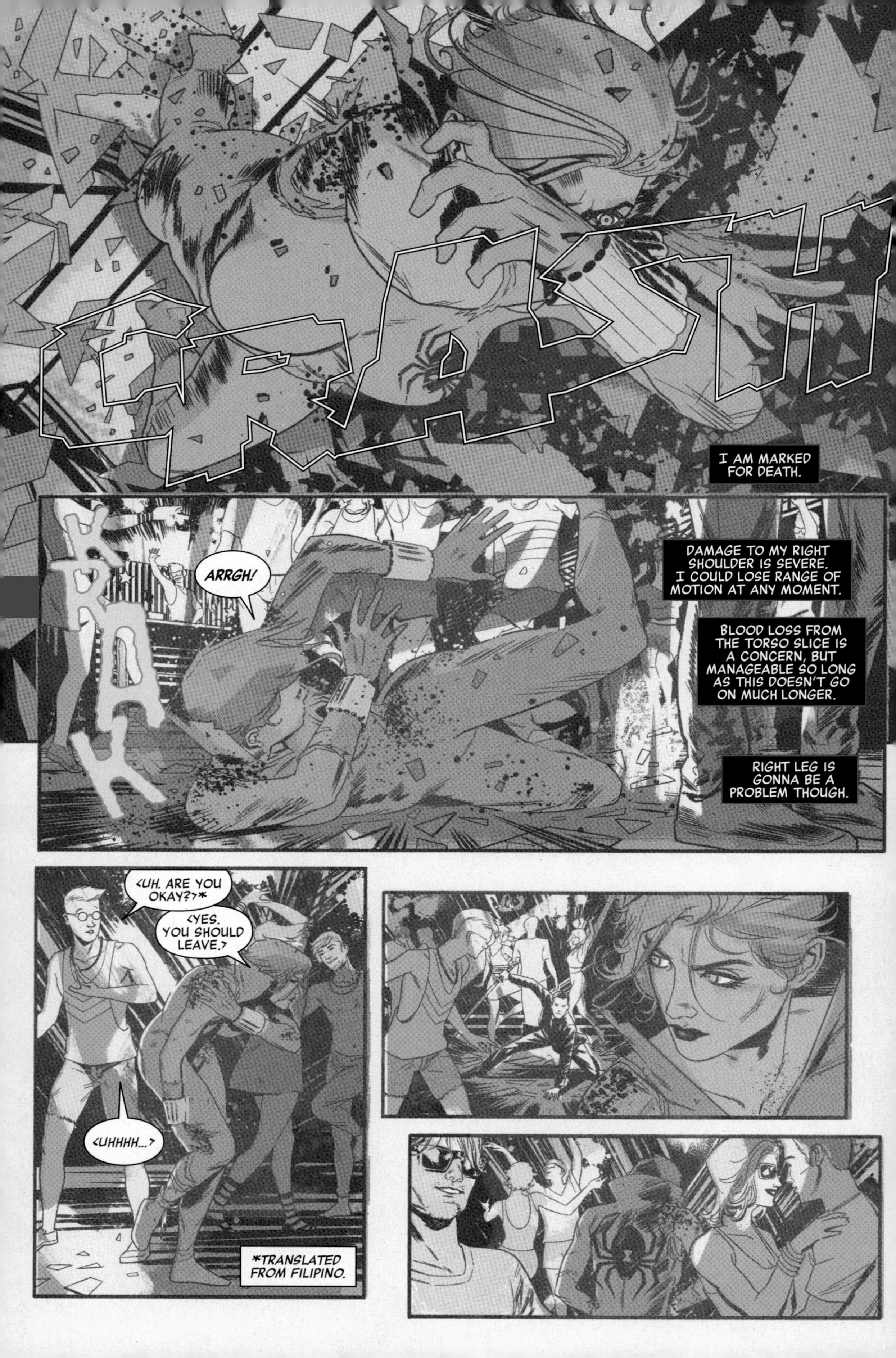
CRASH
I AM MARKED FOR DEATH.
KRAK
ARRGH!
DAMAGE TO MY RIGHT SHOULDER IS SEVERE. I COULD LOSE RANGE OF MOTION AT ANY MOMENT.
BLOOD LOSS FROM THE TORSO SLICE IS A CONCERN, BUT MANAGEABLE SO LONG AS THIS DOESN'T GO ON MUCH LONGER.
RIGHT LEG IS GONNA BE A PROBLEM THOUGH.
<UH. ARE YOU OKAY?>*
<YES. YOU SHOULD LEAVE.>
<UHHHH...>
*TRANSLATED FROM FILIPINO.

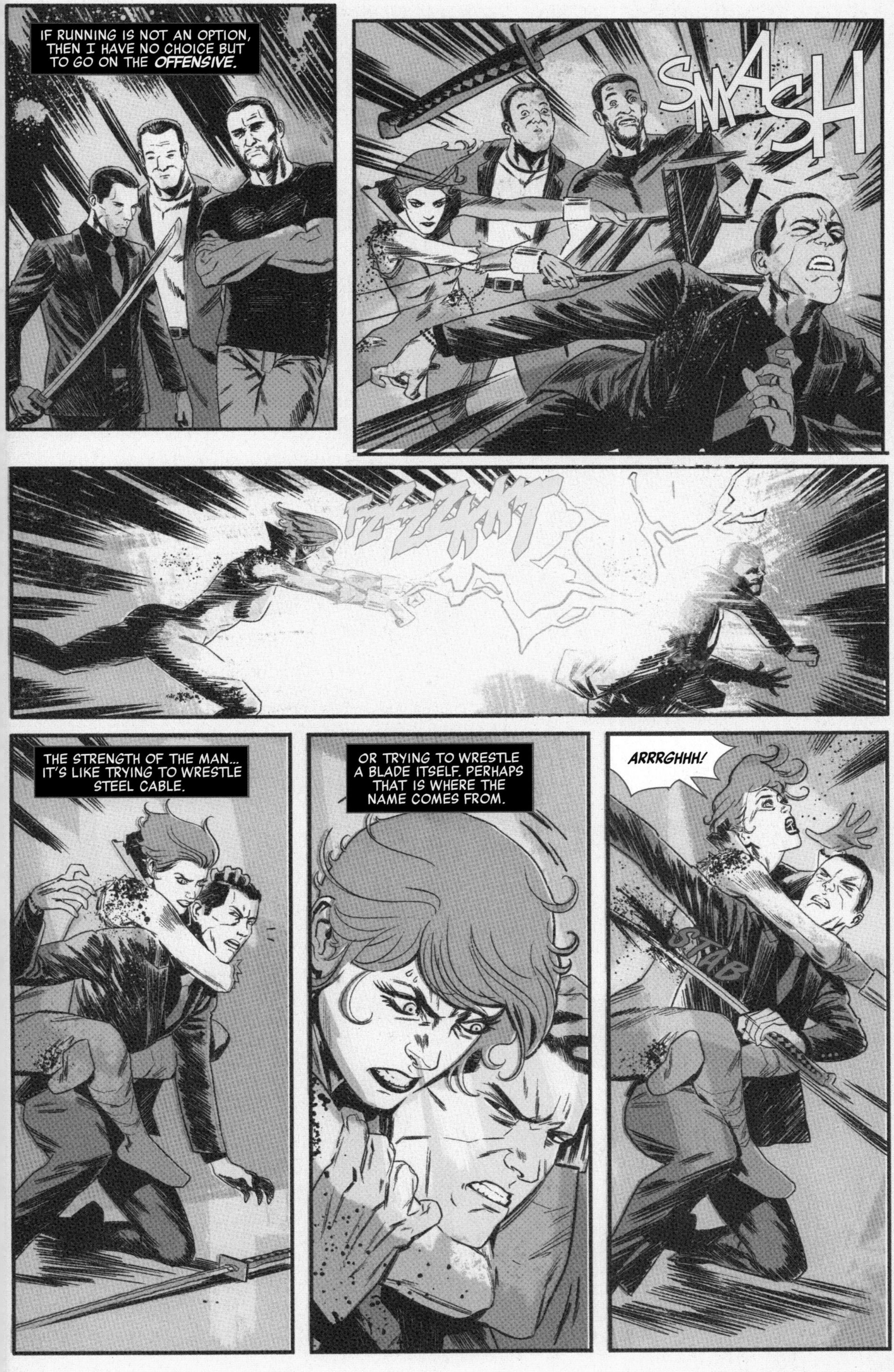
IF RUNNING IS NOT AN OPTION, THEN I HAVE NO CHOICE BUT TO GO ON THE *OFFENSIVE.*
SMASH
FZZZKKT
THE STRENGTH OF THE MAN... IT'S LIKE TRYING TO WRESTLE STEEL CABLE.
OR TRYING TO WRESTLE A BLADE ITSELF. PERHAPS THAT IS WHERE THE NAME COMES FROM.
ARRRGHHH!
STAB

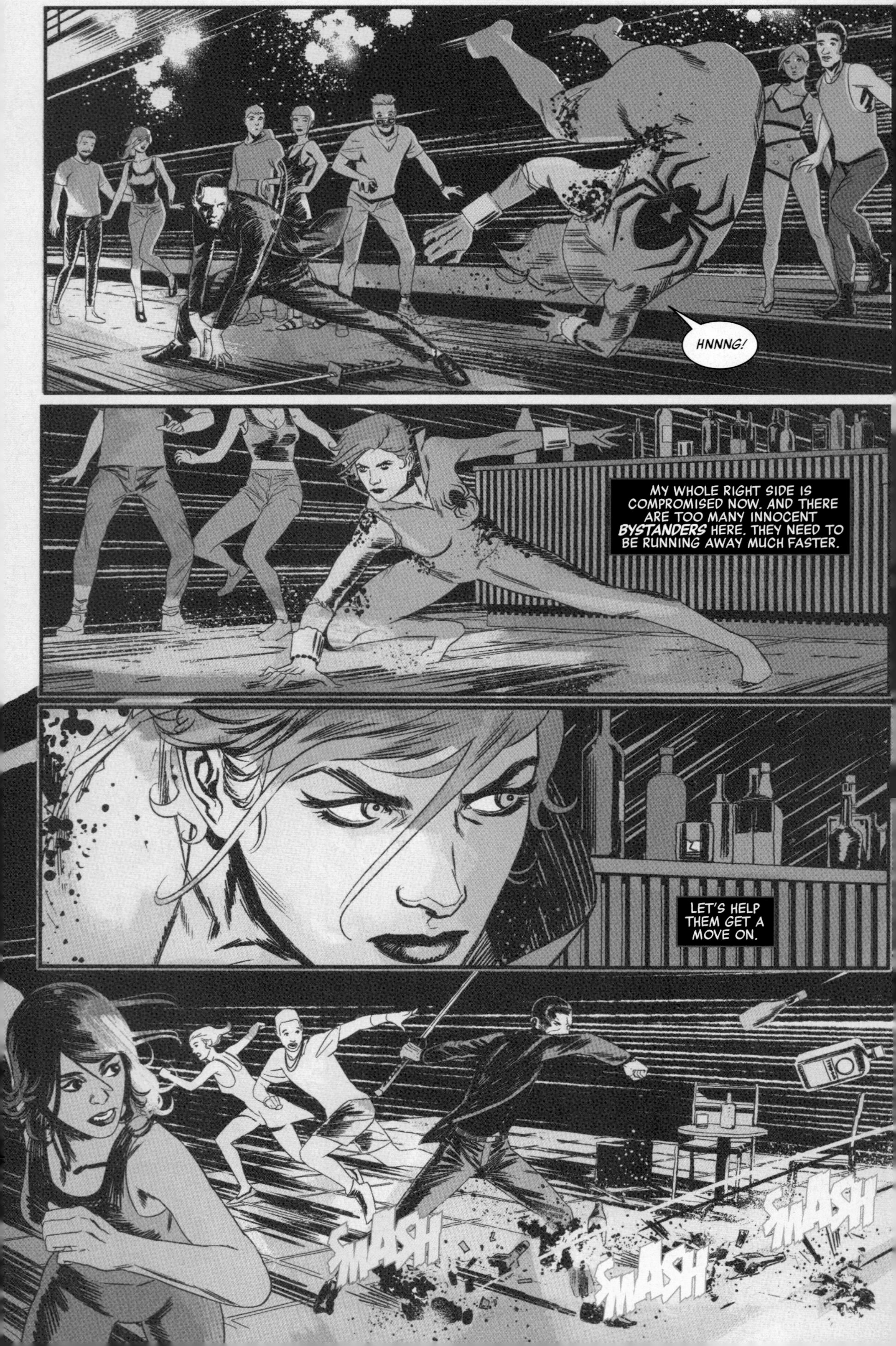
HNNNG!
MY WHOLE RIGHT SIDE IS COMPROMISED NOW. AND THERE ARE TOO MANY INNOCENT BYSTANDERS HERE. THEY NEED TO BE RUNNING AWAY MUCH FASTER.
LET'S HELP THEM GET A MOVE ON.
SMASH
SMASH
SMASH

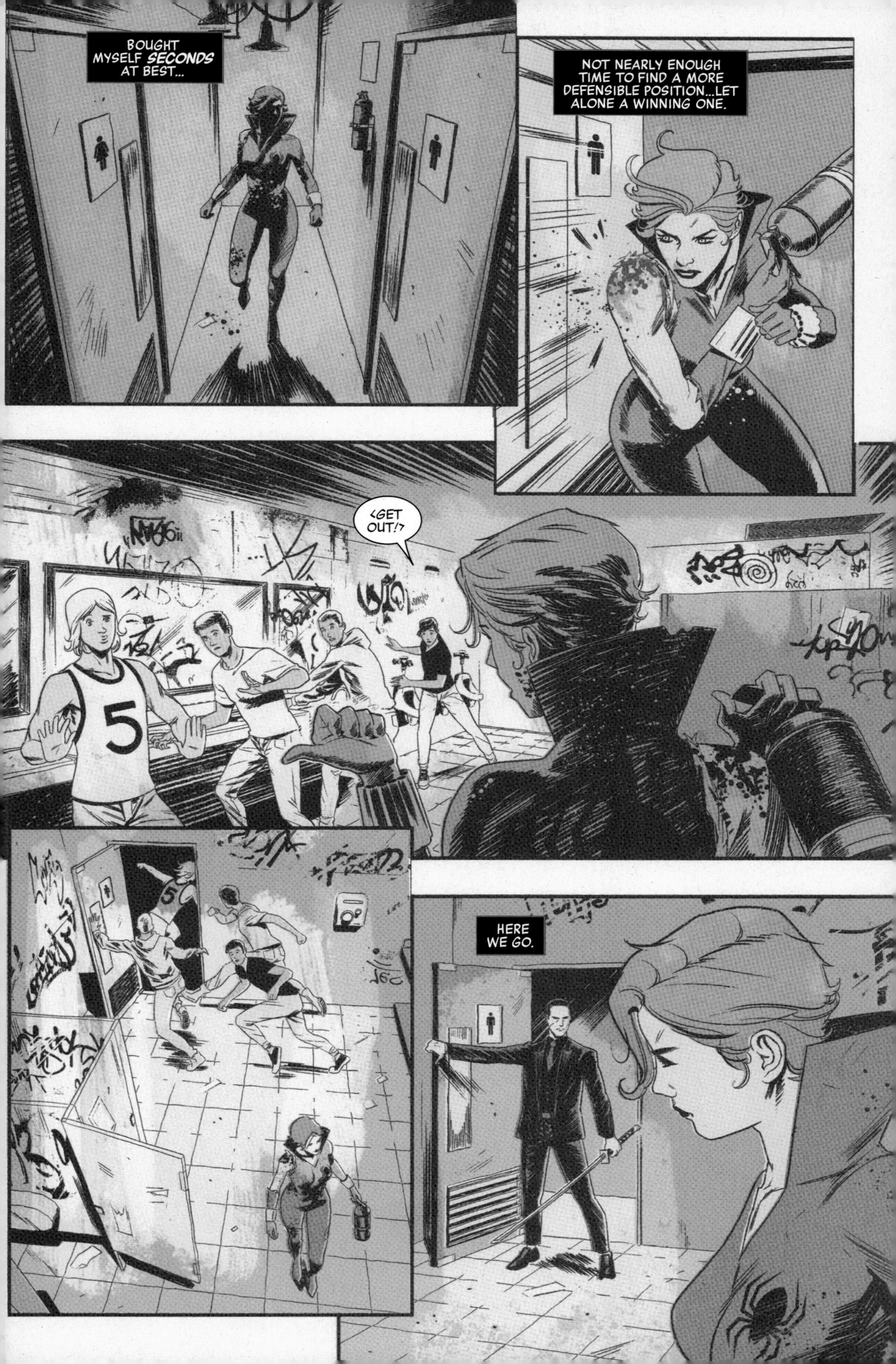
BOUGHT MYSELF SECONDS AT BEST...
NOT NEARLY ENOUGH TIME TO FIND A MORE DEFENSIBLE POSITION...LET ALONE A WINNING ONE.
<GET OUT!>
HERE WE GO.

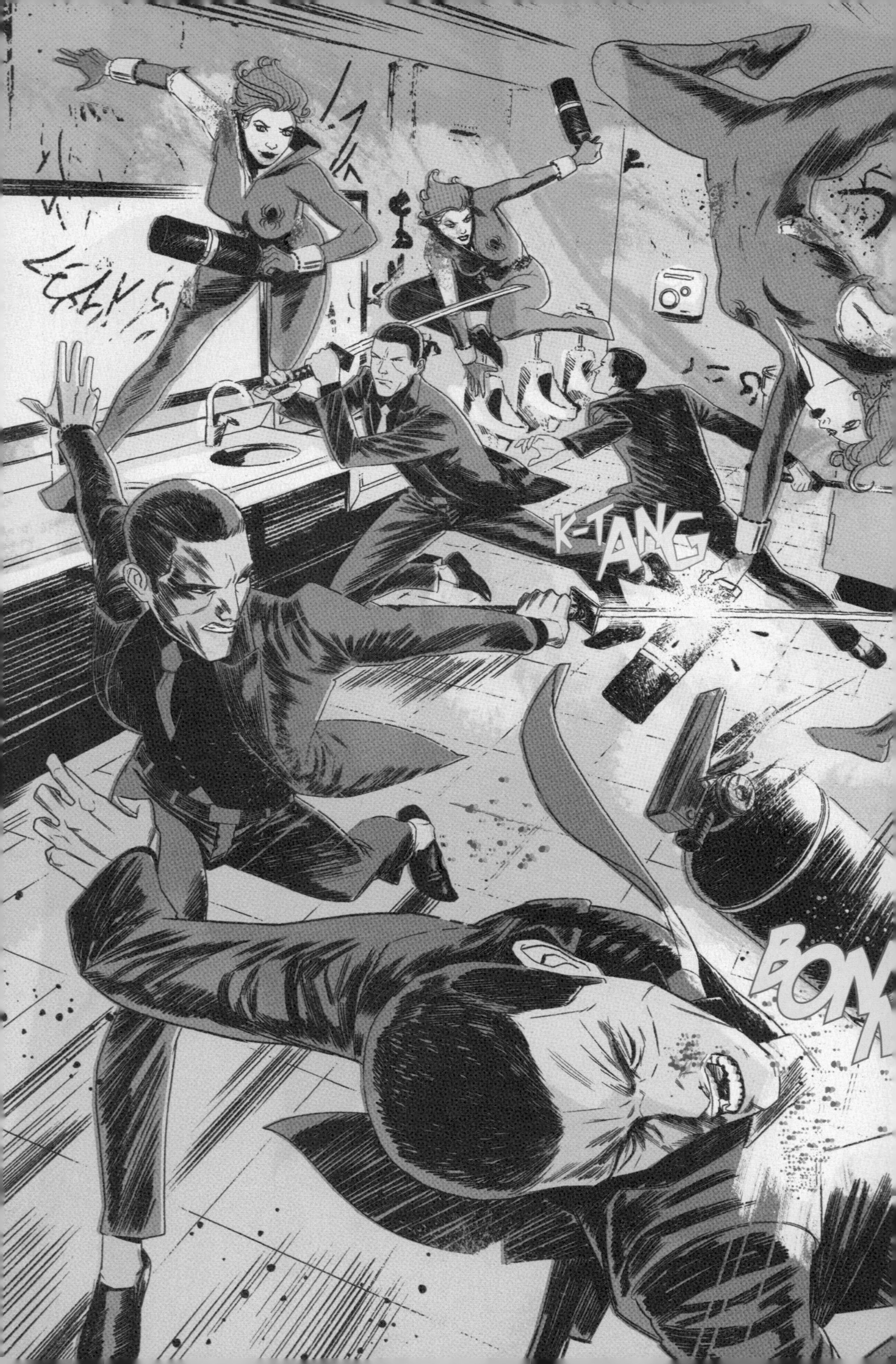

K-TANG
BON

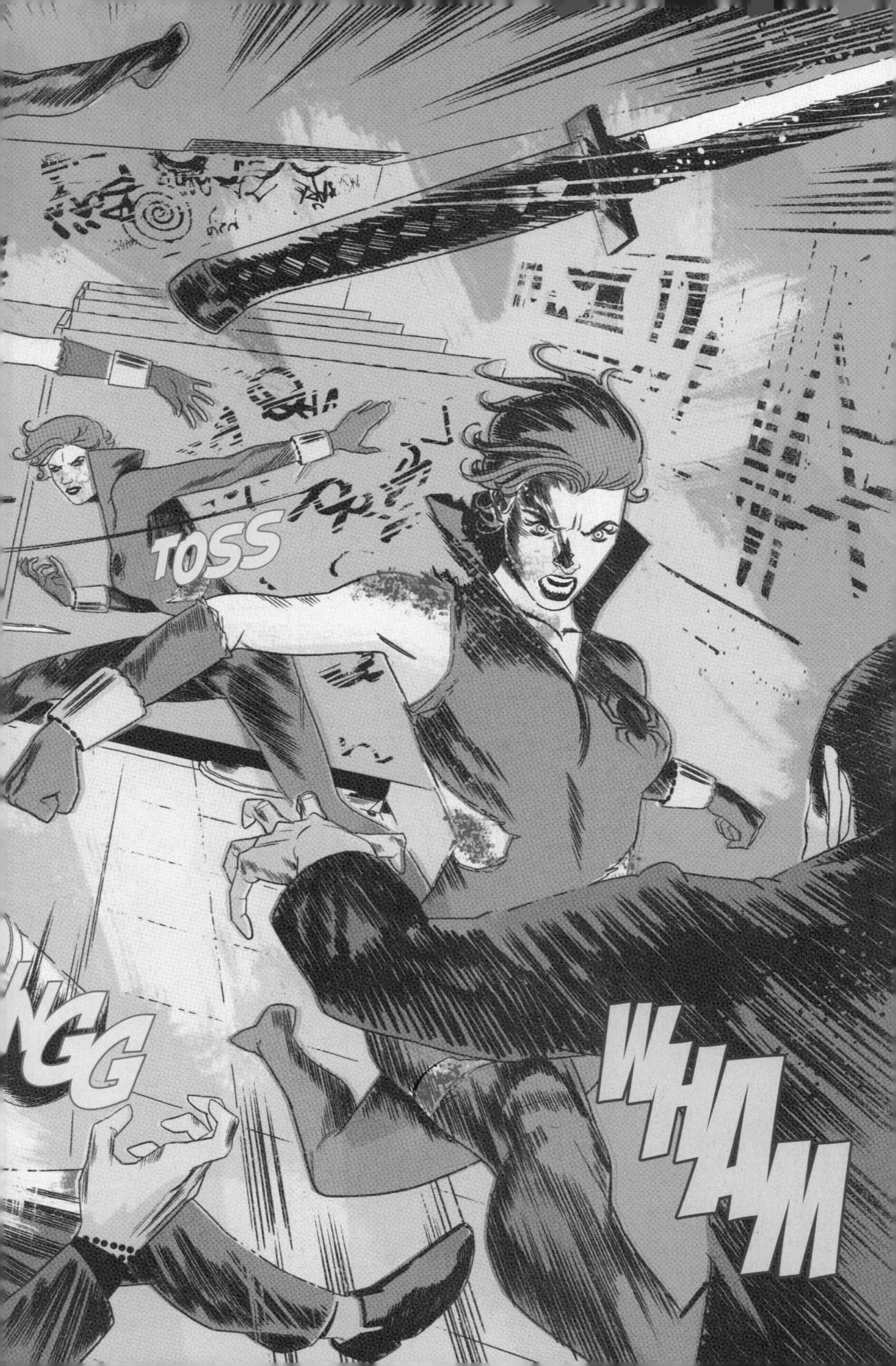
TOSS
NGG
WHAM

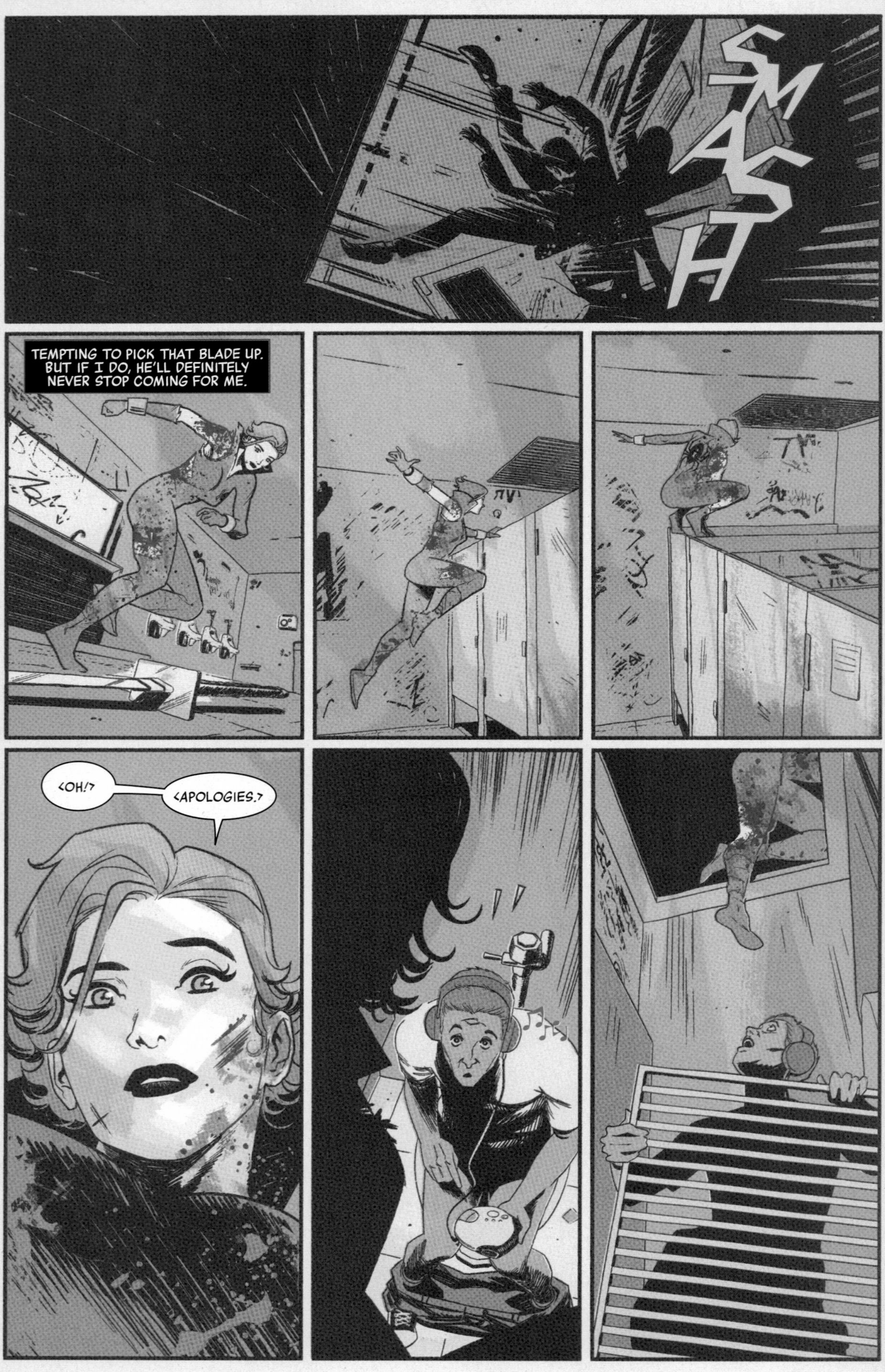
SMASH
TEMPTING TO PICK THAT BLADE UP. BUT IF I DO, HE'LL DEFINITELY NEVER STOP COMING FOR ME.
<OH!>
<APOLOGIES.>

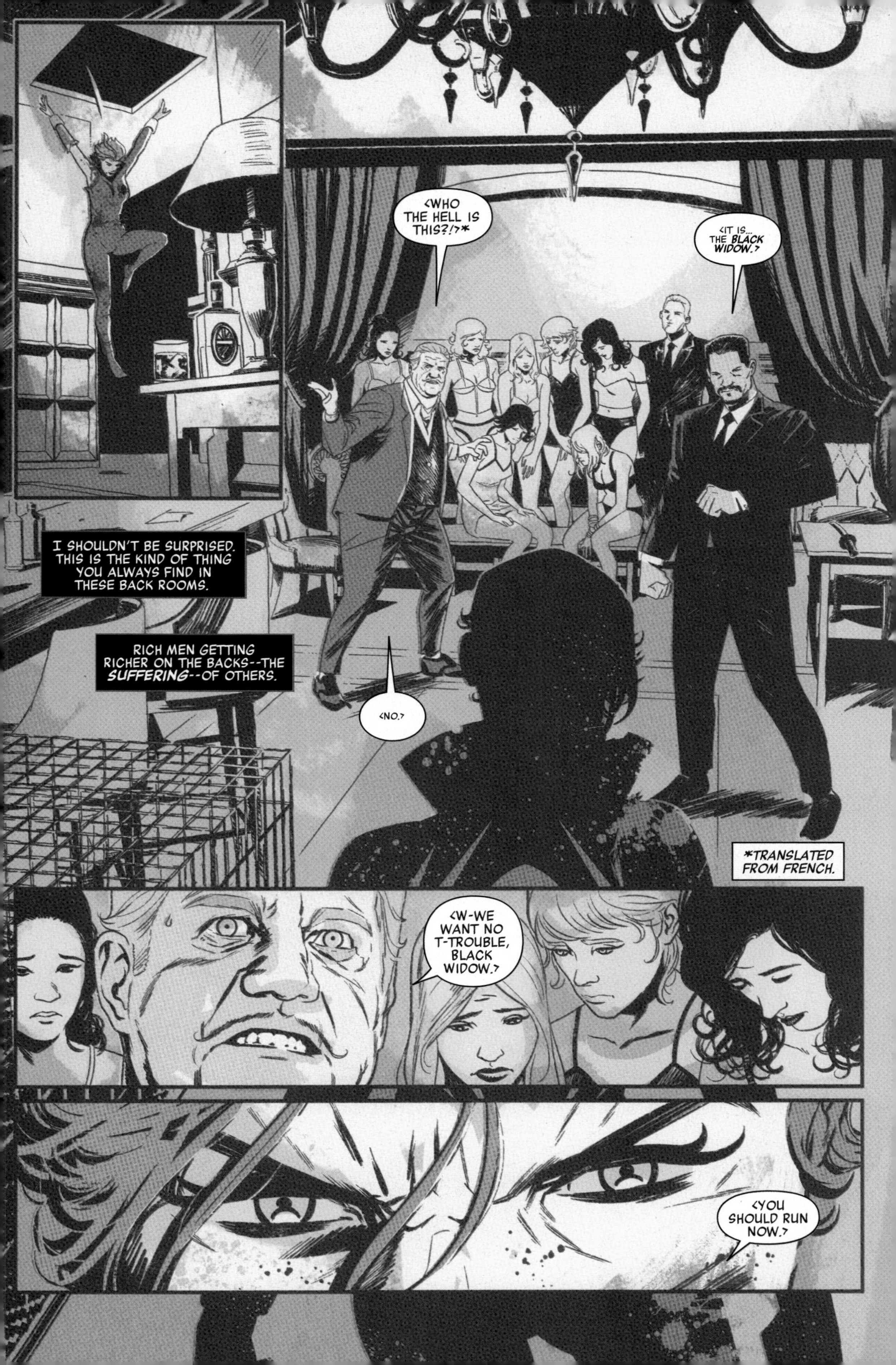

I SHOULDN'T BE SURPRISED. THIS IS THE KIND OF THING YOU ALWAYS FIND IN THESE BACK ROOMS.
RICH MEN GETTING RICHER ON THE BACKS--THE SUFFERING--OF OTHERS.
<WHO THE HELL IS THIS?!>*
<IT IS... THE BLACK WIDOW.>
<NO.>
*TRANSLATED FROM FRENCH.
<W-WE WANT NO T-TROUBLE, BLACK WIDOW.>
<YOU SHOULD RUN NOW.>

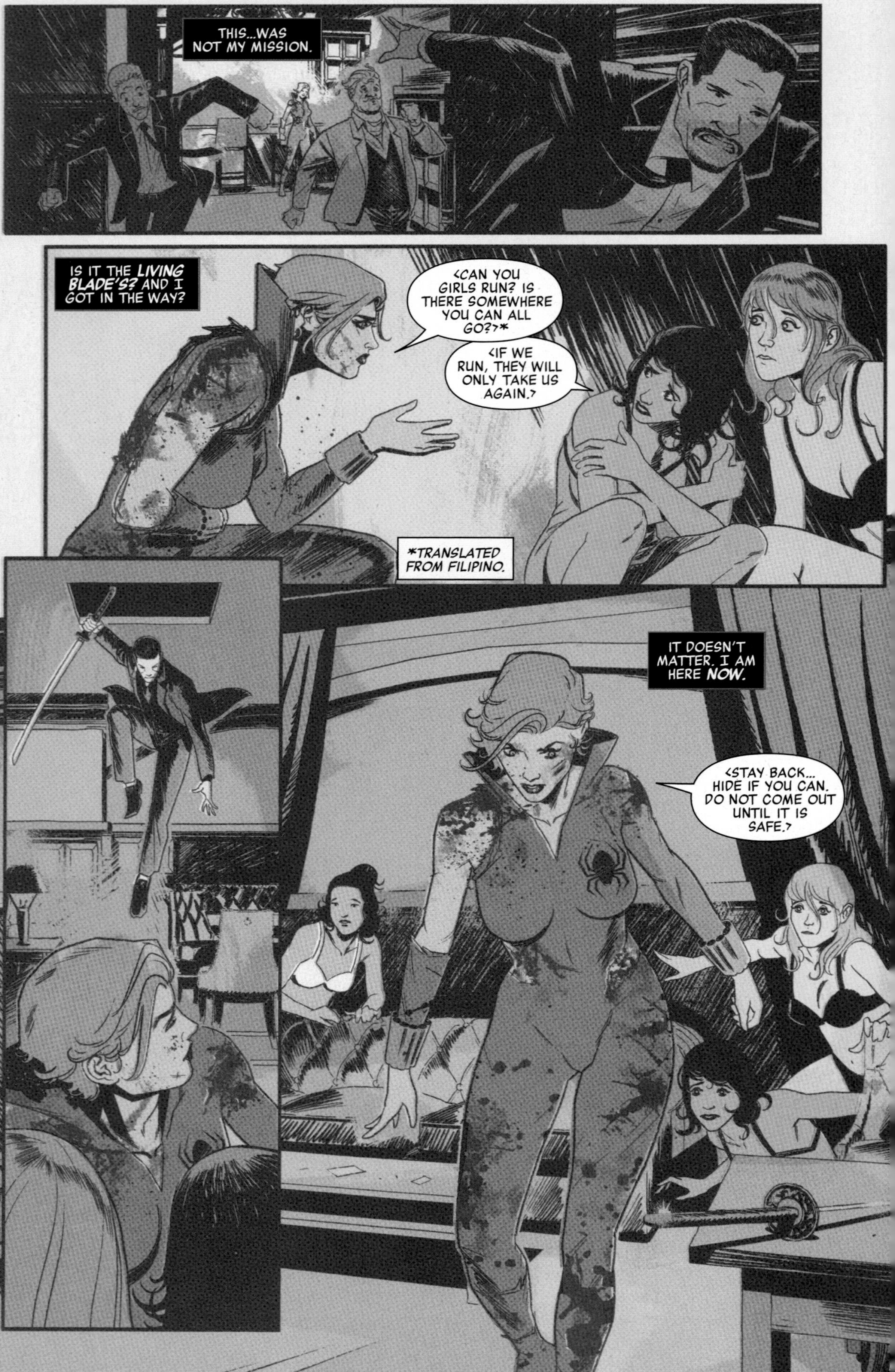
THIS...WAS NOT MY MISSION.
IS IT THE LIVING BLADE'S? AND I GOT IN THE WAY?
<CAN YOU GIRLS RUN? IS THERE SOMEWHERE YOU CAN ALL GO?>*
<IF WE RUN, THEY WILL ONLY TAKE US AGAIN.>
*TRANSLATED FROM FILIPINO.
IT DOESN'T MATTER. I AM HERE NOW.
<STAY BACK... HIDE IF YOU CAN. DO NOT COME OUT UNTIL IT IS SAFE.>

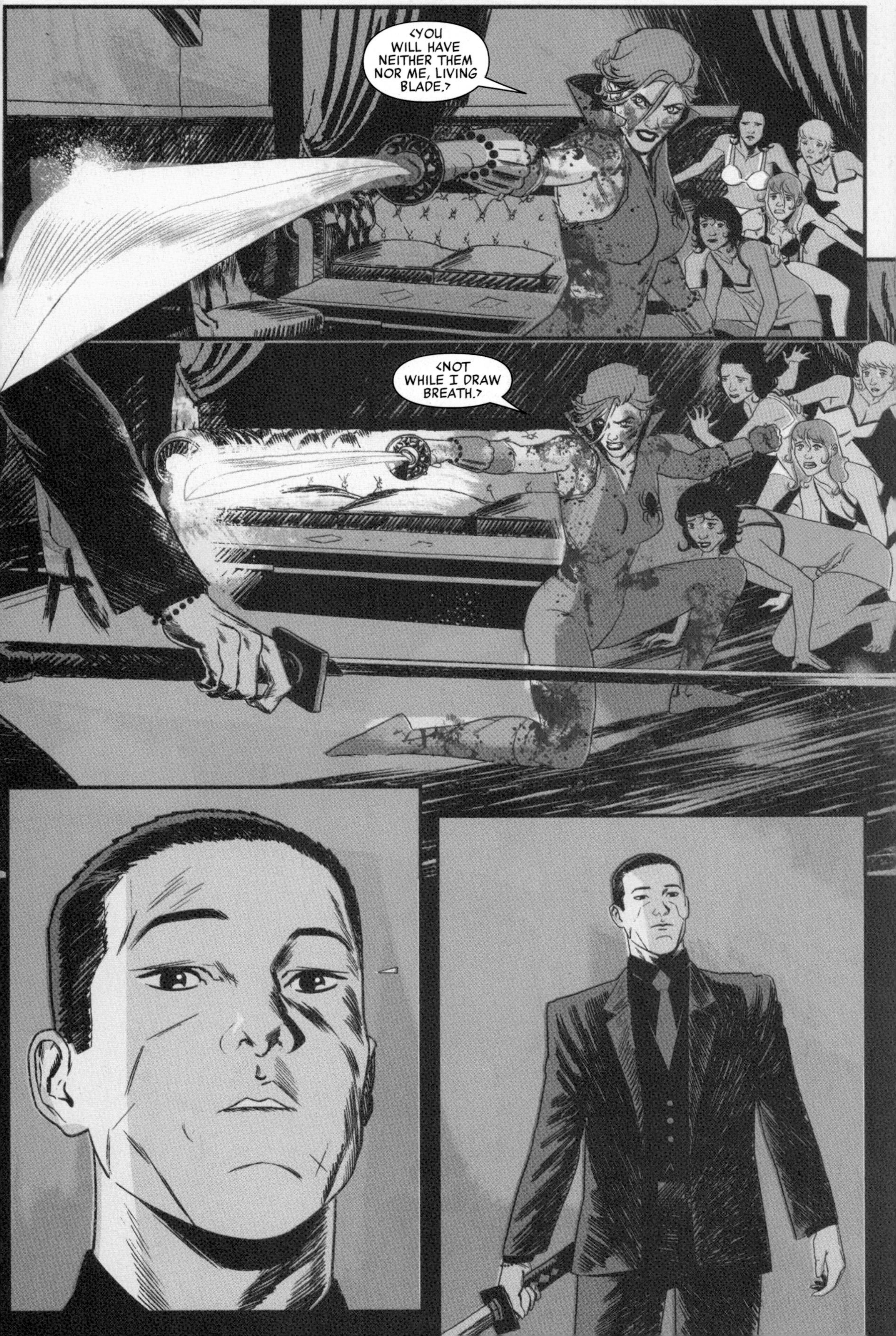
<YOU WILL HAVE NEITHER THEM NOR ME, LIVING BLADE.>
<NOT WHILE I DRAW BREATH.>

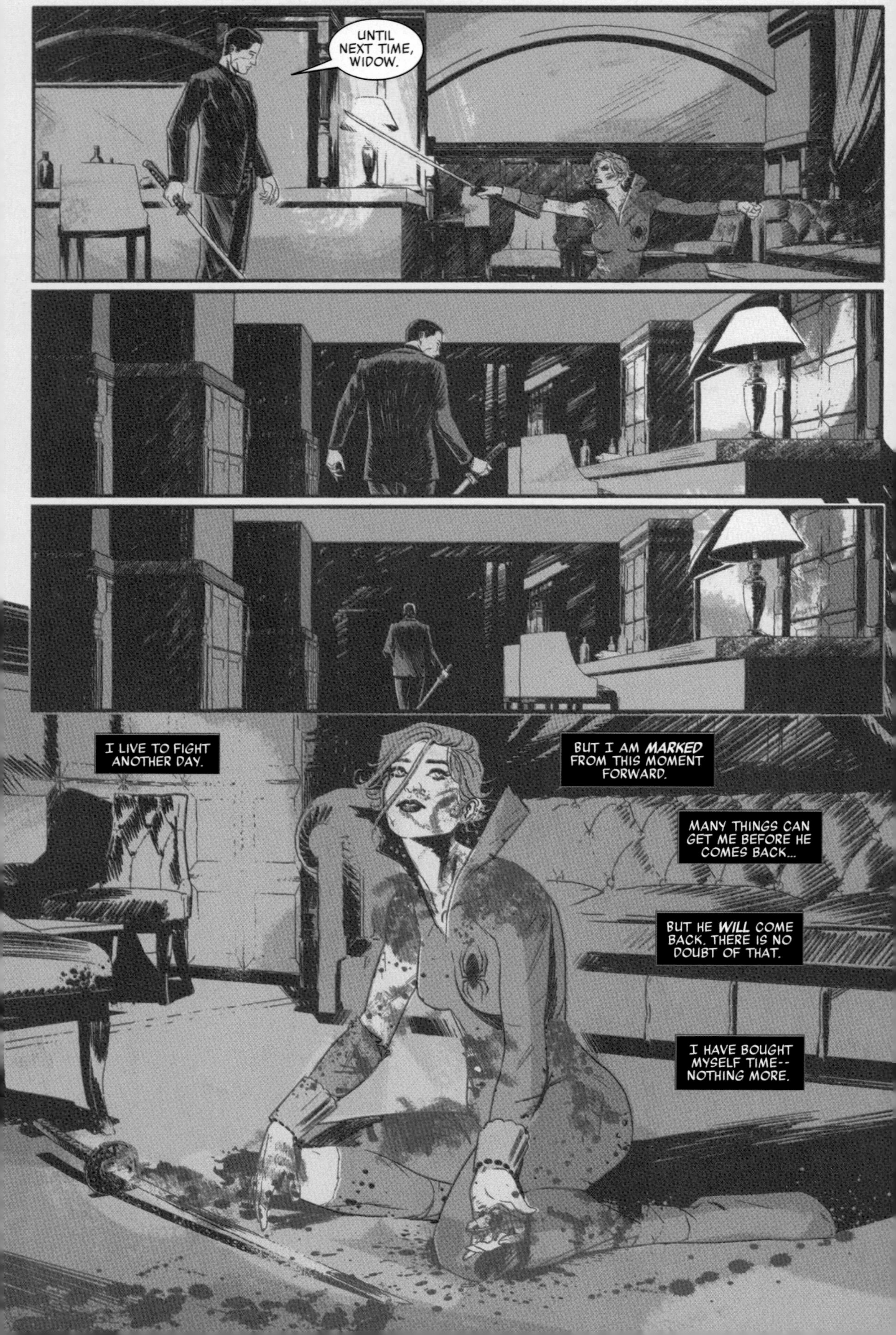
UNTIL NEXT TIME, WIDOW.
I LIVE TO FIGHT ANOTHER DAY.
BUT I AM MARKED FROM THIS MOMENT FORWARD.
MANY THINGS CAN GET ME BEFORE HE COMES BACK...
BUT HE WILL COME BACK. THERE IS NO DOUBT OF THAT.
I HAVE BOUGHT MYSELF TIME-- NOTHING MORE.

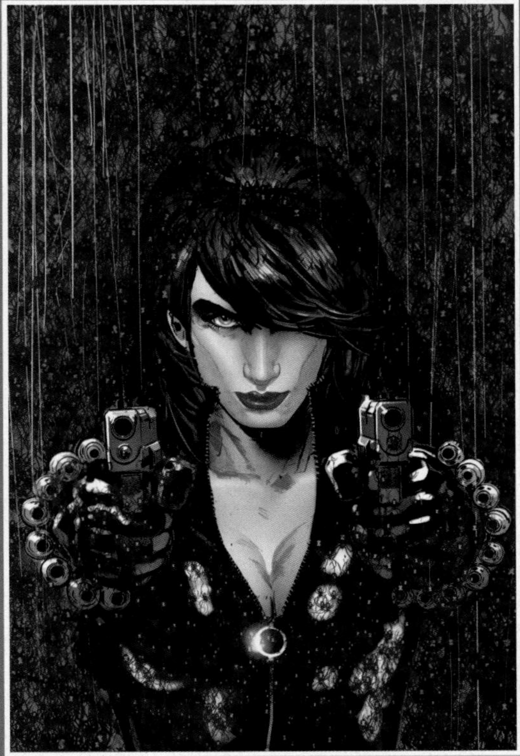

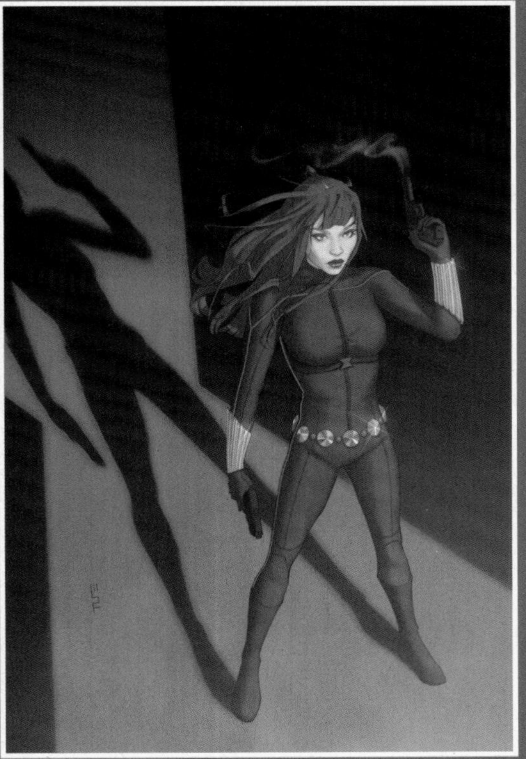

#14 VARIANT BY
PHIL JIMENEZ & MARTE GRACIA

#15 VARIANT BY
W. SCOTT FORBES

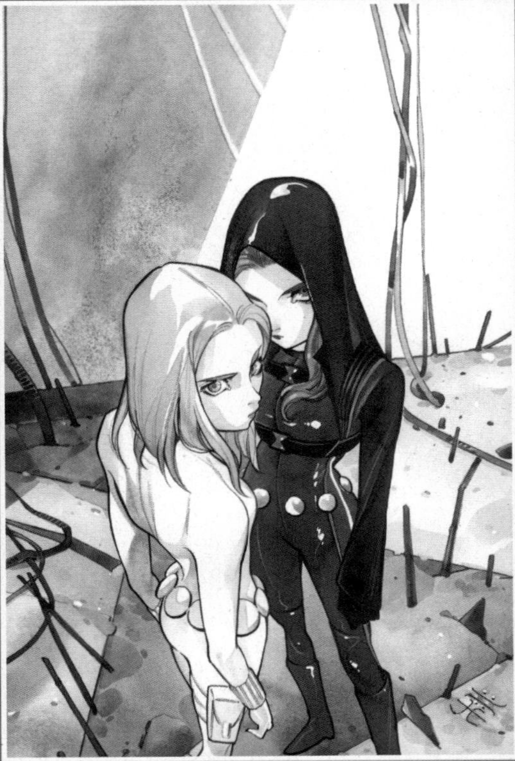

#15 VARIANT BY
PEACH MOMOKO

FOURTEEN

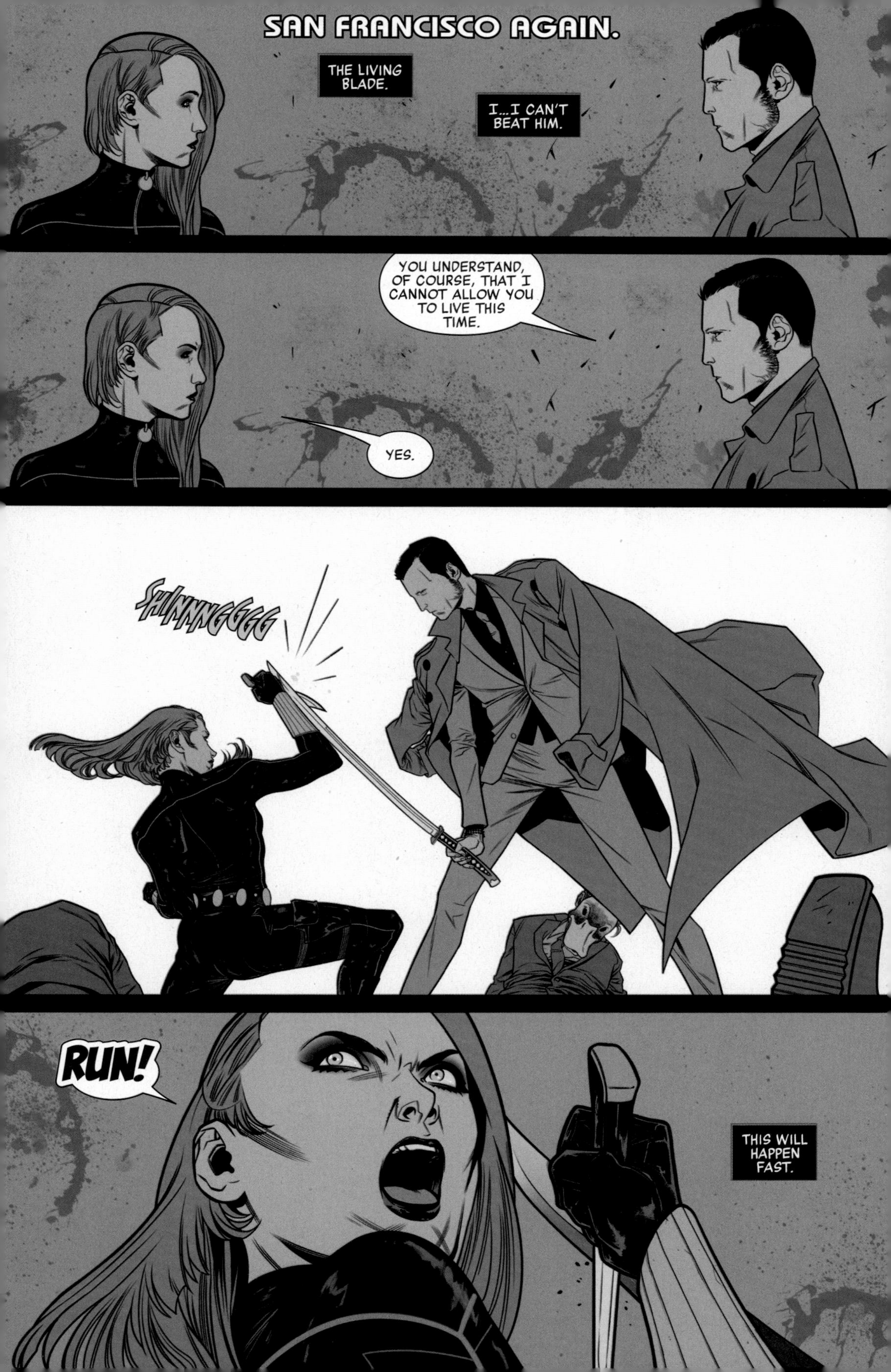
SAN FRANCISCO AGAIN.
THE LIVING BLADE.
I...I CAN'T BEAT HIM.
YOU UNDERSTAND, OF COURSE, THAT I CANNOT ALLOW YOU TO LIVE THIS TIME.
YES.
SHINNNGGGG
RUN!
THIS WILL HAPPEN FAST.

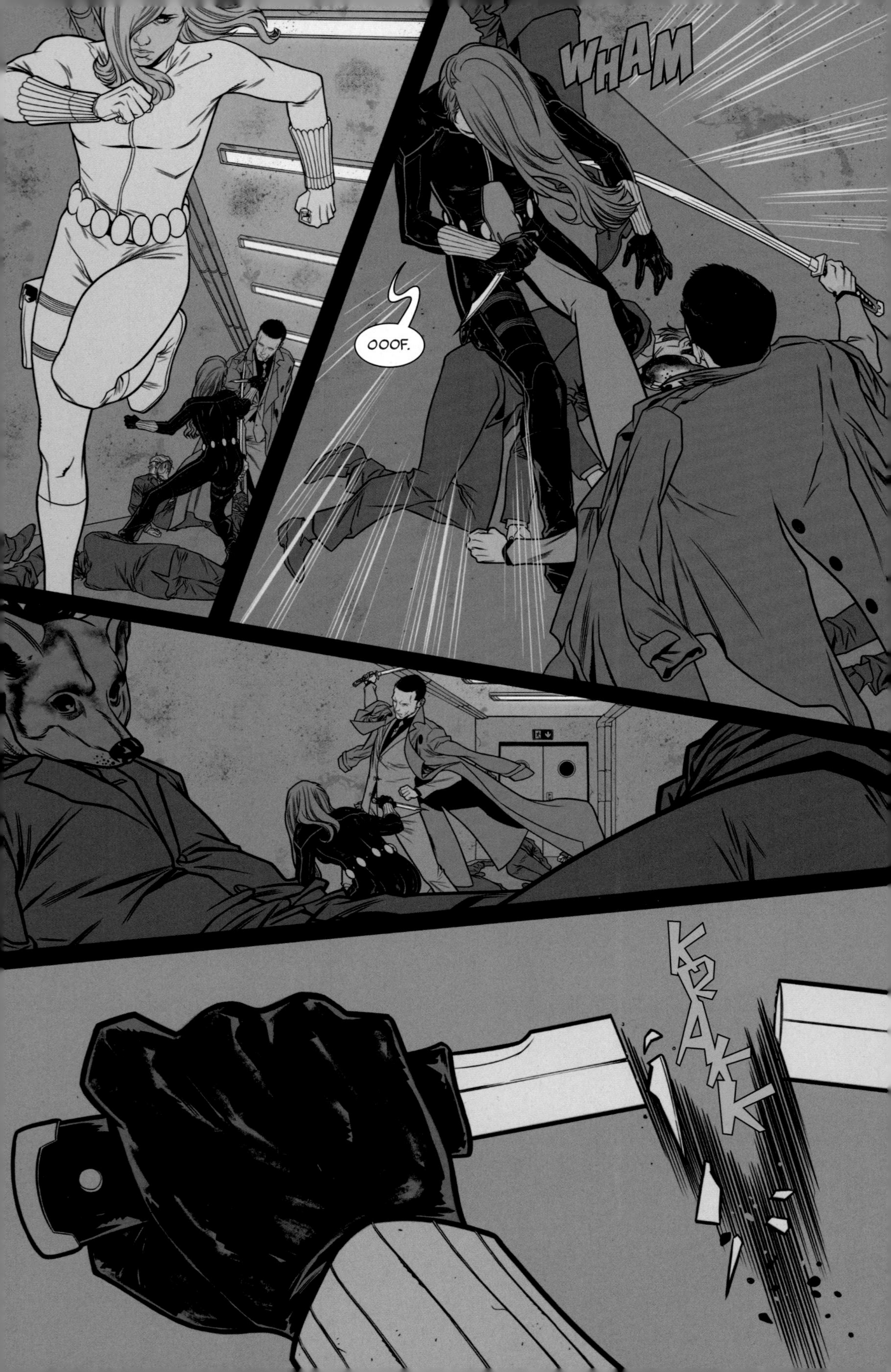
WHAM
OOOF.
KRAKK

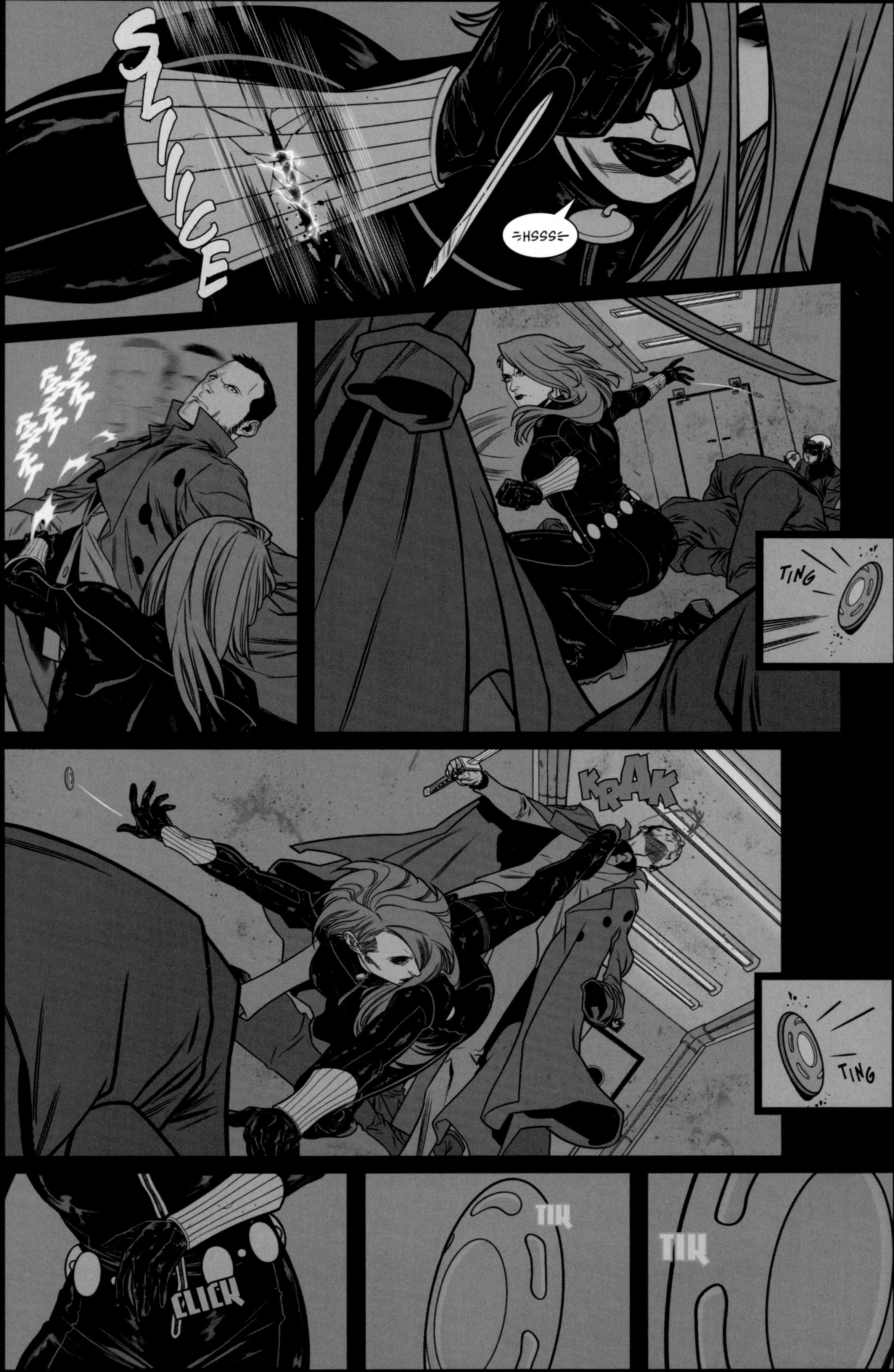
SLIIICE
HSSS
TING
KRAK
TING
CLICK
TIK
TIK

BOOM

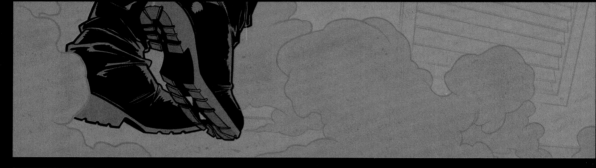

KLANG

STOP. SLOW DOWN.

CONCENTRATE.

YELENA WILL DO WHAT SHE KNOWS TO DO. IT'S FINE.

NOW MOVE.

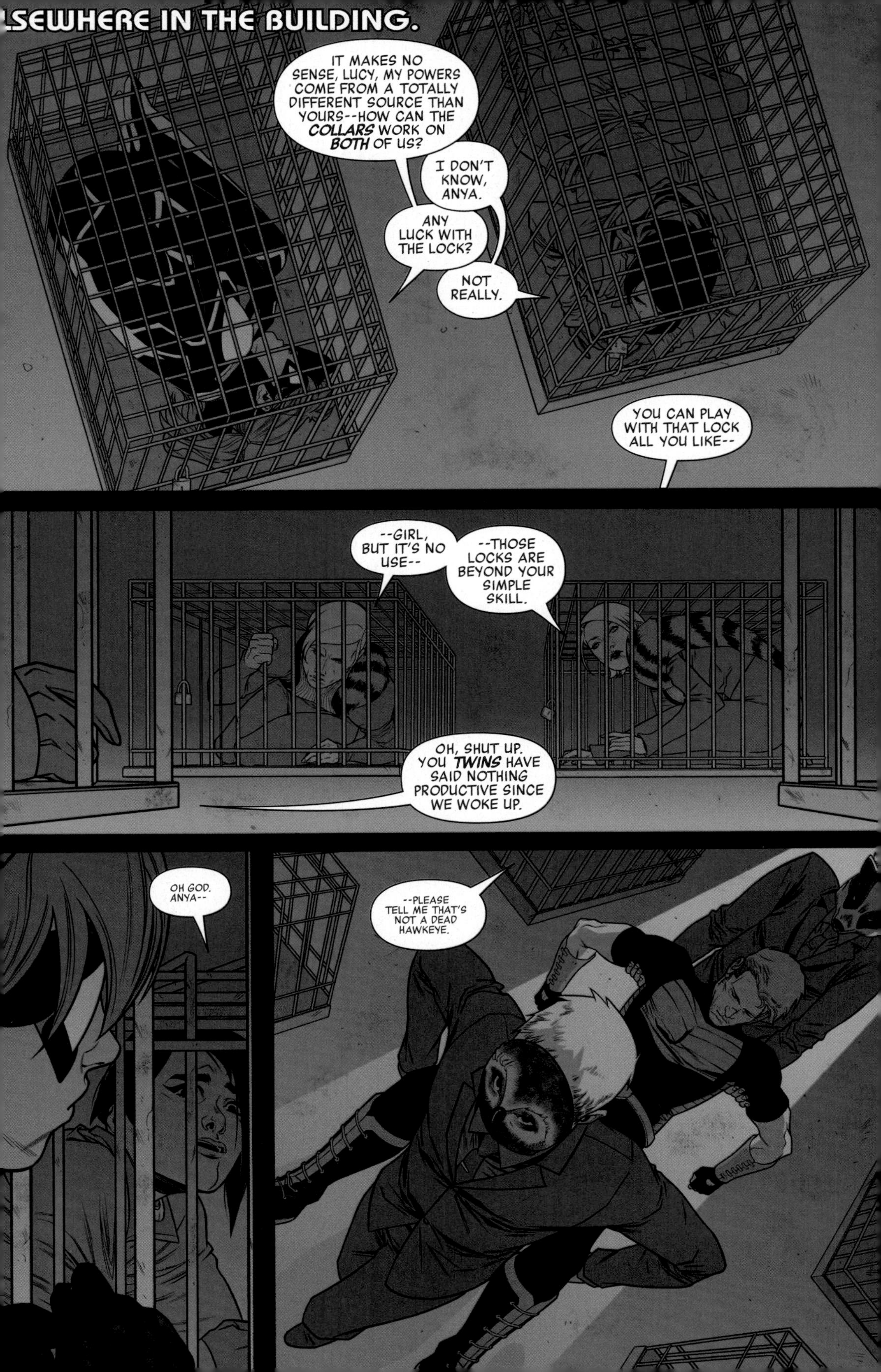
LSEWHERE IN THE BUILDING.
IT MAKES NO SENSE, LUCY, MY POWERS COME FROM A TOTALLY DIFFERENT SOURCE THAN YOURS--HOW CAN THE COLLARS WORK ON BOTH OF US?
I DON'T KNOW, ANYA.
ANY LUCK WITH THE LOCK?
NOT REALLY.
YOU CAN PLAY WITH THAT LOCK ALL YOU LIKE--
--GIRL, BUT IT'S NO USE--
--THOSE LOCKS ARE BEYOND YOUR SIMPLE SKILL.
OH, SHUT UP. YOU TWINS HAVE SAID NOTHING PRODUCTIVE SINCE WE WOKE UP.
OH GOD. ANYA--
--PLEASE TELL ME THAT'S NOT A DEAD HAWKEYE.

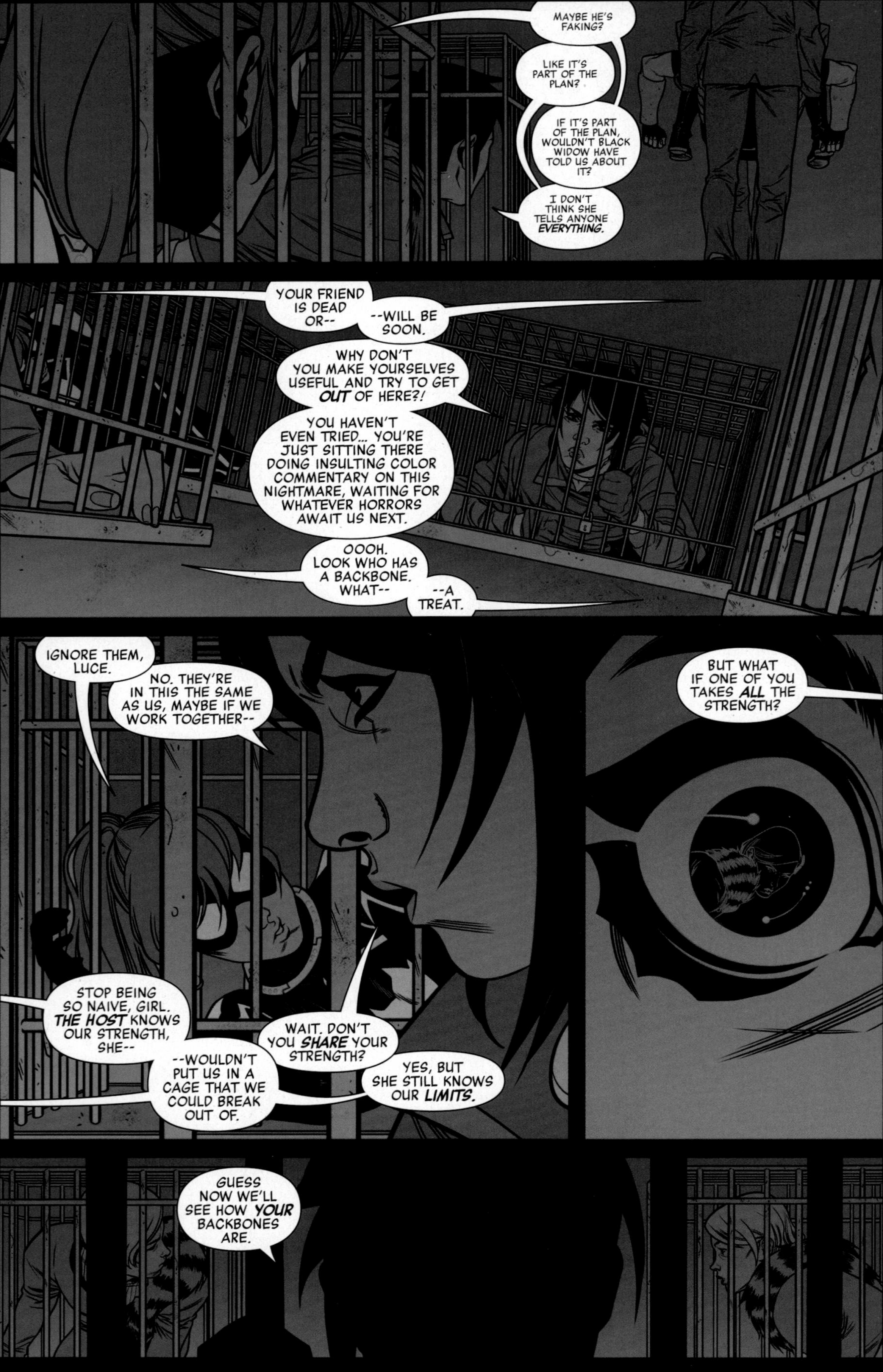
MAYBE HE'S FAKING?
LIKE IT'S PART OF THE PLAN?
IF IT'S PART OF THE PLAN, WOULDN'T BLACK WIDOW HAVE TOLD US ABOUT IT?
I DON'T THINK SHE TELLS ANYONE **EVERYTHING.**
YOUR FRIEND IS DEAD OR--
--WILL BE SOON.
WHY DON'T YOU MAKE YOURSELVES USEFUL AND TRY TO GET ***OUT*** OF HERE?!
YOU HAVEN'T EVEN TRIED... YOU'RE JUST SITTING THERE DOING INSULTING COLOR COMMENTARY ON THIS NIGHTMARE, WAITING FOR WHATEVER HORRORS AWAIT US NEXT.
OOOH. LOOK WHO HAS A BACKBONE. WHAT--
--A TREAT.
IGNORE THEM, LUCE.
NO. THEY'RE IN THIS THE SAME AS US, MAYBE IF WE WORK TOGETHER--
BUT WHAT IF ONE OF YOU TAKES ***ALL*** THE STRENGTH?
STOP BEING SO NAIVE, GIRL. ***THE HOST*** KNOWS OUR STRENGTH, SHE--
--WOULDN'T PUT US IN A CAGE THAT WE COULD BREAK OUT OF.
WAIT. DON'T YOU ***SHARE*** YOUR STRENGTH?
YES, BUT SHE STILL KNOWS OUR ***LIMITS.***
GUESS NOW WE'LL SEE HOW ***YOUR*** BACKBONES ARE.

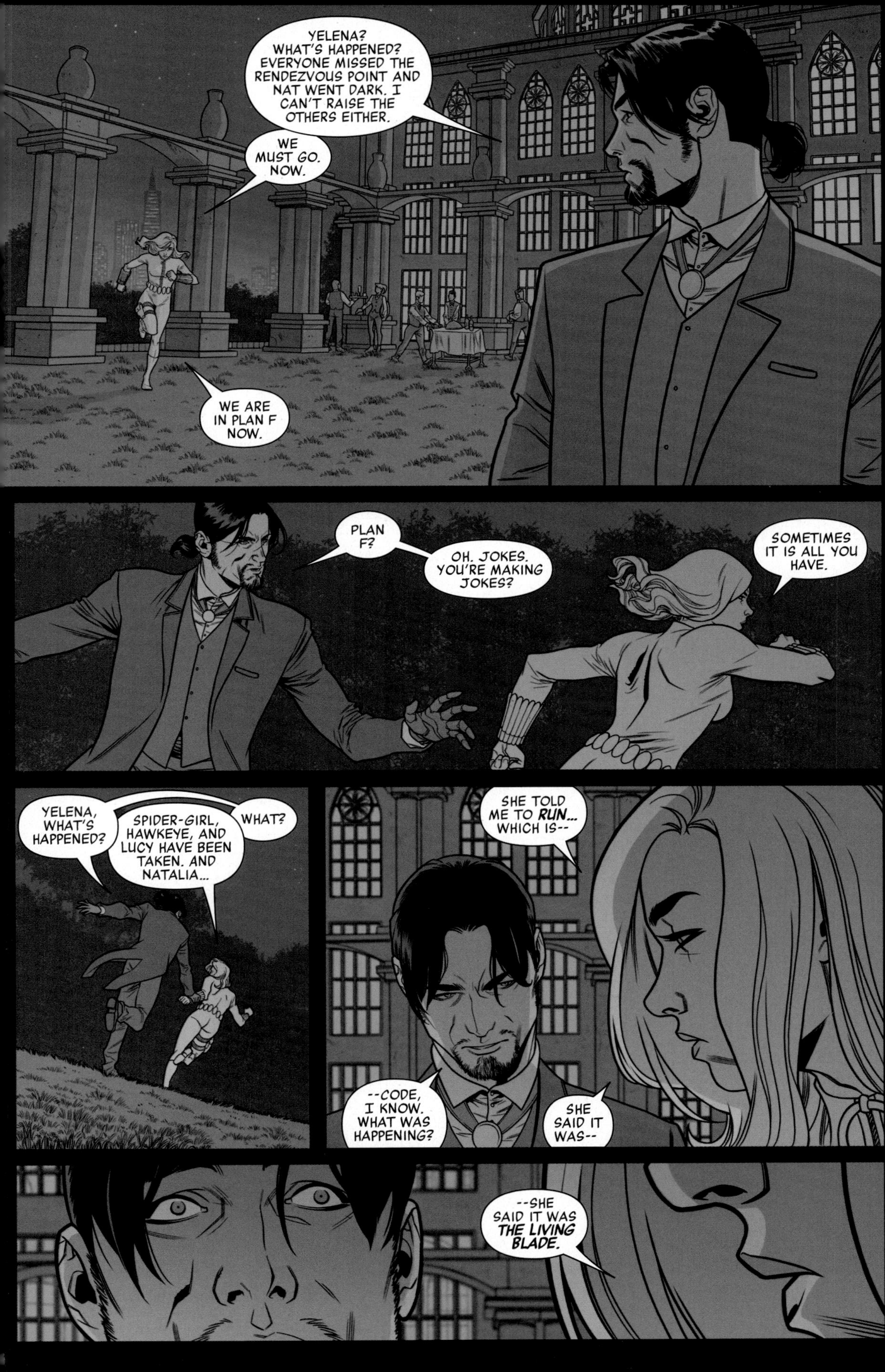
YELENA? WHAT'S HAPPENED? EVERYONE MISSED THE RENDEZVOUS POINT AND NAT WENT DARK. I CAN'T RAISE THE OTHERS EITHER.
WE MUST GO. NOW.
WE ARE IN PLAN F NOW.
PLAN F?
OH. JOKES. YOU'RE MAKING JOKES?
SOMETIMES IT IS ALL YOU HAVE.
YELENA, WHAT'S HAPPENED?
SPIDER-GIRL, HAWKEYE, AND LUCY HAVE BEEN TAKEN. AND NATALIA...
WHAT?
SHE TOLD ME TO RUN... WHICH IS--
--CODE, I KNOW. WHAT WAS HAPPENING?
SHE SAID IT WAS--
--SHE SAID IT WAS THE LIVING BLADE.

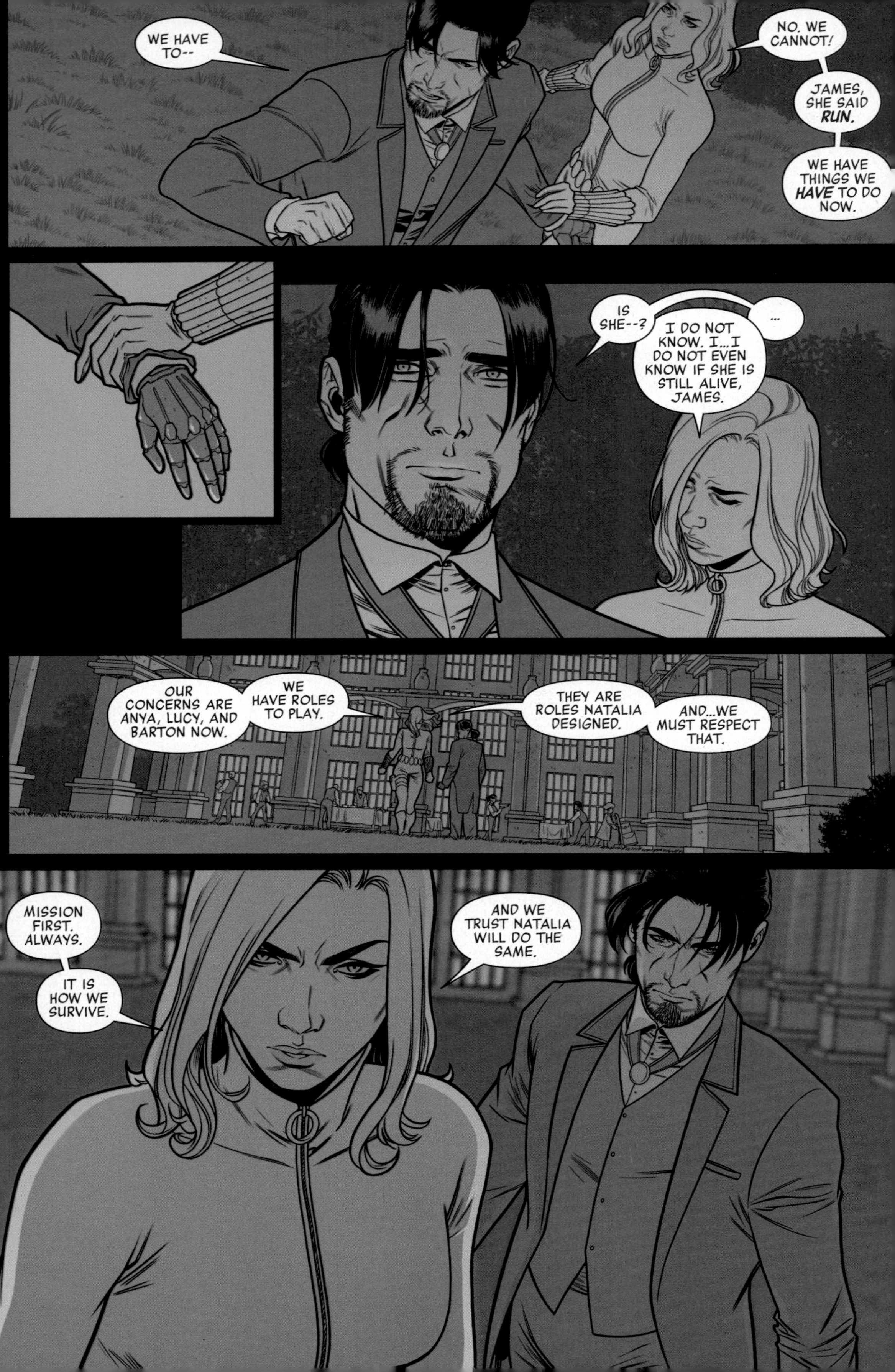
WE HAVE TO--
NO. WE CANNOT!
JAMES, SHE SAID RUN.
WE HAVE THINGS WE HAVE TO DO NOW.
IS SHE--?
...
I DO NOT KNOW. I...I DO NOT EVEN KNOW IF SHE IS STILL ALIVE, JAMES.
OUR CONCERNS ARE ANYA, LUCY, AND BARTON NOW.
WE HAVE ROLES TO PLAY.
THEY ARE ROLES NATALIA DESIGNED.
AND...WE MUST RESPECT THAT.
MISSION FIRST. ALWAYS.
IT IS HOW WE SURVIVE.
AND WE TRUST NATALIA WILL DO THE SAME.

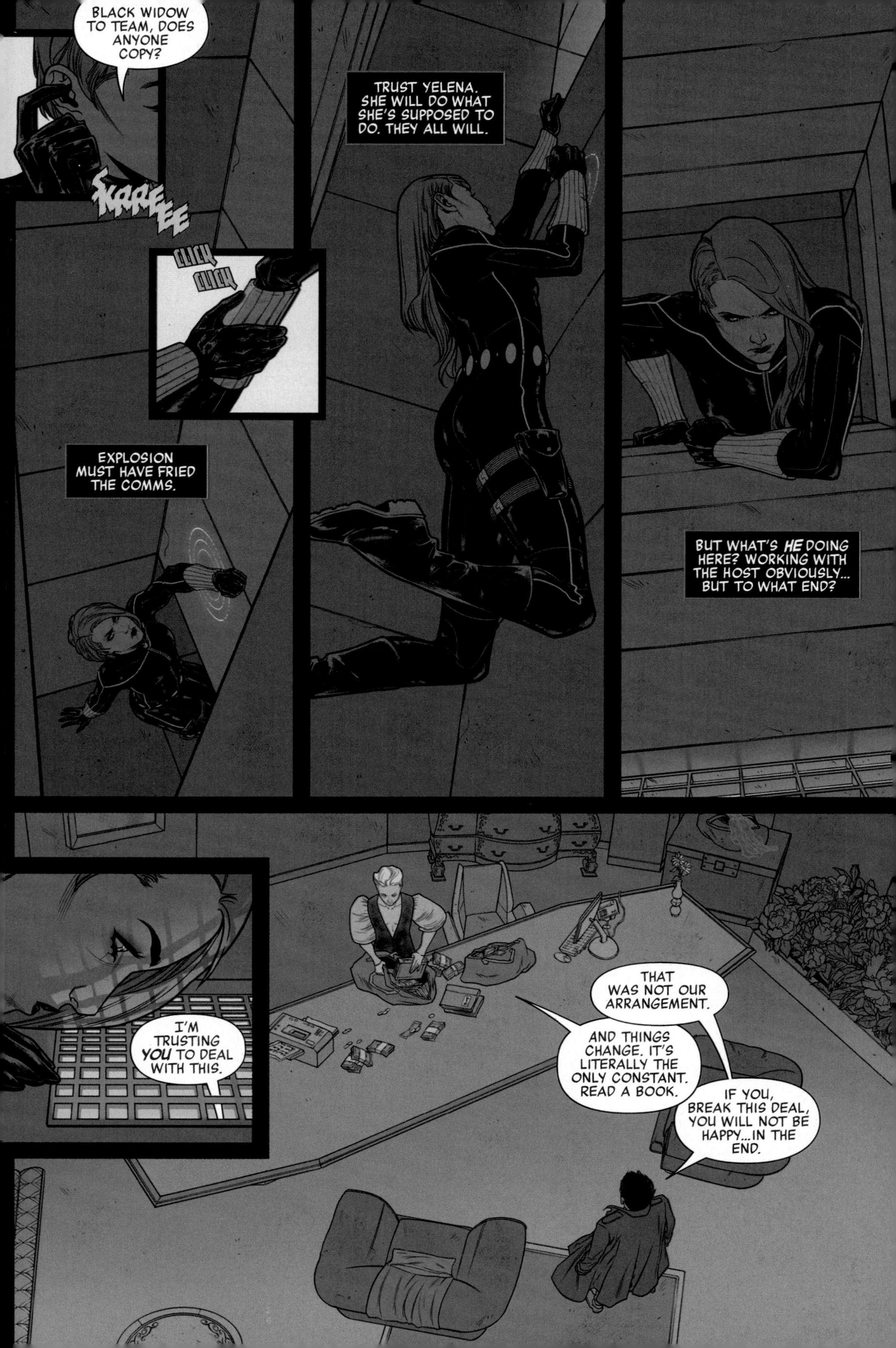

BLACK WIDOW TO TEAM, DOES ANYONE COPY?
SKREEEE
CLICK CLICK
EXPLOSION MUST HAVE FRIED THE COMMS.
TRUST YELENA. SHE WILL DO WHAT SHE'S SUPPOSED TO DO. THEY ALL WILL.
BUT WHAT'S *HE* DOING HERE? WORKING WITH THE HOST OBVIOUSLY... BUT TO WHAT END?
I'M TRUSTING *YOU* TO DEAL WITH THIS.
THAT WAS NOT OUR ARRANGEMENT.
AND THINGS CHANGE. IT'S LITERALLY THE ONLY CONSTANT. READ A BOOK.
IF YOU, BREAK THIS DEAL, YOU WILL NOT BE HAPPY...IN THE END.

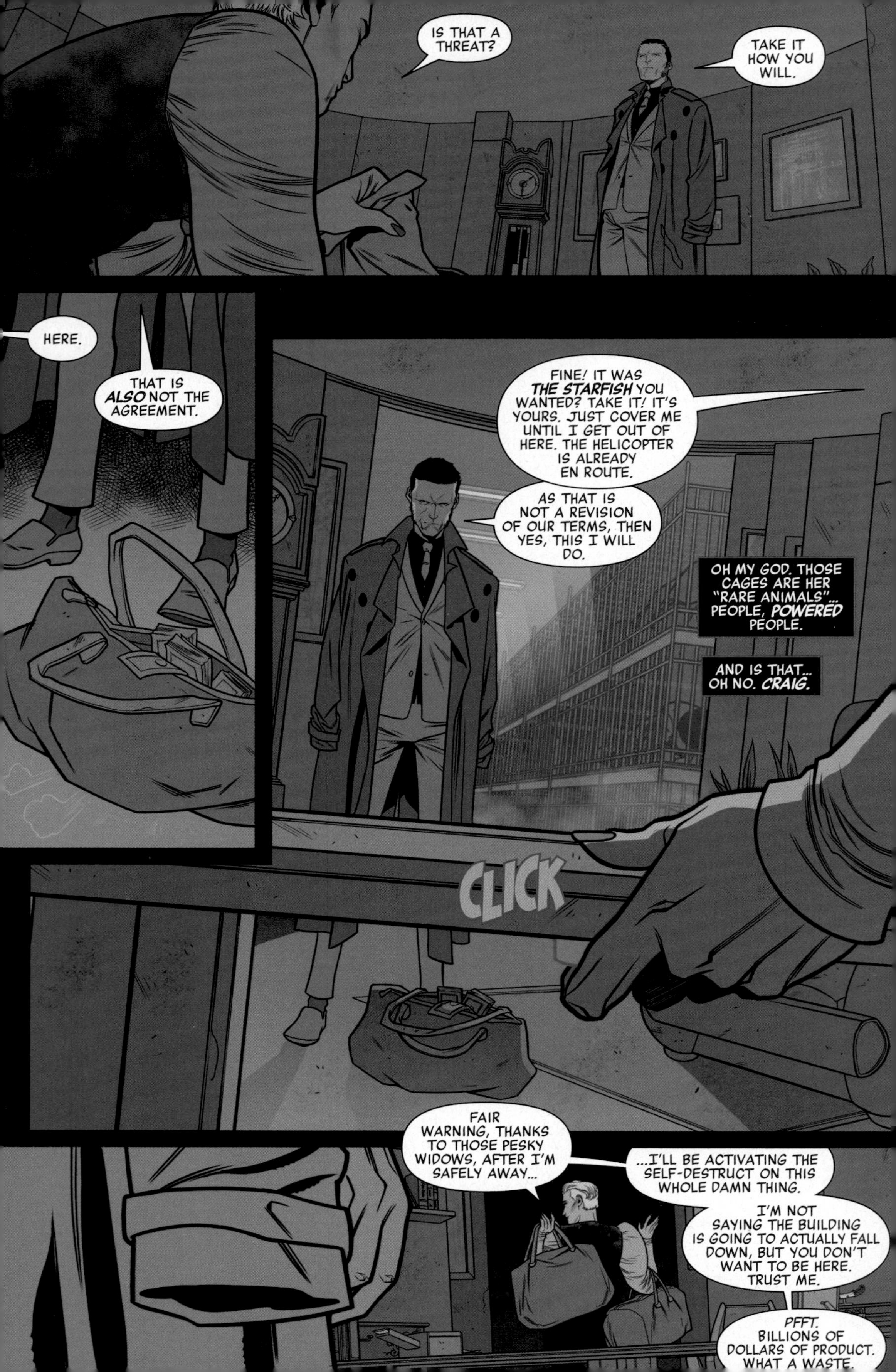
IS THAT A THREAT?
TAKE IT HOW YOU WILL.
HERE.
THAT IS ALSO NOT THE AGREEMENT.
FINE! IT WAS THE STARFISH YOU WANTED? TAKE IT! IT'S YOURS. JUST COVER ME UNTIL I GET OUT OF HERE. THE HELICOPTER IS ALREADY EN ROUTE.
AS THAT IS NOT A REVISION OF OUR TERMS, THEN YES, THIS I WILL DO.
OH MY GOD. THOSE CAGES ARE HER "RARE ANIMALS"... PEOPLE, POWERED PEOPLE.
AND IS THAT... OH NO. CRAIG.
CLICK
FAIR WARNING, THANKS TO THOSE PESKY WIDOWS, AFTER I'M SAFELY AWAY...
...I'LL BE ACTIVATING THE SELF-DESTRUCT ON THIS WHOLE DAMN THING.
I'M NOT SAYING THE BUILDING IS GOING TO ACTUALLY FALL DOWN, BUT YOU DON'T WANT TO BE HERE. TRUST ME.
PFFT. BILLIONS OF DOLLARS OF PRODUCT. WHAT A WASTE.

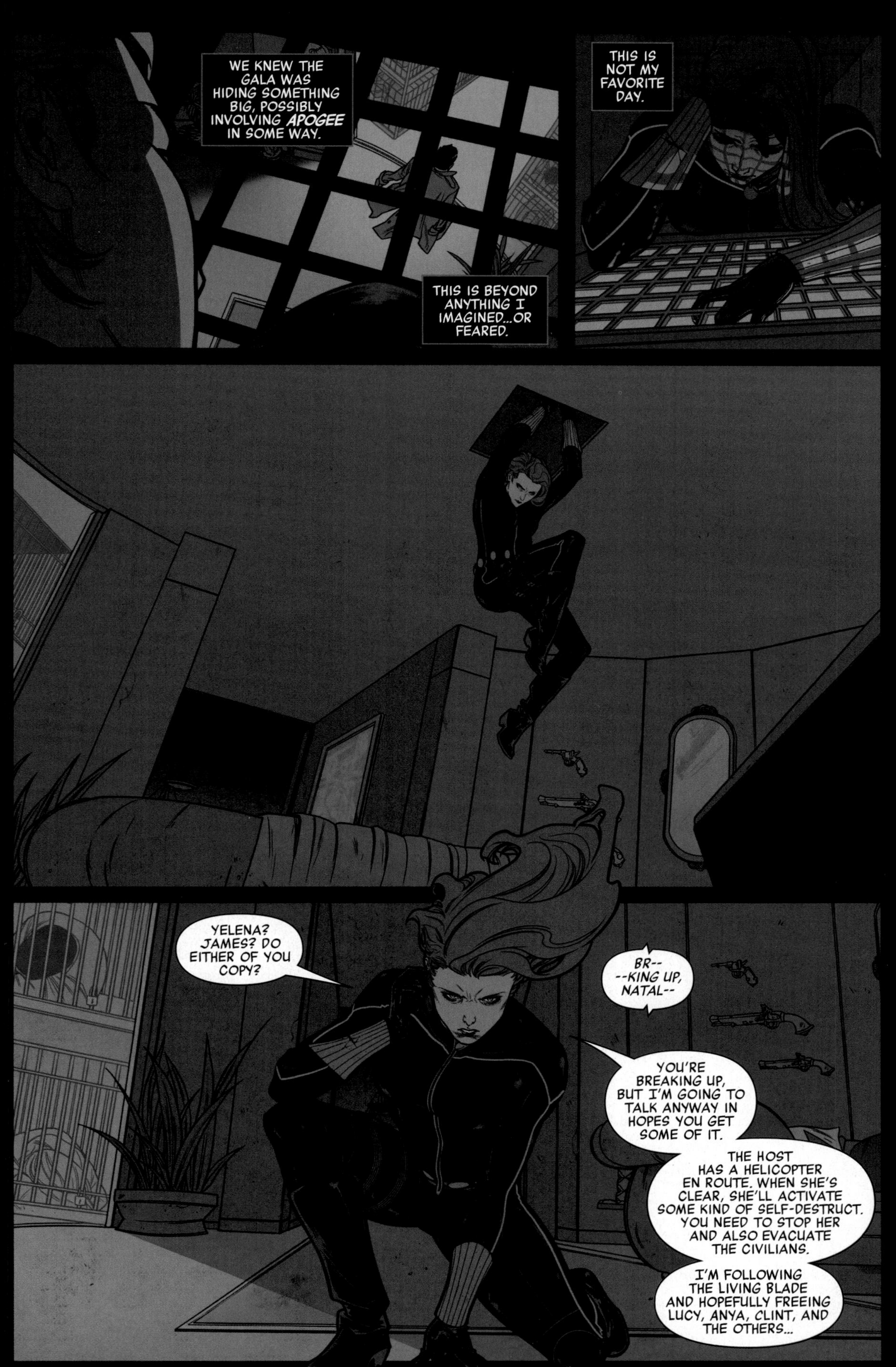
WE KNEW THE GALA WAS HIDING SOMETHING BIG, POSSIBLY INVOLVING APOGEE IN SOME WAY.
THIS IS BEYOND ANYTHING I IMAGINED...OR FEARED.
THIS IS NOT MY FAVORITE DAY.
YELENA? JAMES? DO EITHER OF YOU COPY?
BR-- --KING UP, NATAL--
YOU'RE BREAKING UP, BUT I'M GOING TO TALK ANYWAY IN HOPES YOU GET SOME OF IT.
THE HOST HAS A HELICOPTER EN ROUTE. WHEN SHE'S CLEAR, SHE'LL ACTIVATE SOME KIND OF SELF-DESTRUCT. YOU NEED TO STOP HER AND ALSO EVACUATE THE CIVILIANS.
I'M FOLLOWING THE LIVING BLADE AND HOPEFULLY FREEING LUCY, ANYA, CLINT, AND THE OTHERS...

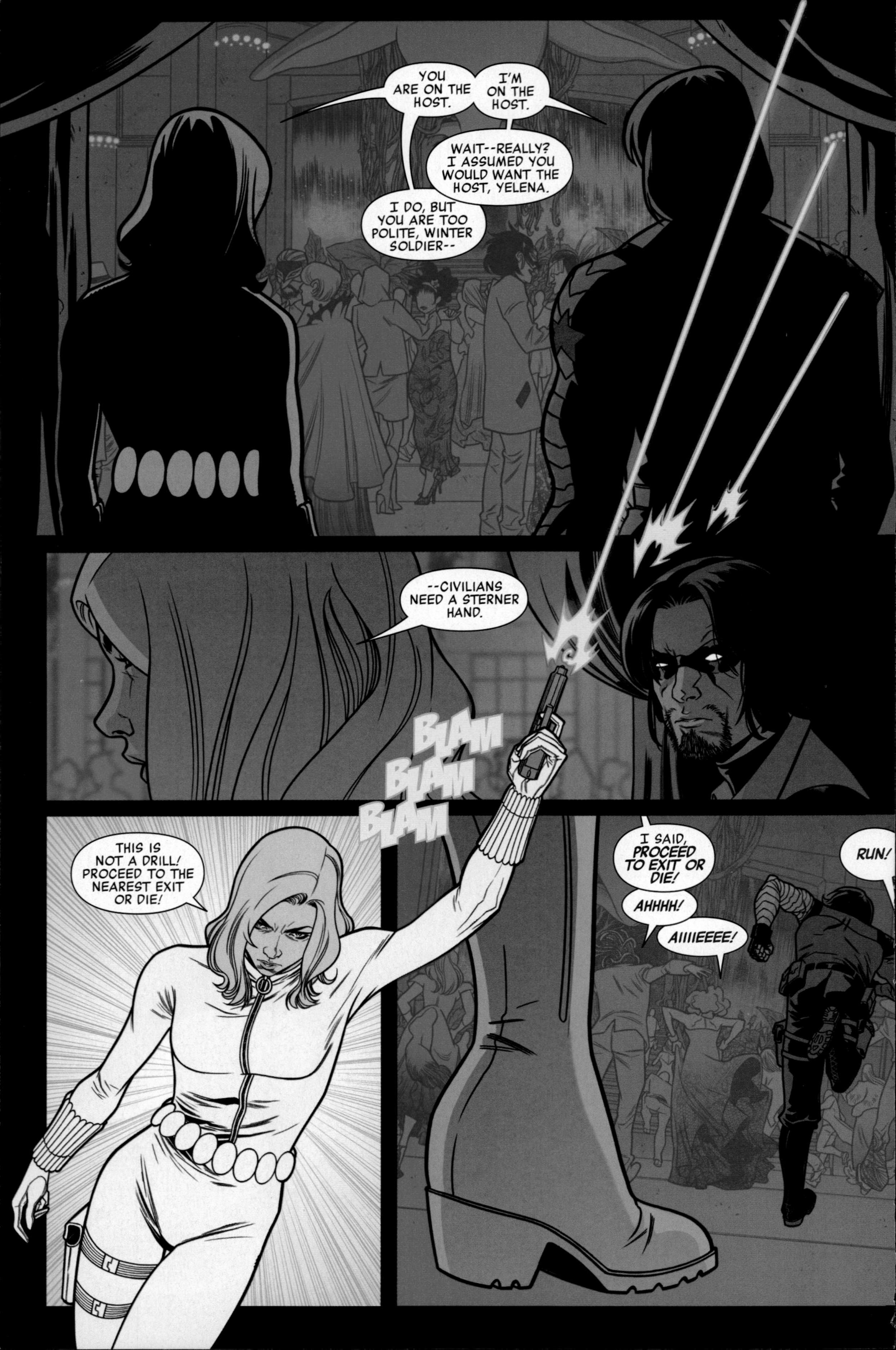
YOU ARE ON THE HOST.
I'M ON THE HOST.
WAIT--REALLY? I ASSUMED YOU WOULD WANT THE HOST, YELENA.
I DO, BUT YOU ARE TOO POLITE, WINTER SOLDIER--
--CIVILIANS NEED A STERNER HAND.
BLAM BLAM BLAM
THIS IS NOT A DRILL! PROCEED TO THE NEAREST EXIT OR DIE!
I SAID, PROCEED TO EXIT OR DIE!
AHHHH!
AIIIEEEE!
RUN!

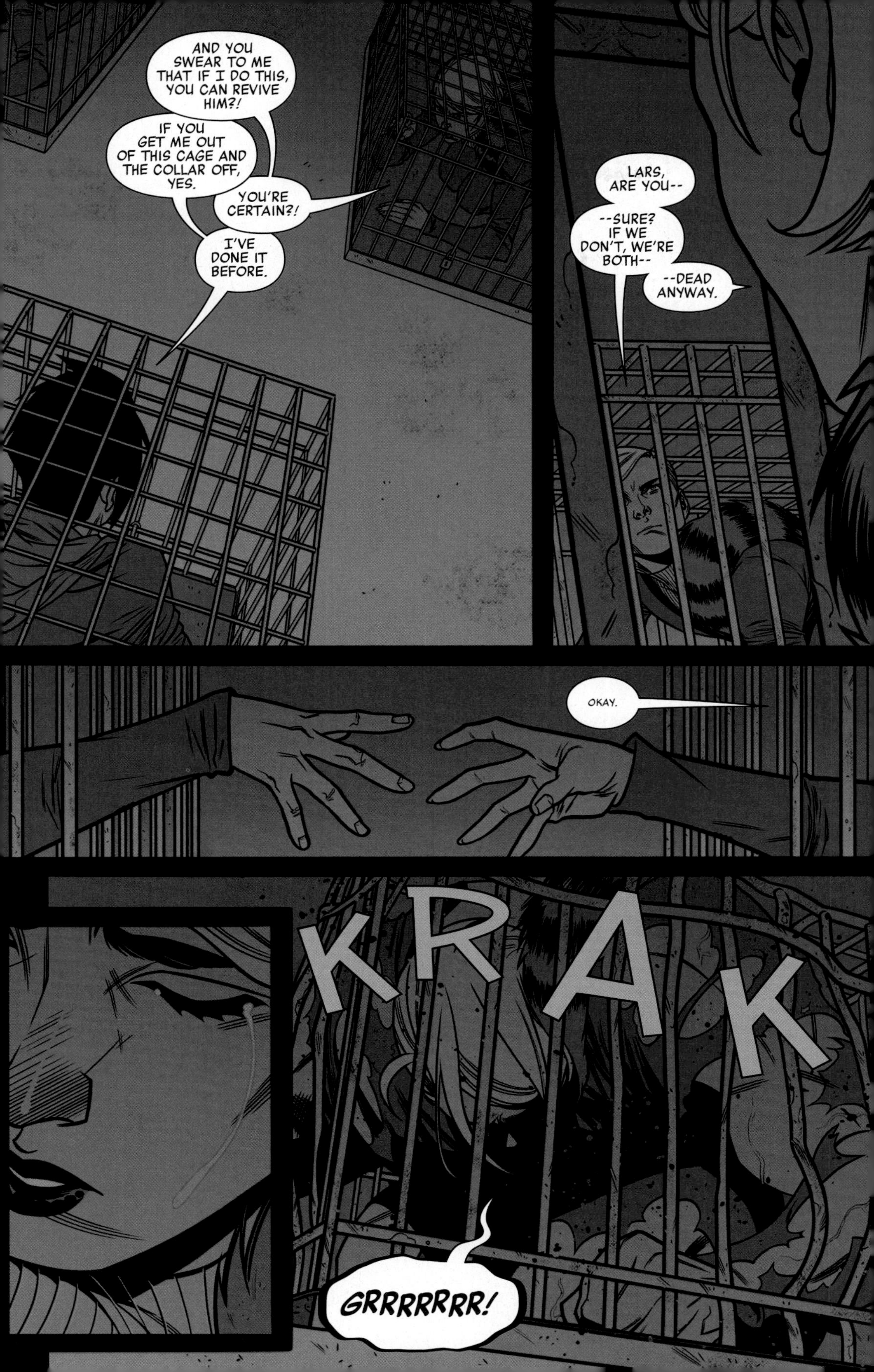
AND YOU SWEAR TO ME THAT IF I DO THIS, YOU CAN REVIVE HIM?!
IF YOU GET ME OUT OF THIS CAGE AND THE COLLAR OFF, YES.
YOU'RE CERTAIN?!
I'VE DONE IT BEFORE.
LARS, ARE YOU--
--SURE? IF WE DON'T, WE'RE BOTH--
--DEAD ANYWAY.
OKAY.
KRAK
GRRRRRRR!

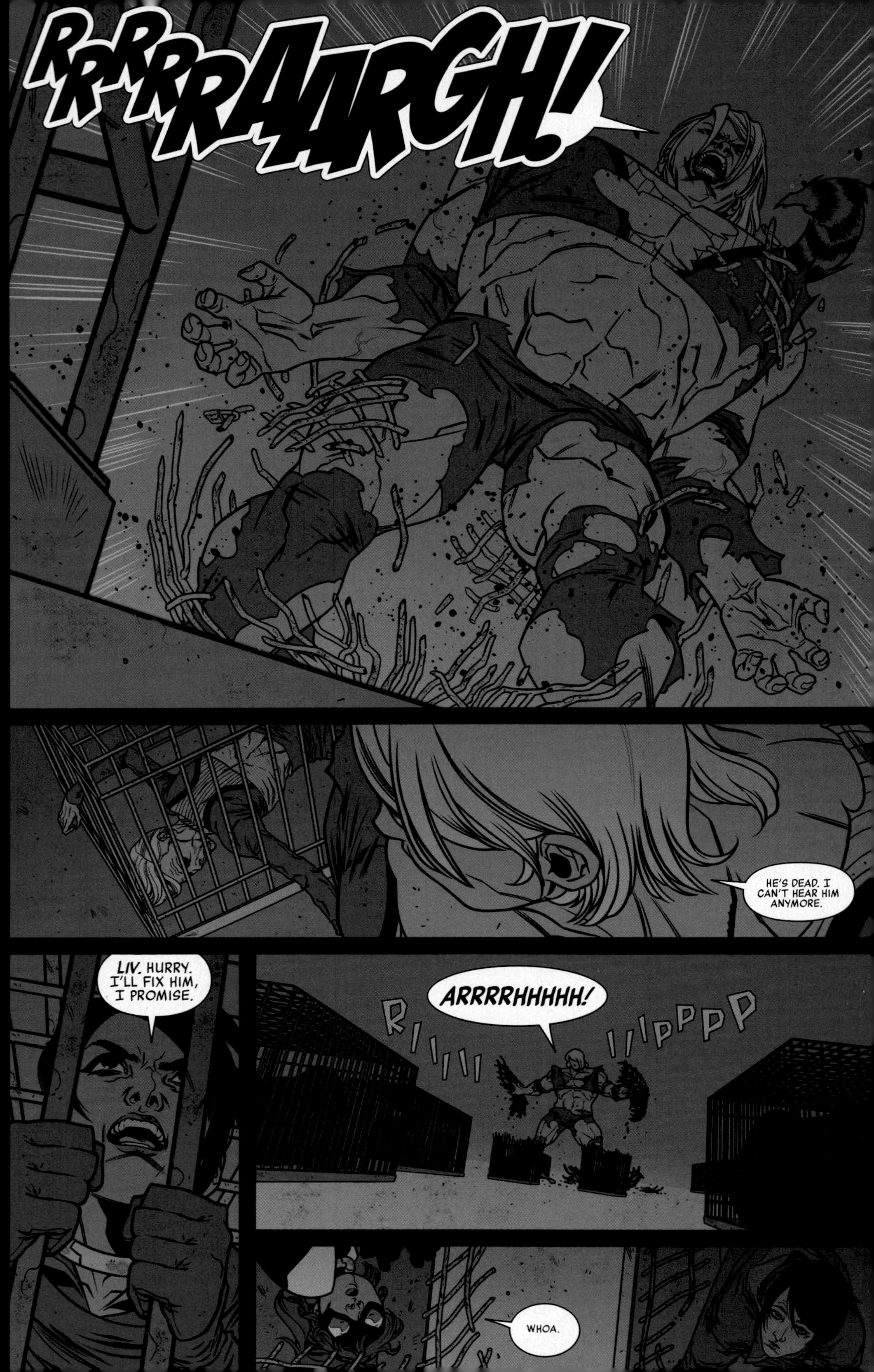

RRRRRAARGH!
HE'S DEAD. I CAN'T HEAR HIM ANYMORE.
LIV. HURRY. I'LL FIX HIM, I PROMISE.
ARRRRHHHHH!
RIIIII IIIPPPP
WHOA.

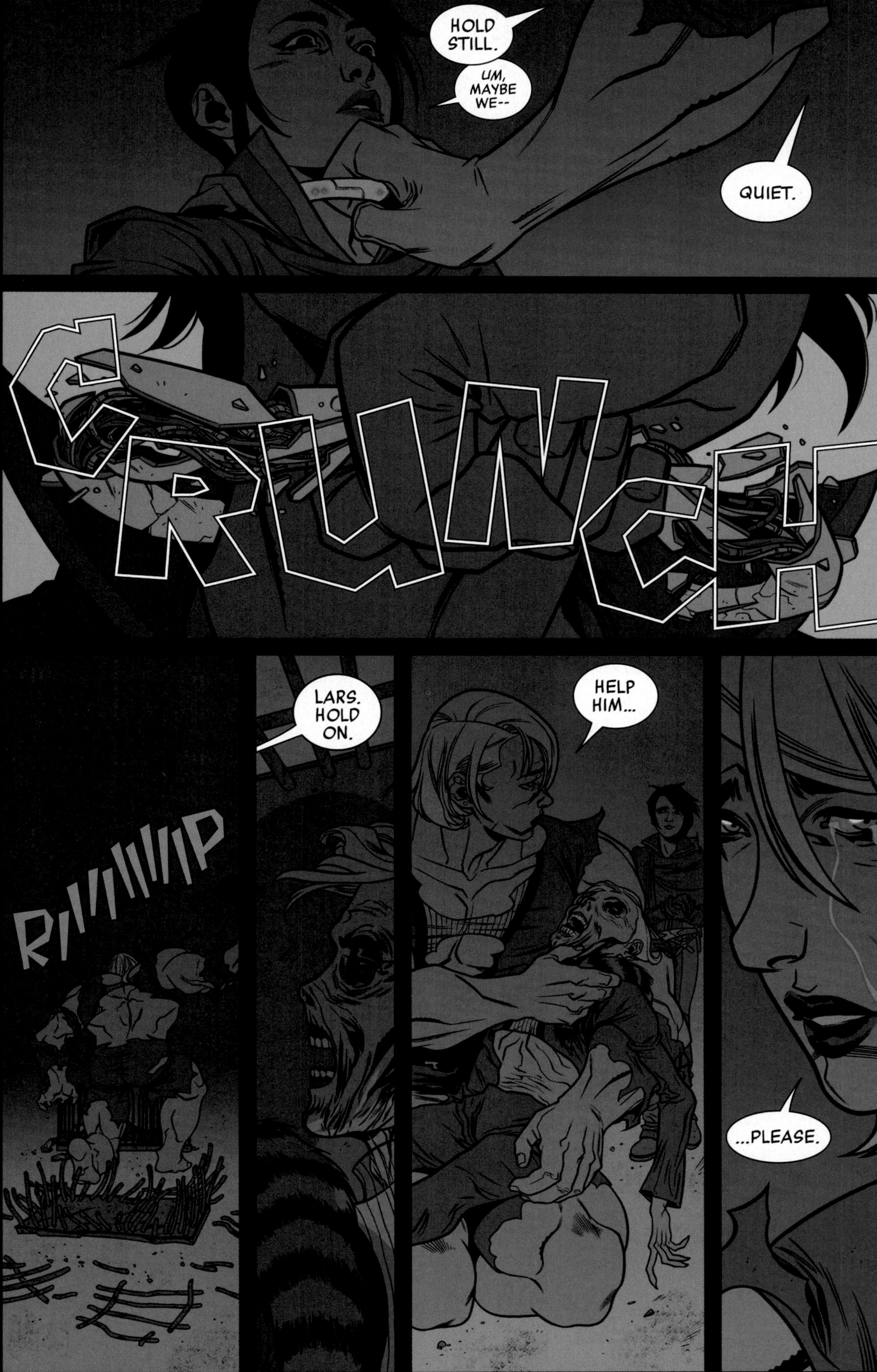

HOLD STILL.
UM, MAYBE WE--
QUIET.
CRUNCH
RIIIIIIIP
LARS. HOLD ON.
HELP HIM...
...PLEASE.

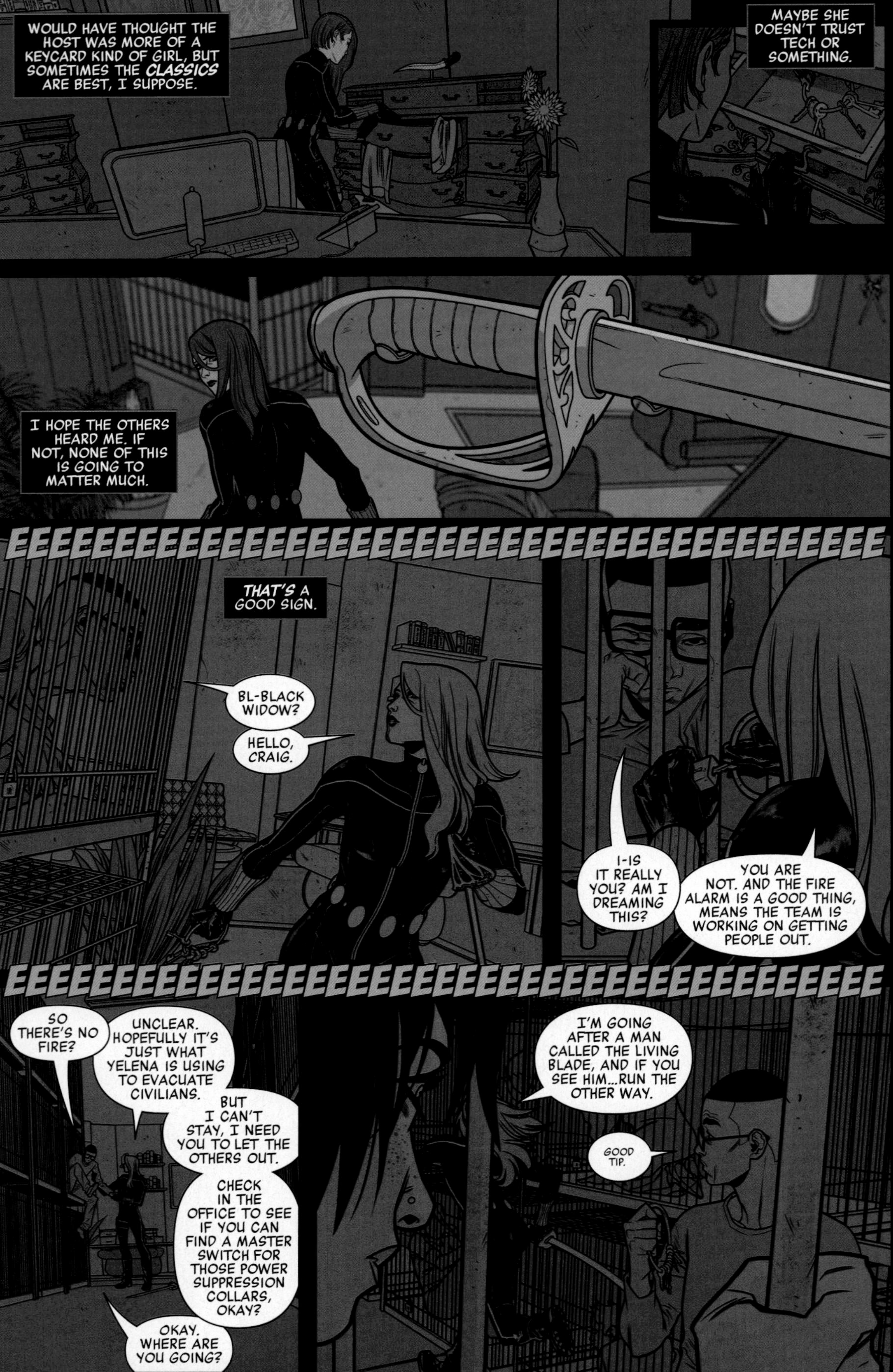

WOULD HAVE THOUGHT THE HOST WAS MORE OF A KEYCARD KIND OF GIRL, BUT SOMETIMES THE *CLASSICS* ARE BEST, I SUPPOSE.
MAYBE SHE DOESN'T TRUST TECH OR SOMETHING.
I HOPE THE OTHERS HEARD ME. IF NOT, NONE OF THIS IS GOING TO MATTER MUCH.
EEEEEEEEEEEEEEEEEEEEEEEEEEEEEEEEEEEEEEEEEE
THAT'S A GOOD SIGN.
BL-BLACK WIDOW?
HELLO, CRAIG.
I-IS IT REALLY YOU? AM I DREAMING THIS?
YOU ARE NOT. AND THE FIRE ALARM IS A GOOD THING, MEANS THE TEAM IS WORKING ON GETTING PEOPLE OUT.
EEEEEEEEEEEEEEEEEEEEEEEEEEEEEEEEEEEEEEEEEE
SO THERE'S NO FIRE?
UNCLEAR. HOPEFULLY IT'S JUST WHAT YELENA IS USING TO EVACUATE CIVILIANS.
BUT I CAN'T STAY, I NEED YOU TO LET THE OTHERS OUT.
CHECK IN THE OFFICE TO SEE IF YOU CAN FIND A MASTER SWITCH FOR THOSE POWER SUPPRESSION COLLARS, OKAY?
OKAY. WHERE ARE YOU GOING?
I'M GOING AFTER A MAN CALLED THE LIVING BLADE, AND IF YOU SEE HIM...RUN THE OTHER WAY.
GOOD TIP.

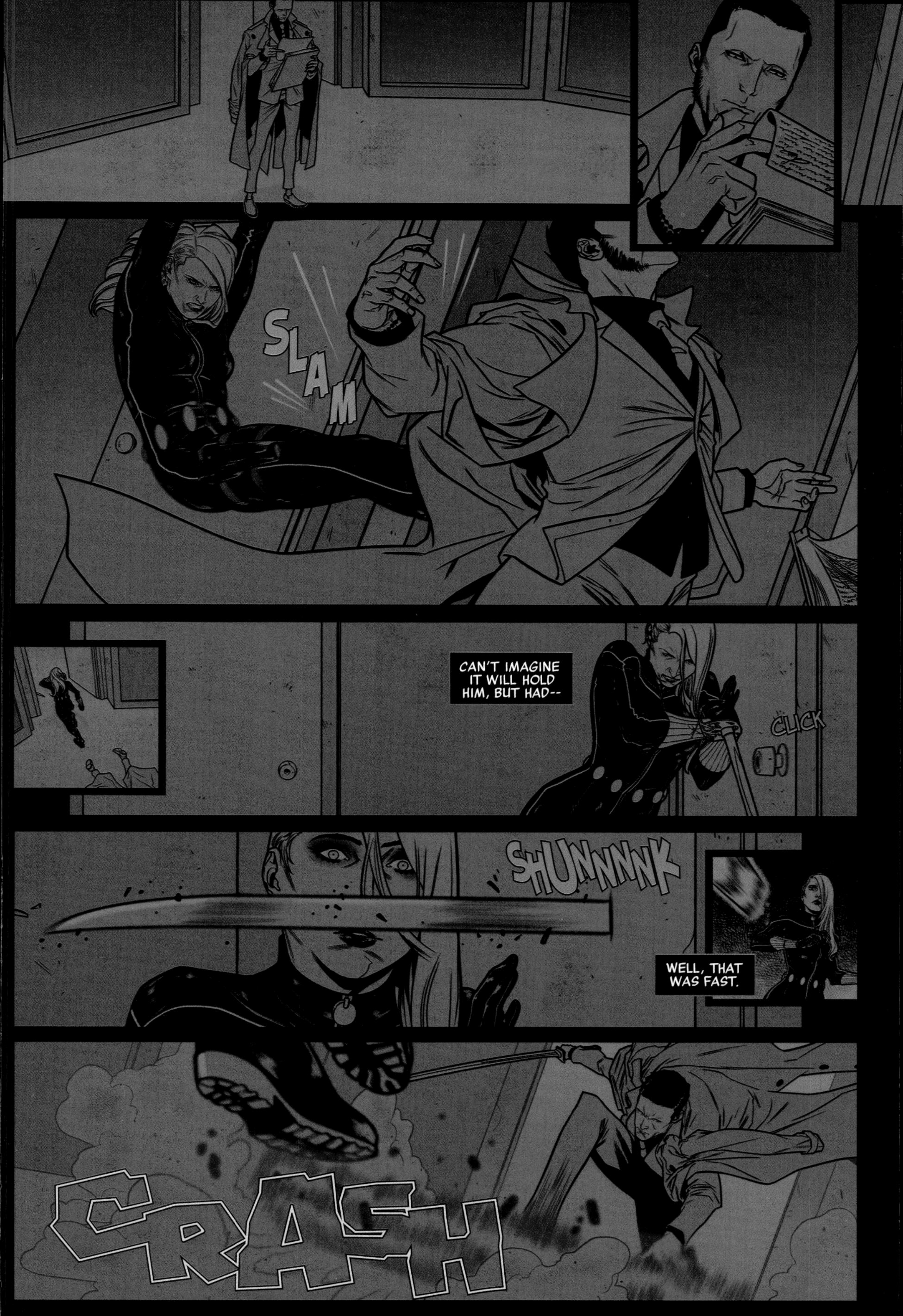
SLAM
CAN'T IMAGINE IT WILL HOLD HIM, BUT HAD--
CLICK
SHUNNNNK
WELL, THAT WAS FAST.
CRASH

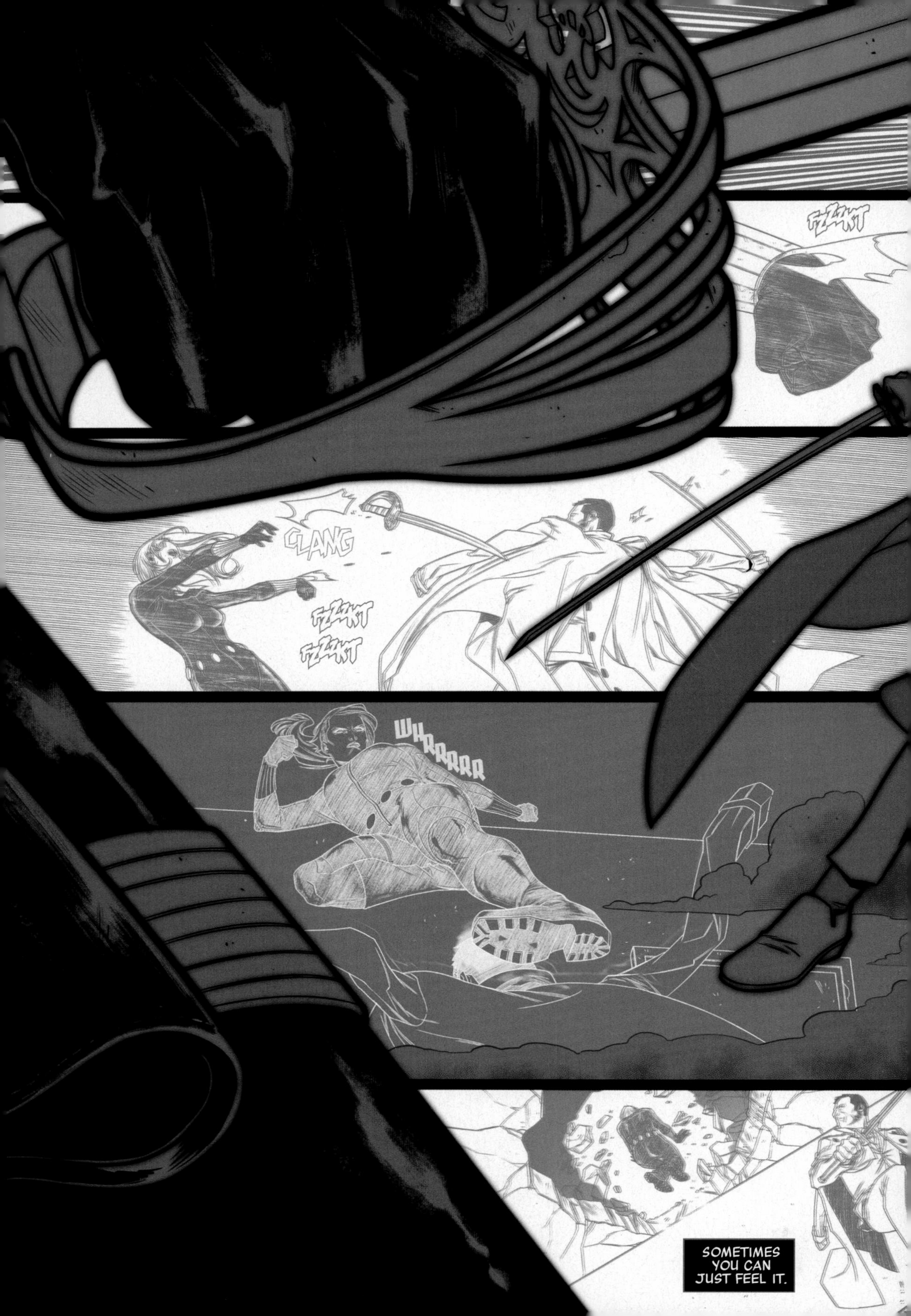

FZZZKT
CLANG
FZZZKT
FZZZKT
WHRRRRRR
SOMETIMES YOU CAN JUST FEEL IT.

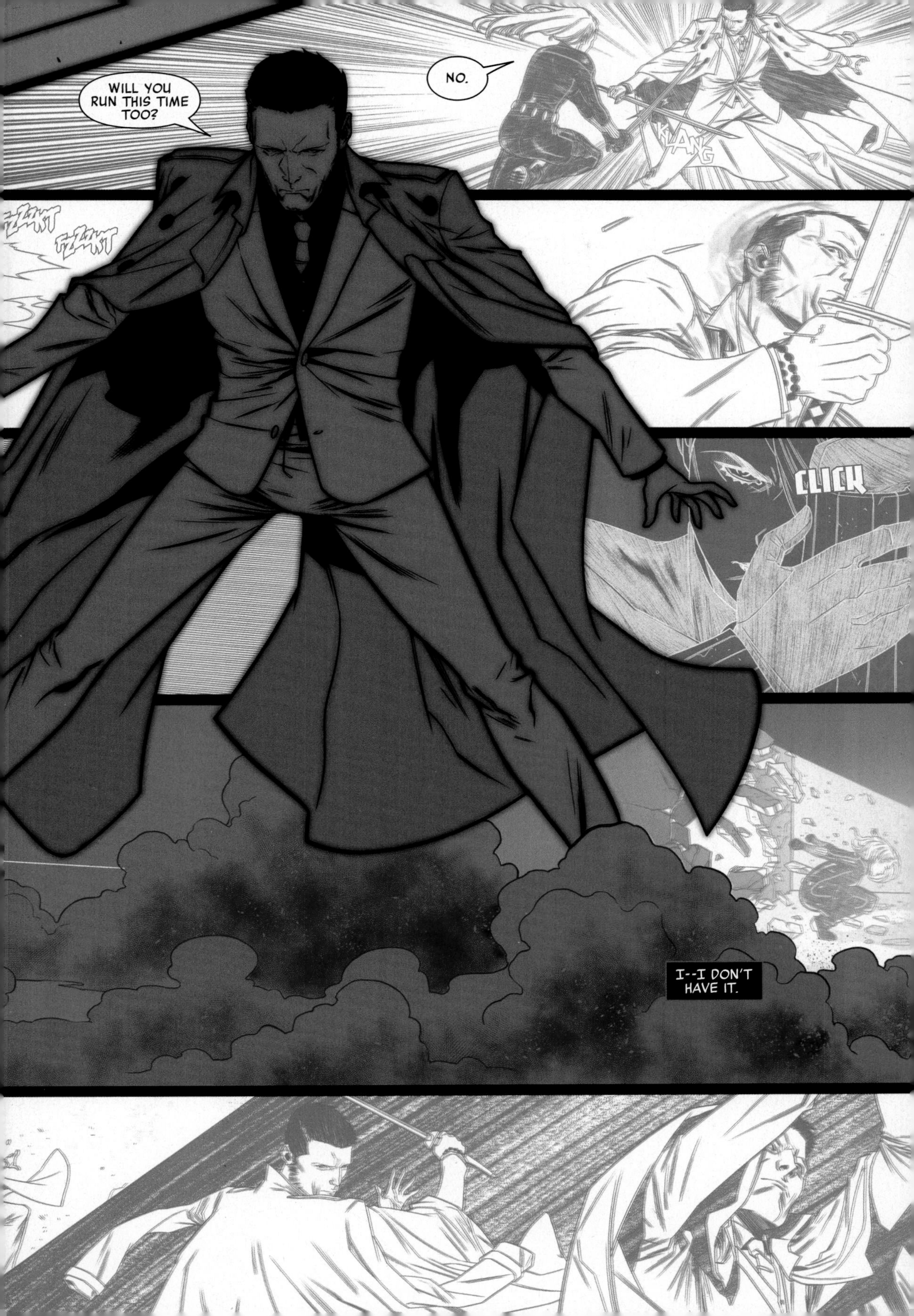
WILL YOU RUN THIS TIME TOO?
NO.
KLANG
FZZZT
FZZZT
CLICK
I--I DON'T HAVE IT.

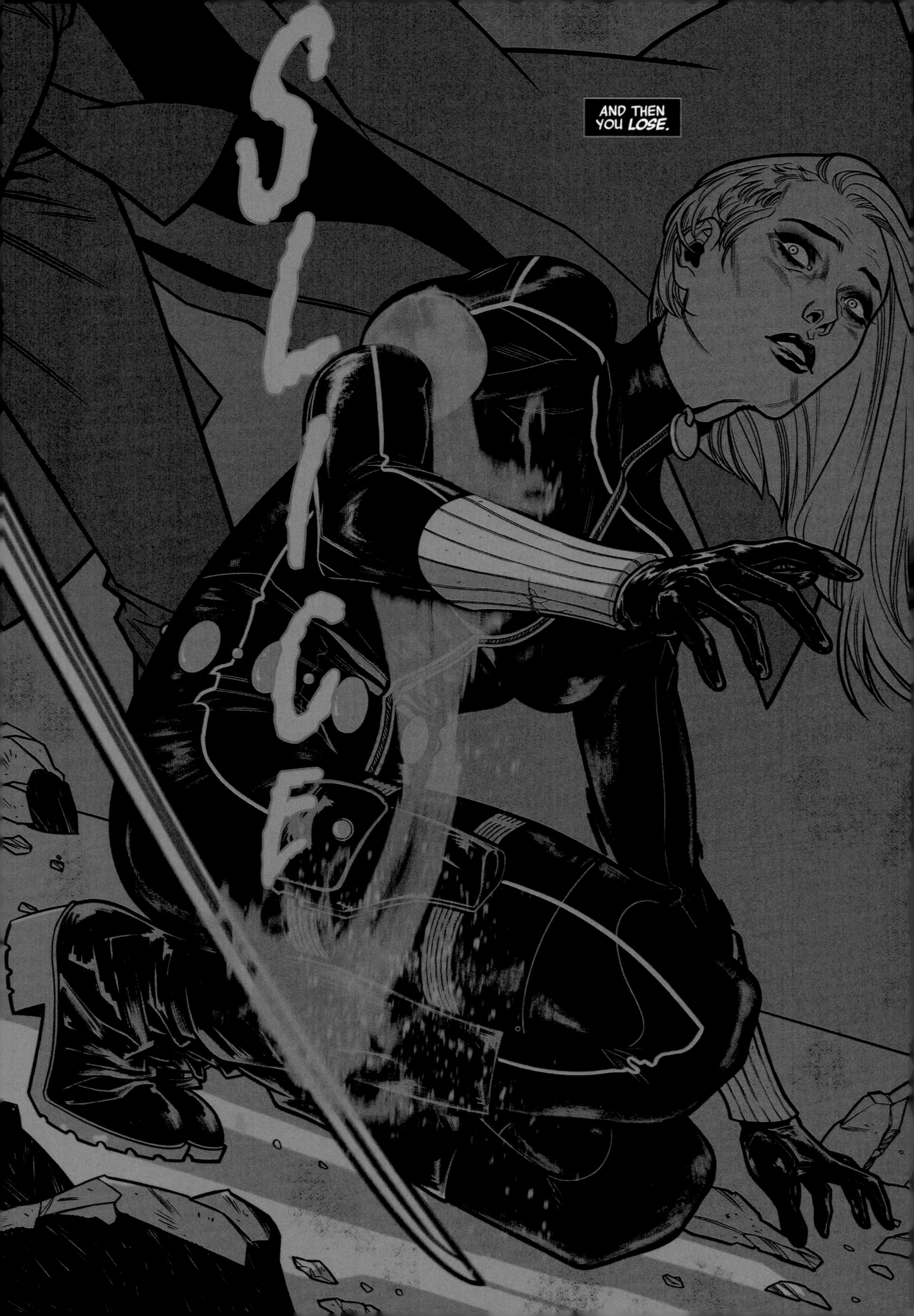
AND THEN YOU *LOSE.*
SLICE

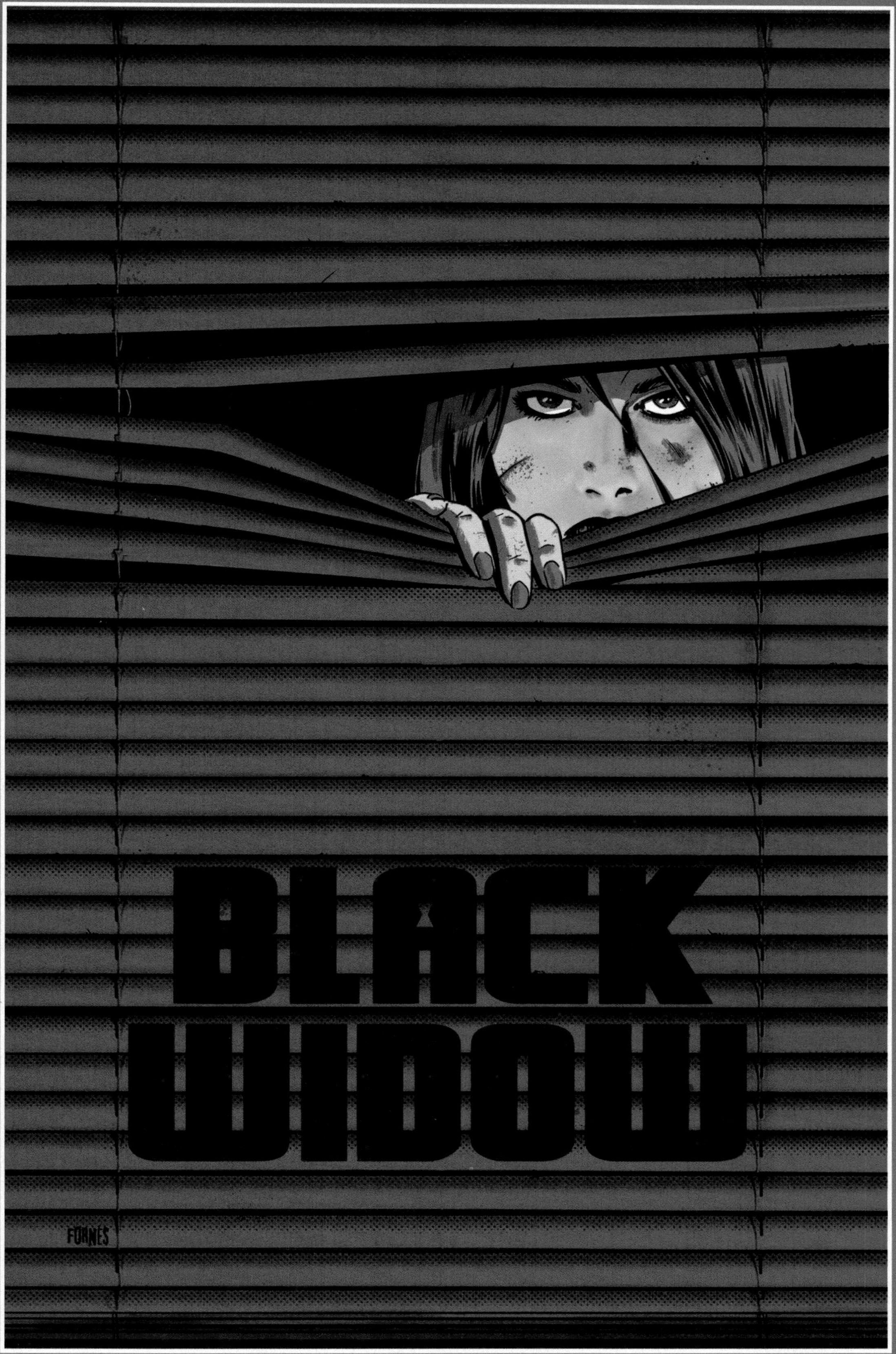
BLACK
WIDOW
FORNÉS

#15 VARIANT BY **JORGE FORNÉS**

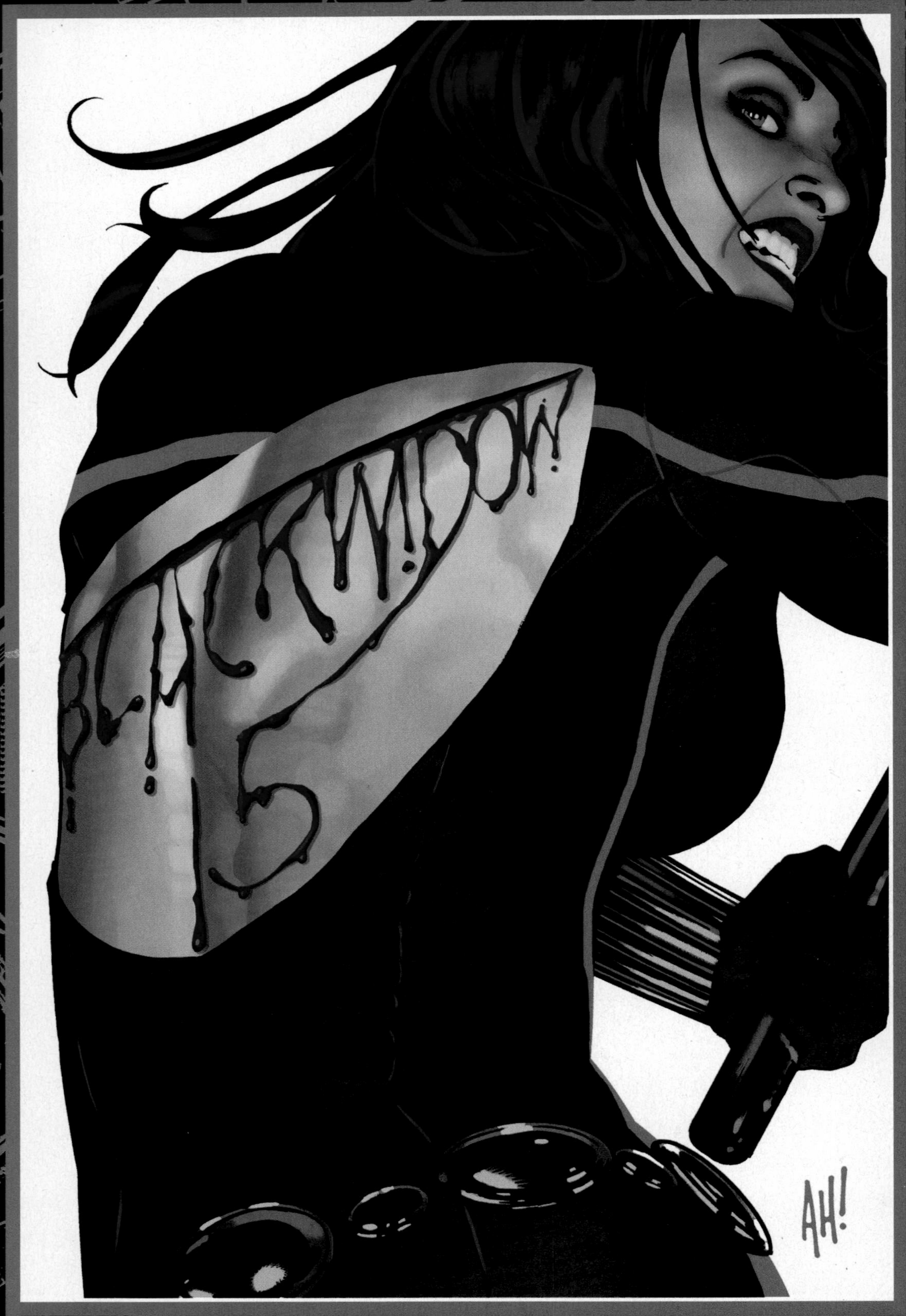
BLACK WIDOW
15
AH!

FIFTEEN

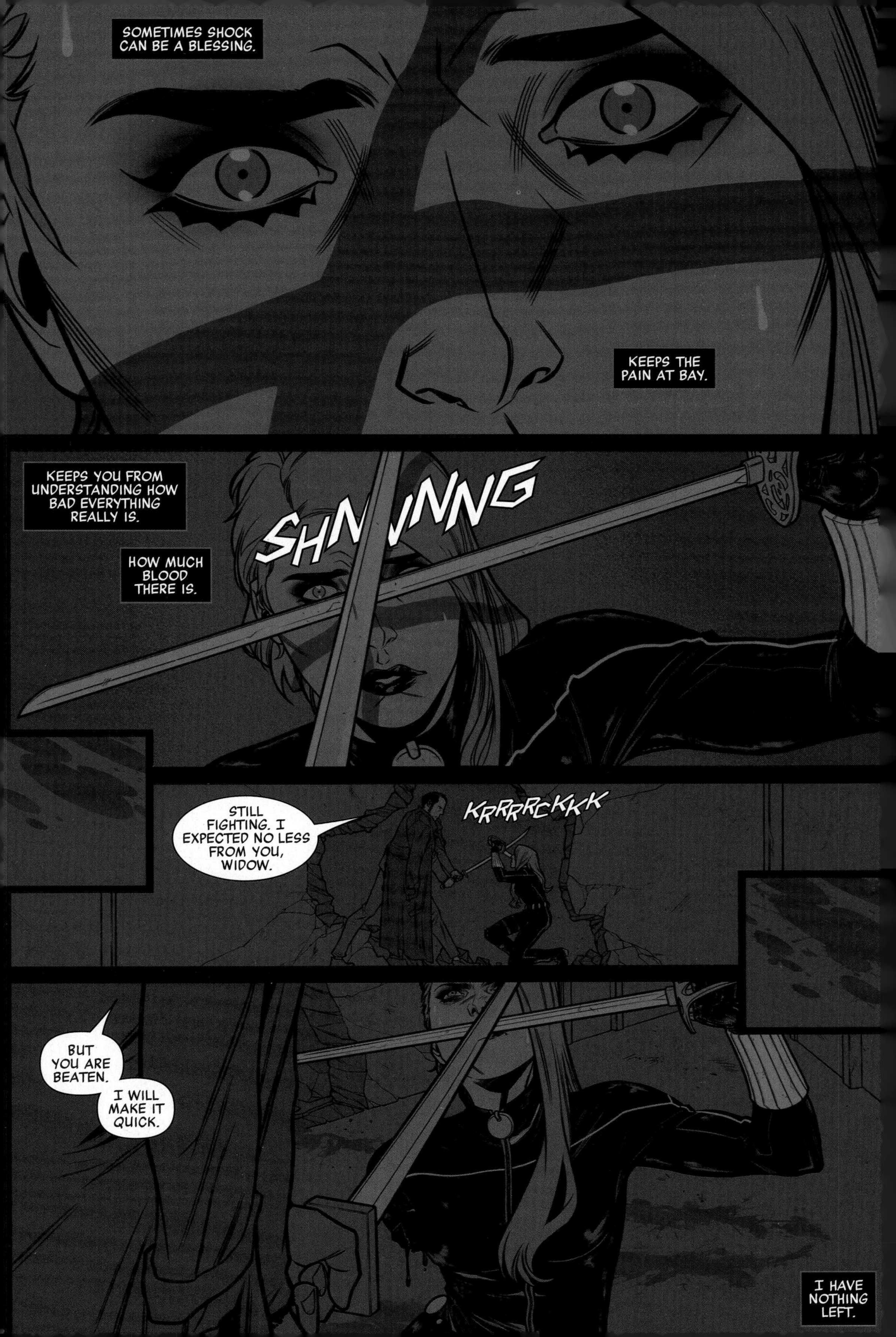
SOMETIMES SHOCK CAN BE A BLESSING.
KEEPS THE PAIN AT BAY.
KEEPS YOU FROM UNDERSTANDING HOW BAD EVERYTHING REALLY IS.
HOW MUCH BLOOD THERE IS.
SHNNNG
STILL FIGHTING. I EXPECTED NO LESS FROM YOU, WIDOW.
KRRRRCKKK
BUT YOU ARE BEATEN.
I WILL MAKE IT QUICK.
I HAVE NOTHING LEFT.

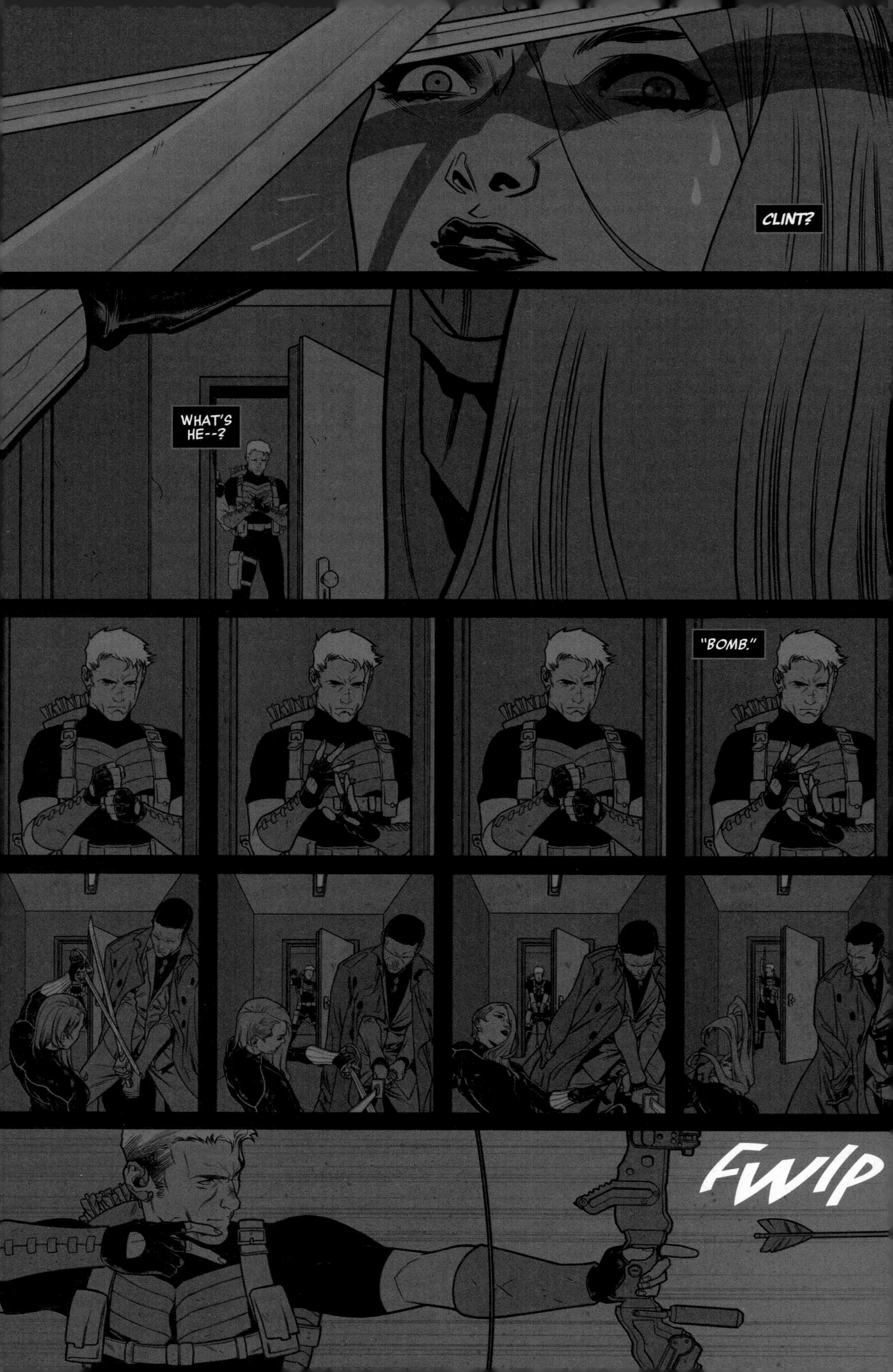
CLINT?
WHAT'S HE--?
"BOMB."
FWIP

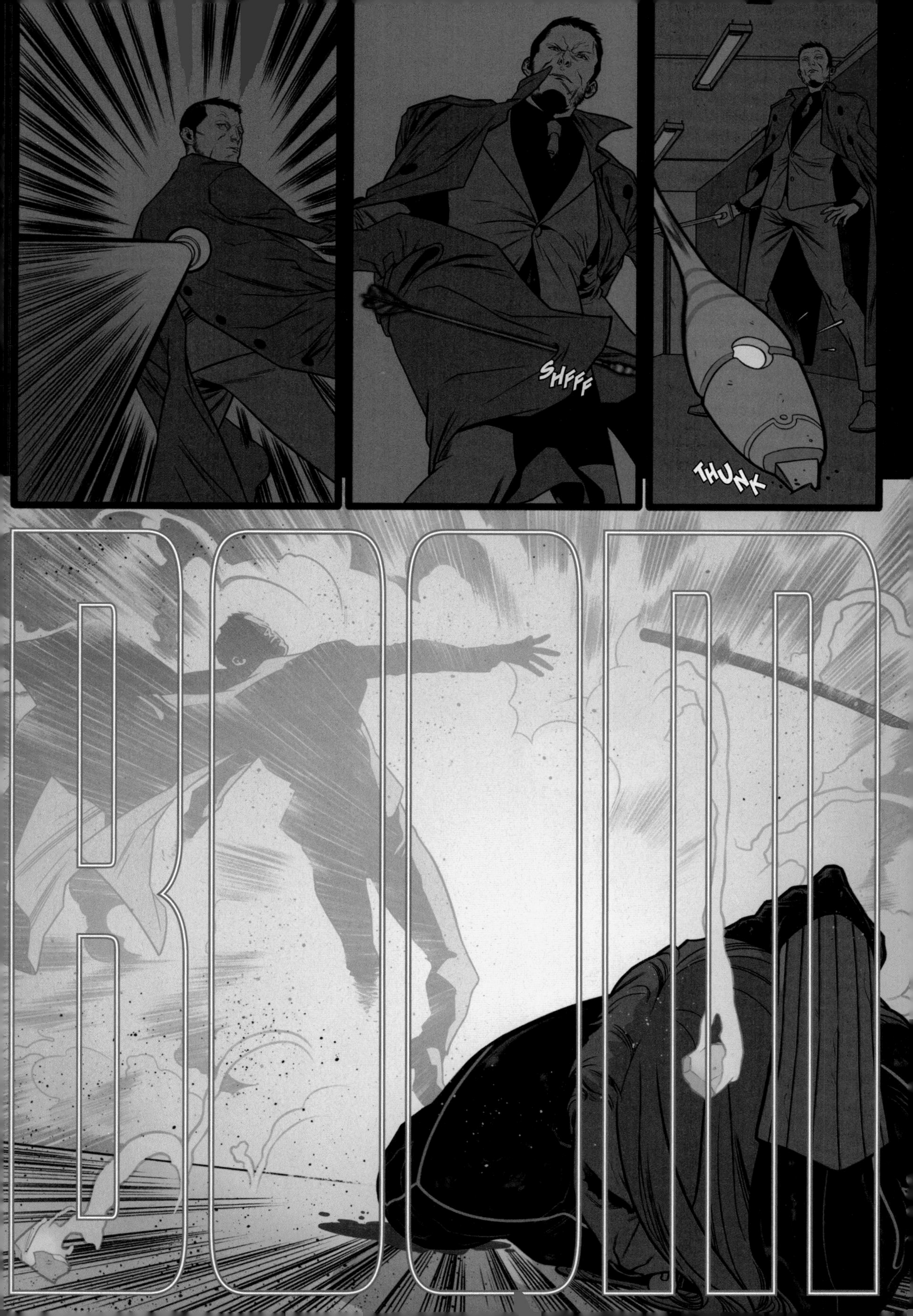
SHFFF
THUNK
BOOM

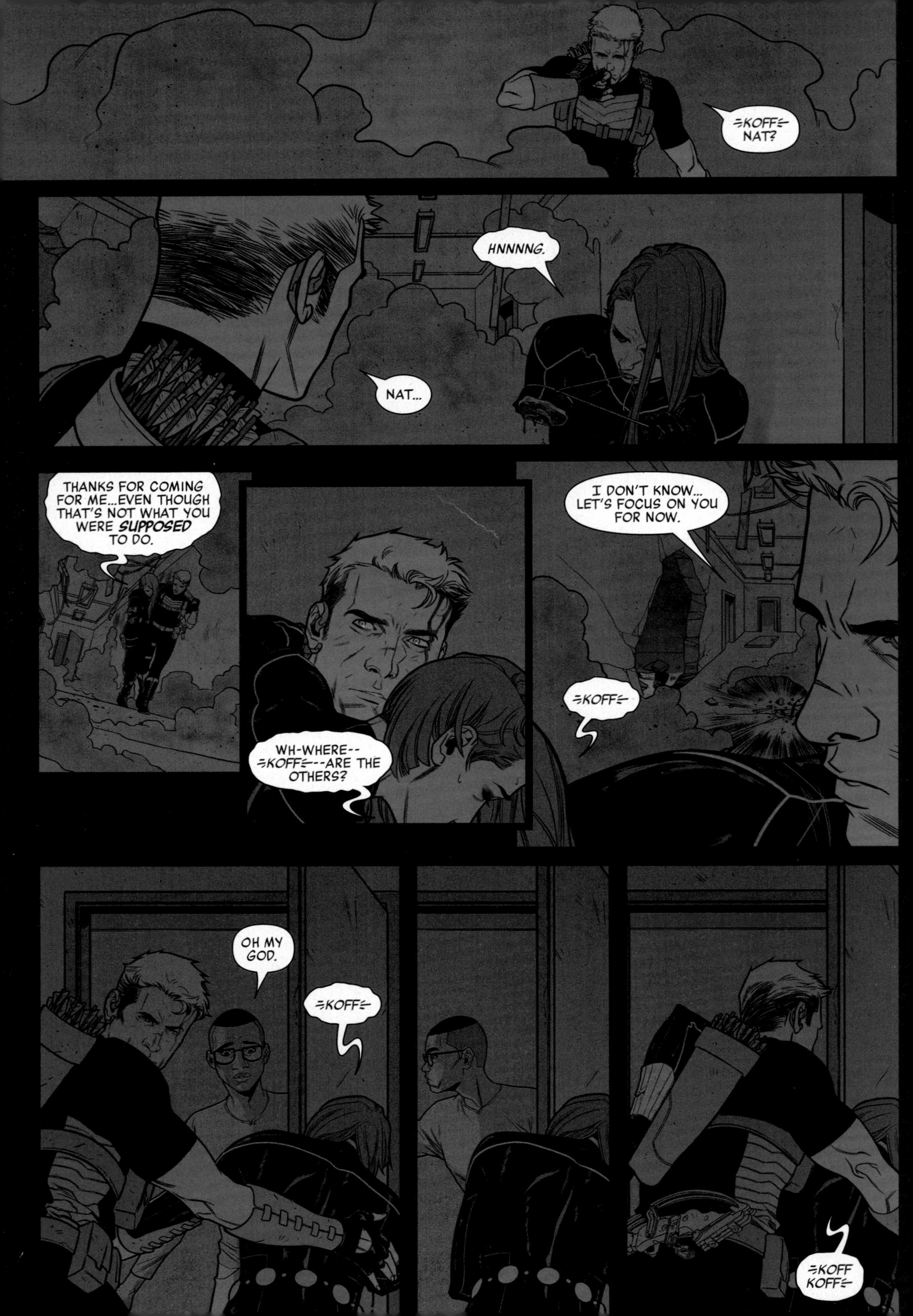

=KOFF= NAT?
HNNNNG.
NAT...
THANKS FOR COMING FOR ME...EVEN THOUGH THAT'S NOT WHAT YOU WERE *SUPPOSED* TO DO.
WH-WHERE-- =KOFF= --ARE THE OTHERS?
I DON'T KNOW... LET'S FOCUS ON YOU FOR NOW.
=KOFF=
OH MY GOD.
=KOFF=
=KOFF KOFF=

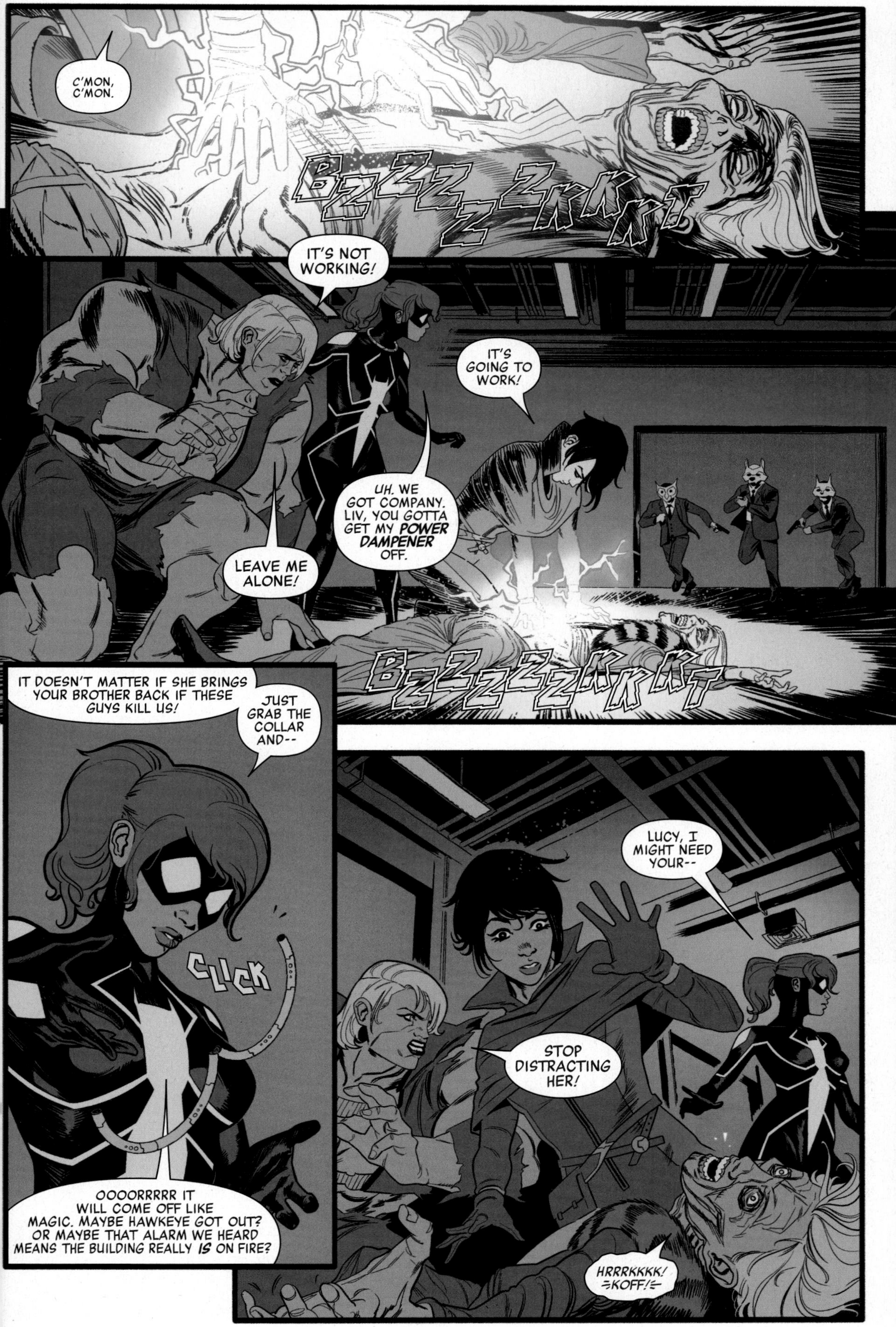
C'MON, C'MON.
BZZZZZZRKRT
IT'S NOT WORKING!
IT'S GOING TO WORK!
LEAVE ME ALONE!
UH. WE GOT COMPANY. LIV, YOU GOTTA GET MY POWER DAMPENER OFF.
BZZZZZZRKRT
IT DOESN'T MATTER IF SHE BRINGS YOUR BROTHER BACK IF THESE GUYS KILL US!
JUST GRAB THE COLLAR AND--
CLICK
OOOORRRRR IT WILL COME OFF LIKE MAGIC. MAYBE HAWKEYE GOT OUT? OR MAYBE THAT ALARM WE HEARD MEANS THE BUILDING REALLY IS ON FIRE?
LUCY, I MIGHT NEED YOUR--
STOP DISTRACTING HER!
HRRRKKKK! KOFF!

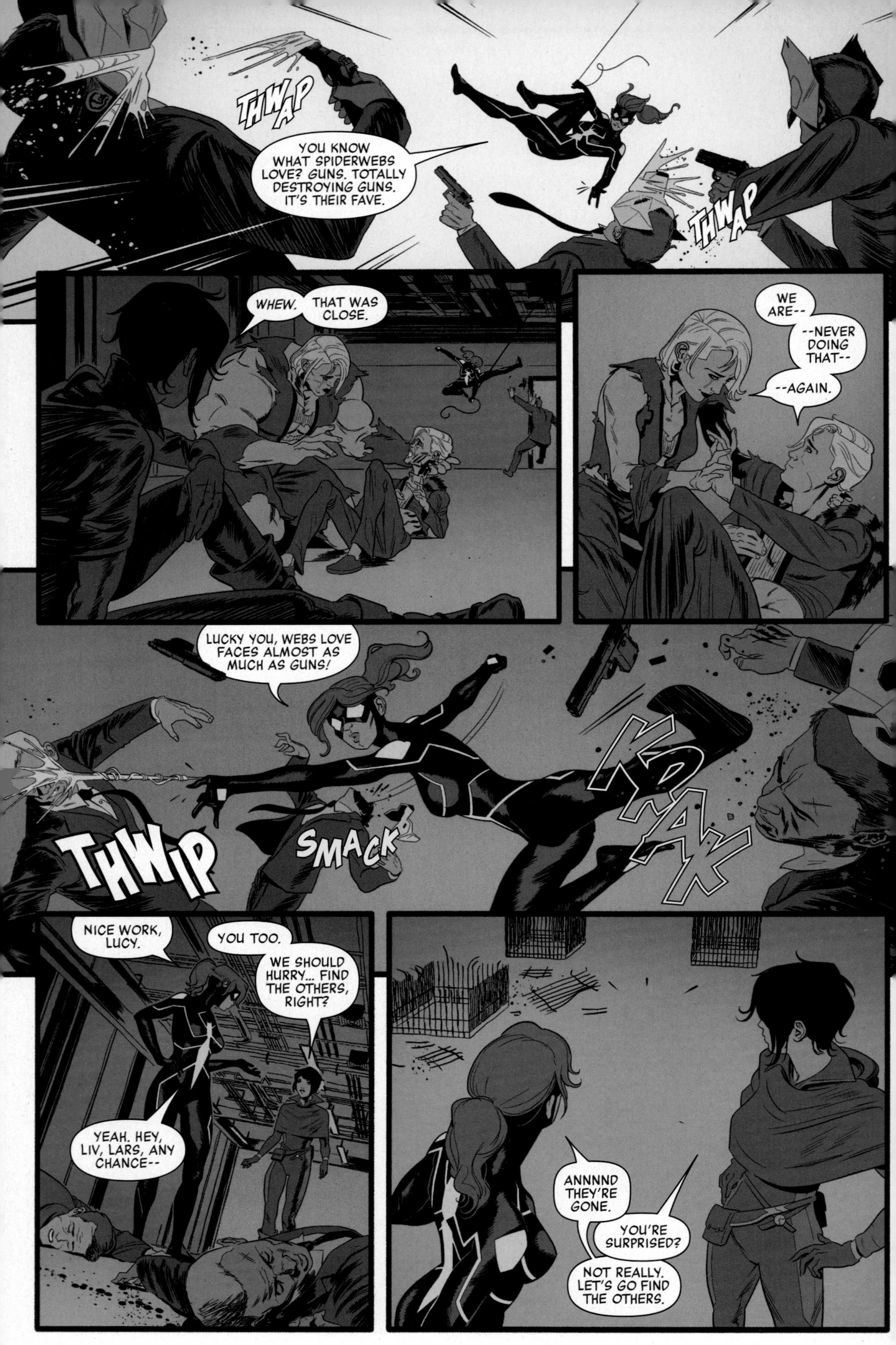
THWAP
YOU KNOW WHAT SPIDERWEBS LOVE? GUNS. TOTALLY DESTROYING GUNS. IT'S THEIR FAVE.
THWAP
WHEW. THAT WAS CLOSE.
WE ARE--
--NEVER DOING THAT--
--AGAIN.
LUCKY YOU, WEBS LOVE FACES ALMOST AS MUCH AS GUNS!
KRAK
THWIP
SMACK
NICE WORK, LUCY.
YOU TOO.
WE SHOULD HURRY... FIND THE OTHERS, RIGHT?
YEAH. HEY, LIV, LARS, ANY CHANCE--
ANNNND THEY'RE GONE.
YOU'RE SURPRISED?
NOT REALLY. LET'S GO FIND THE OTHERS.

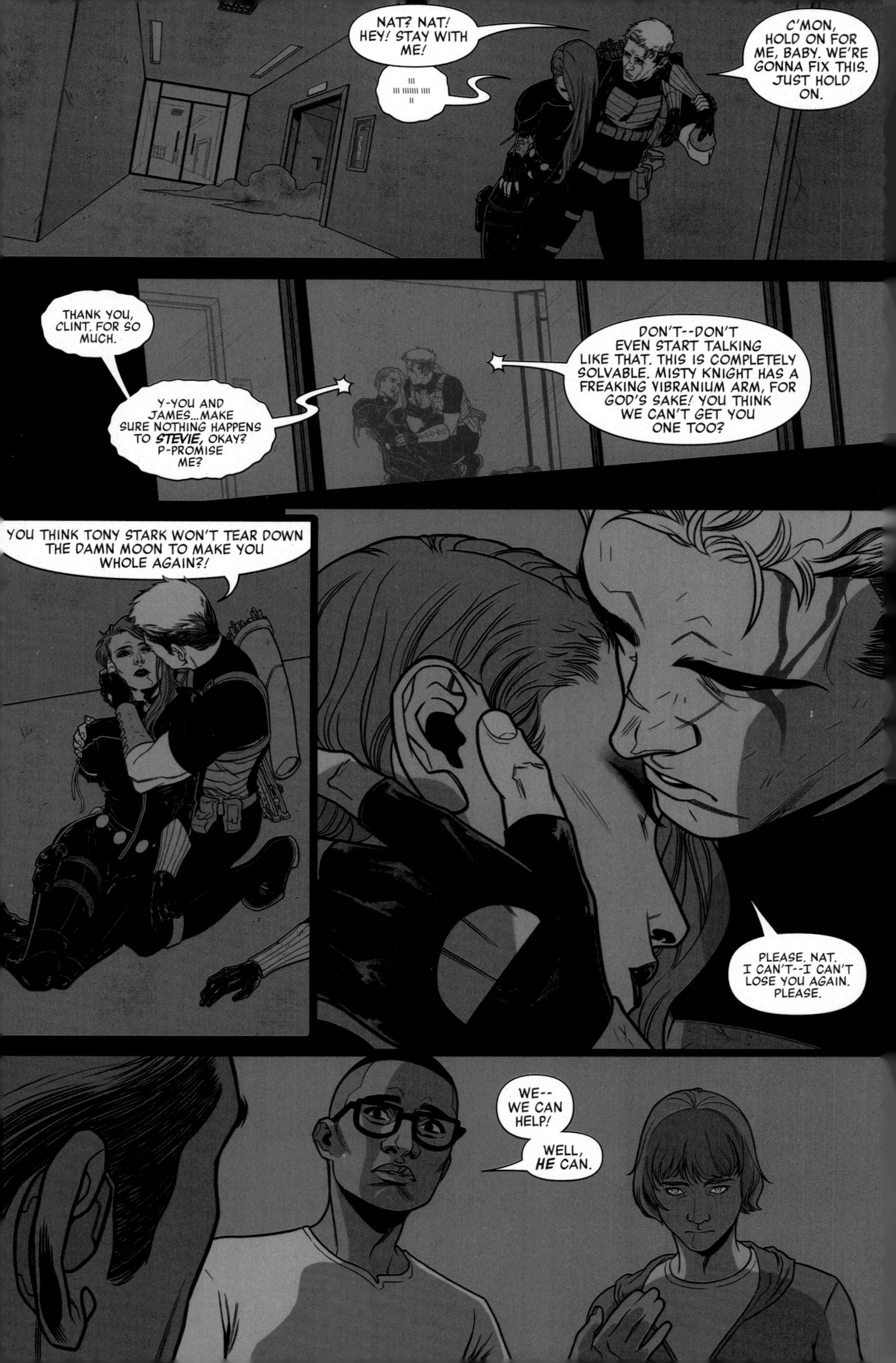

NAT? NAT! HEY! STAY WITH ME!
C'MON, HOLD ON FOR ME, BABY. WE'RE GONNA FIX THIS. JUST HOLD ON.
THANK YOU, CLINT. FOR SO MUCH.
Y-YOU AND JAMES...MAKE SURE NOTHING HAPPENS TO STEVIE, OKAY? P-PROMISE ME?
DON'T--DON'T EVEN START TALKING LIKE THAT. THIS IS COMPLETELY SOLVABLE. MISTY KNIGHT HAS A FREAKING VIBRANIUM ARM, FOR GOD'S SAKE! YOU THINK WE CAN'T GET YOU ONE TOO?
YOU THINK TONY STARK WON'T TEAR DOWN THE DAMN MOON TO MAKE YOU WHOLE AGAIN?!
PLEASE. NAT. I CAN'T--I CAN'T LOSE YOU AGAIN. PLEASE.
WE--WE CAN HELP!
WELL, HE CAN.

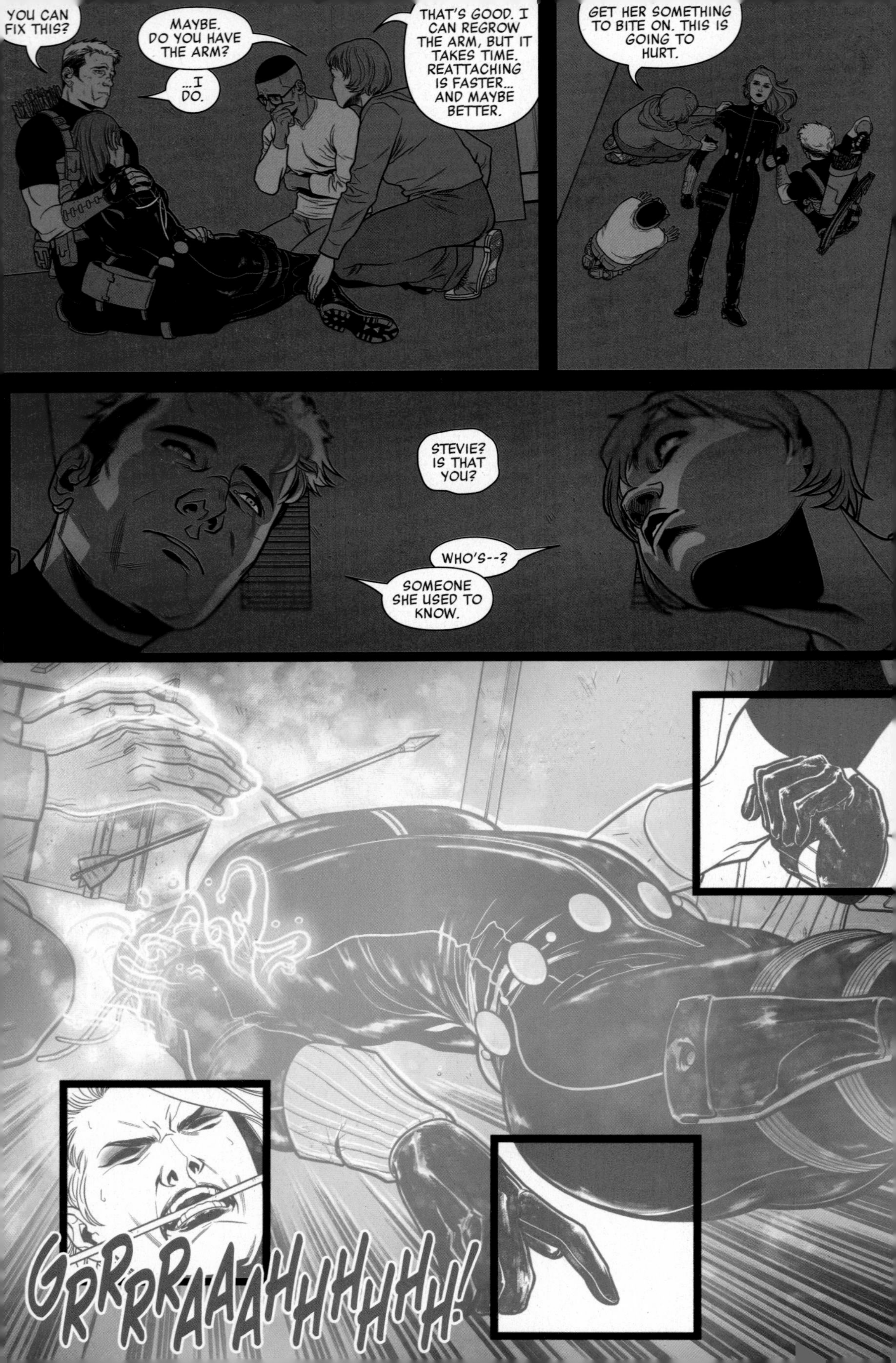
YOU CAN FIX THIS?
MAYBE. DO YOU HAVE THE ARM?
...I DO.
THAT'S GOOD. I CAN REGROW THE ARM, BUT IT TAKES TIME. REATTACHING IS FASTER... AND MAYBE BETTER.
GET HER SOMETHING TO BITE ON. THIS IS GOING TO HURT.
STEVIE? IS THAT YOU?
WHO'S--?
SOMEONE SHE USED TO KNOW.
GRRRRAAAHHHHHH!

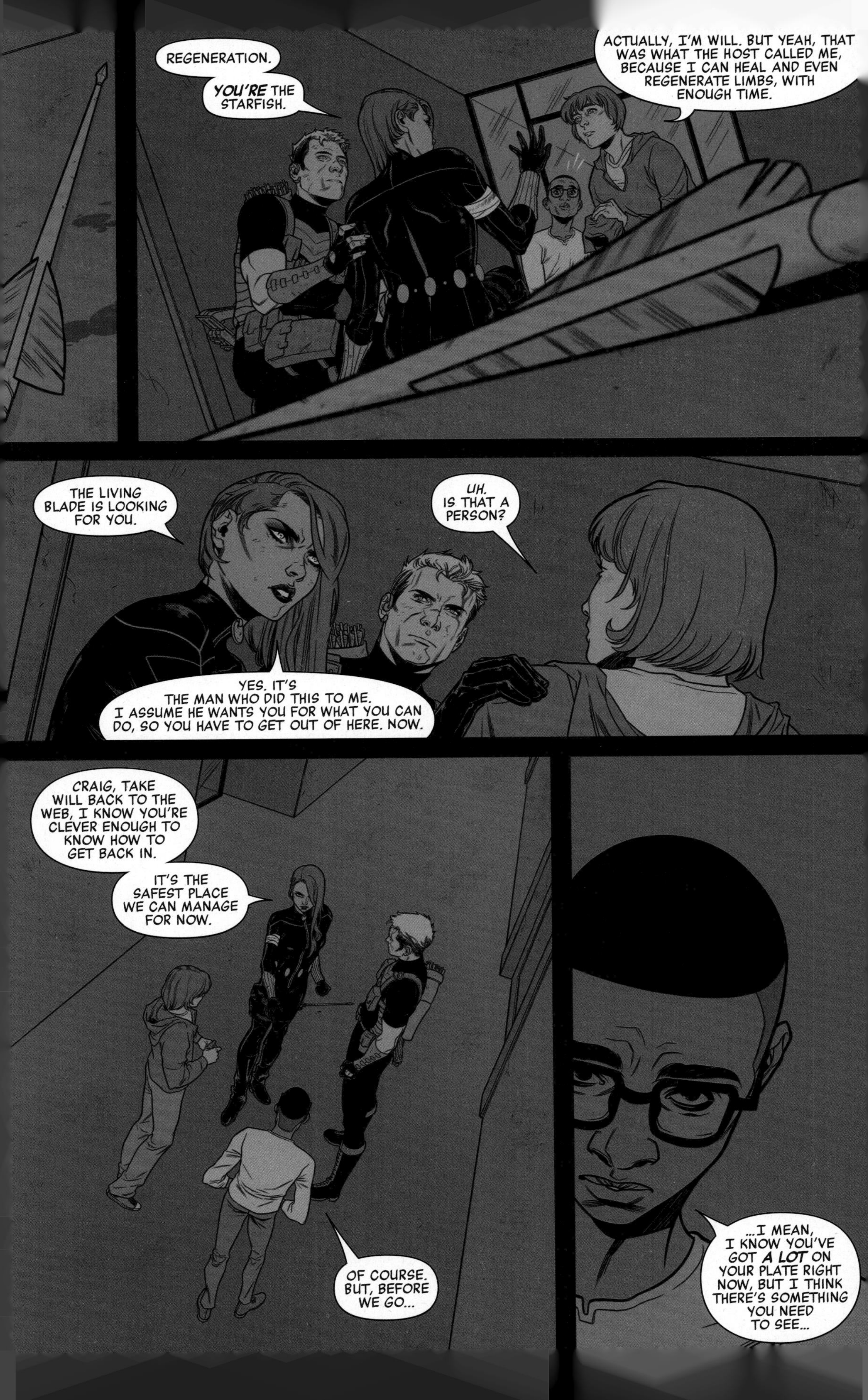
REGENERATION.
YOU'RE THE STARFISH.
ACTUALLY, I'M WILL. BUT YEAH, THAT WAS WHAT THE HOST CALLED ME, BECAUSE I CAN HEAL AND EVEN REGENERATE LIMBS, WITH ENOUGH TIME.
THE LIVING BLADE IS LOOKING FOR YOU.
UH. IS THAT A PERSON?
YES. IT'S THE MAN WHO DID THIS TO ME. I ASSUME HE WANTS YOU FOR WHAT YOU CAN DO, SO YOU HAVE TO GET OUT OF HERE. NOW.
CRAIG, TAKE WILL BACK TO THE WEB, I KNOW YOU'RE CLEVER ENOUGH TO KNOW HOW TO GET BACK IN.
IT'S THE SAFEST PLACE WE CAN MANAGE FOR NOW.
OF COURSE. BUT, BEFORE WE GO...
...I MEAN, I KNOW YOU'VE GOT A LOT ON YOUR PLATE RIGHT NOW, BUT I THINK THERE'S SOMETHING YOU NEED TO SEE...

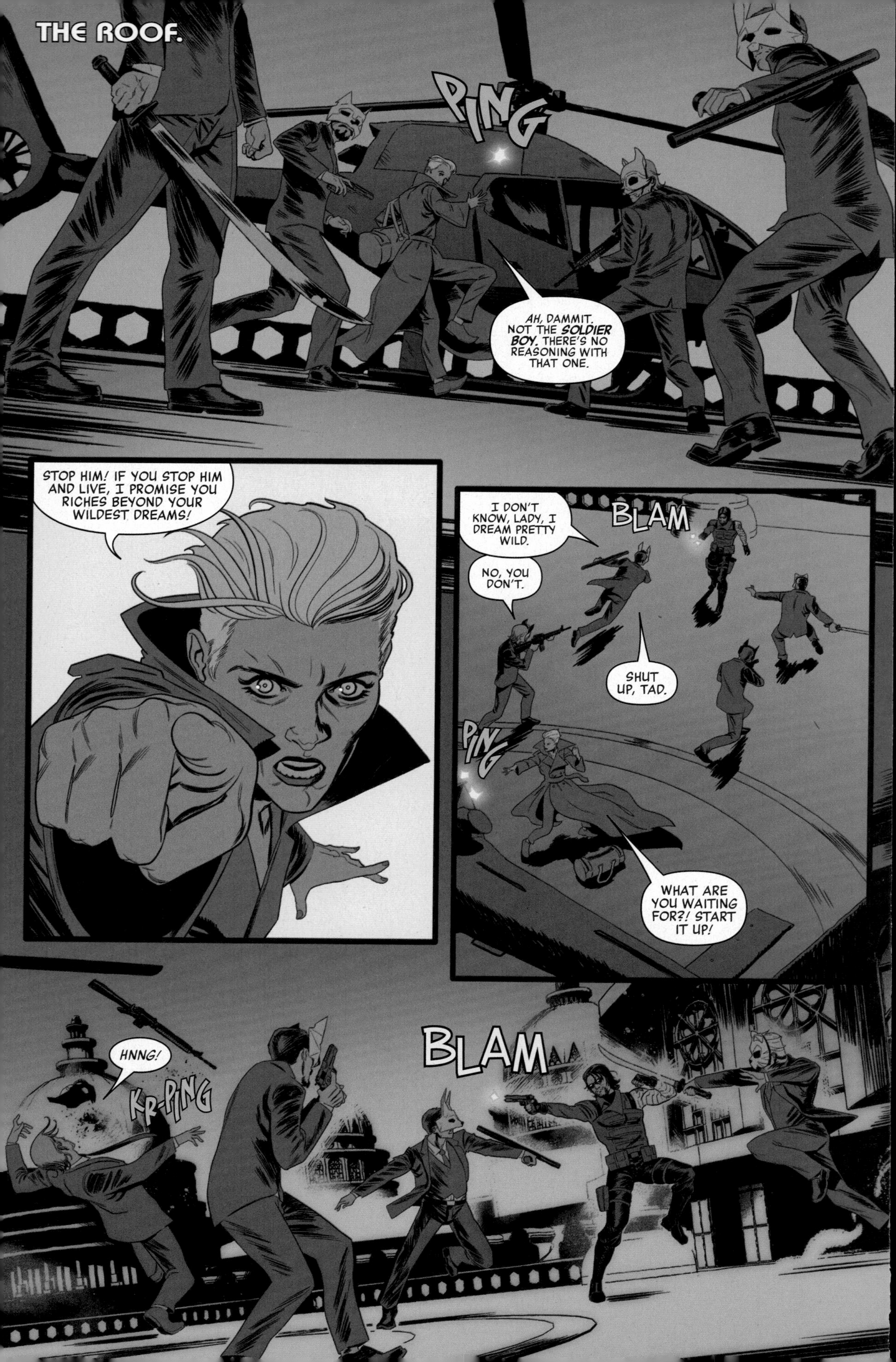
THE ROOF.
PING
AH, DAMMIT. NOT THE SOLDIER BOY. THERE'S NO REASONING WITH THAT ONE.
STOP HIM! IF YOU STOP HIM AND LIVE, I PROMISE YOU RICHES BEYOND YOUR WILDEST DREAMS!
I DON'T KNOW, LADY, I DREAM PRETTY WILD.
BLAM
NO, YOU DON'T.
SHUT UP, TAD.
PING
WHAT ARE YOU WAITING FOR?! START IT UP!
BLAM
HNNG!
KR-PING

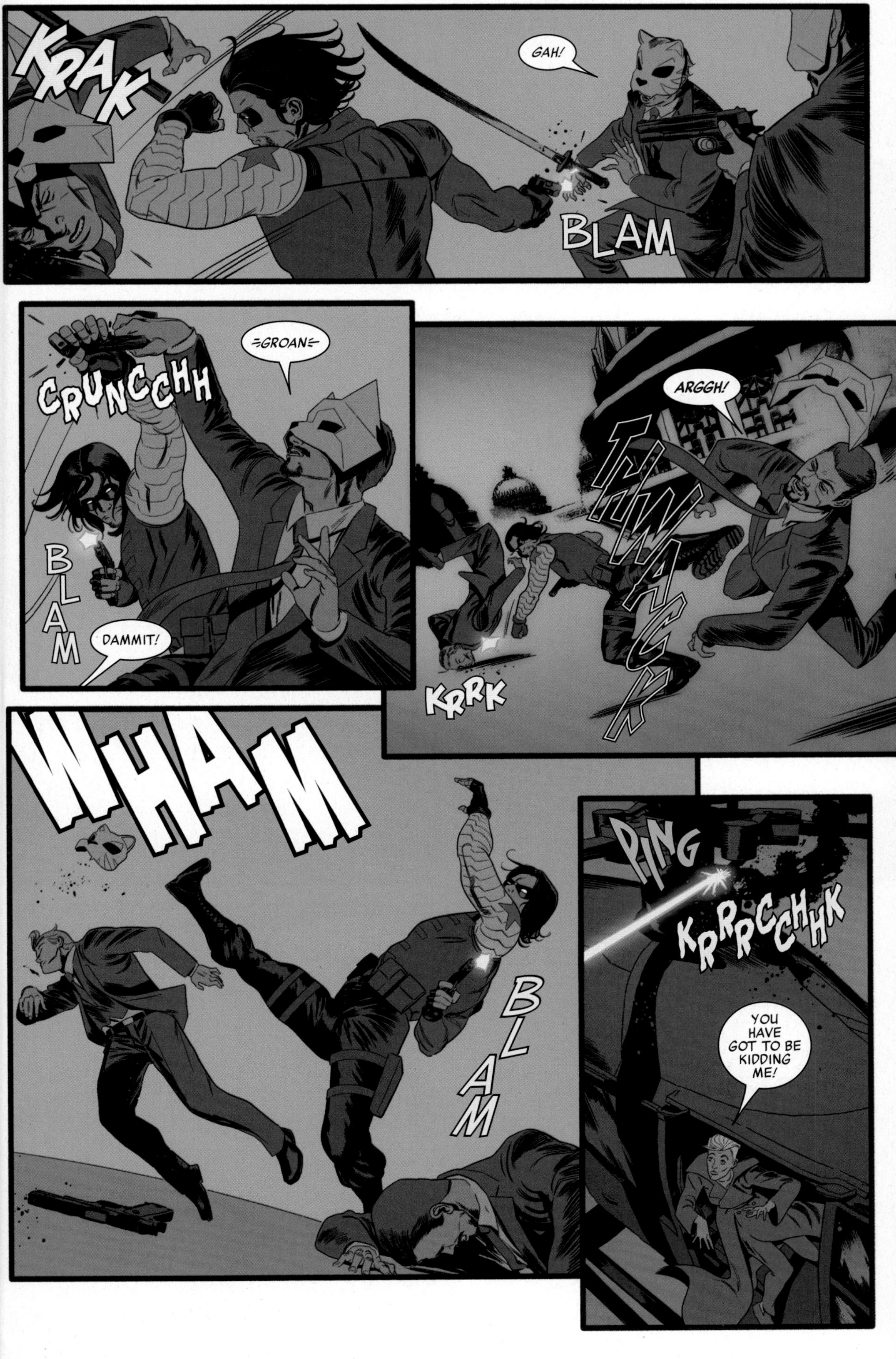
KRAK
GAH!
BLAM
CRUNCCHH
GROAN
BLAM
DAMMIT!
ARGGH!
THWACK
KRRK
WHAM
BLAM
PING
KRRRCHHK
YOU HAVE GOT TO BE KIDDING ME!

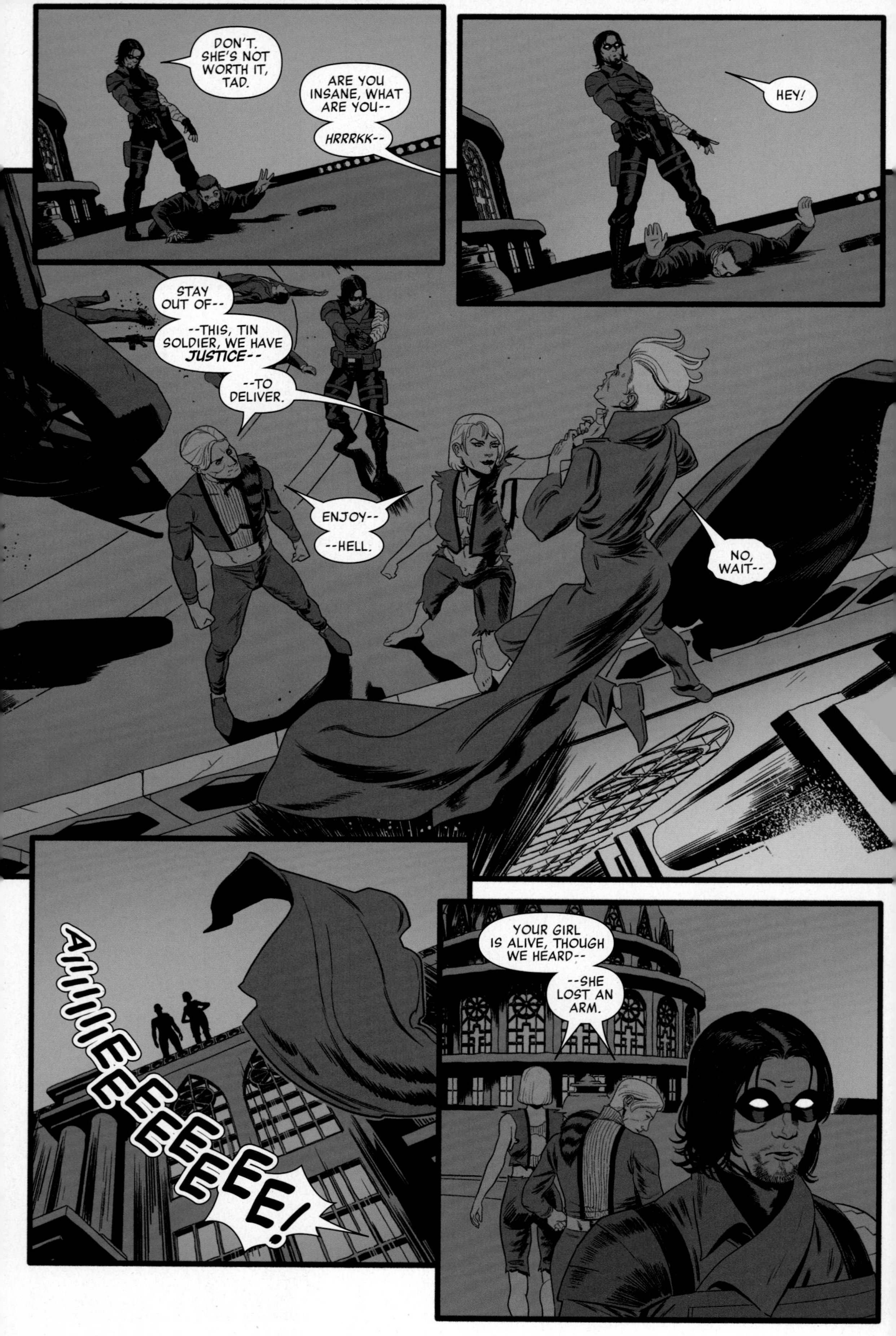
DON'T. SHE'S NOT WORTH IT, TAD.
ARE YOU INSANE, WHAT ARE YOU--
HRRRKK--
HEY!
STAY OUT OF--
--THIS, TIN SOLDIER, WE HAVE JUSTICE--
--TO DELIVER.
ENJOY--
--HELL.
NO, WAIT--
AIIIIIEEEEEEEE!
YOUR GIRL IS ALIVE, THOUGH WE HEARD--
--SHE LOST AN ARM.

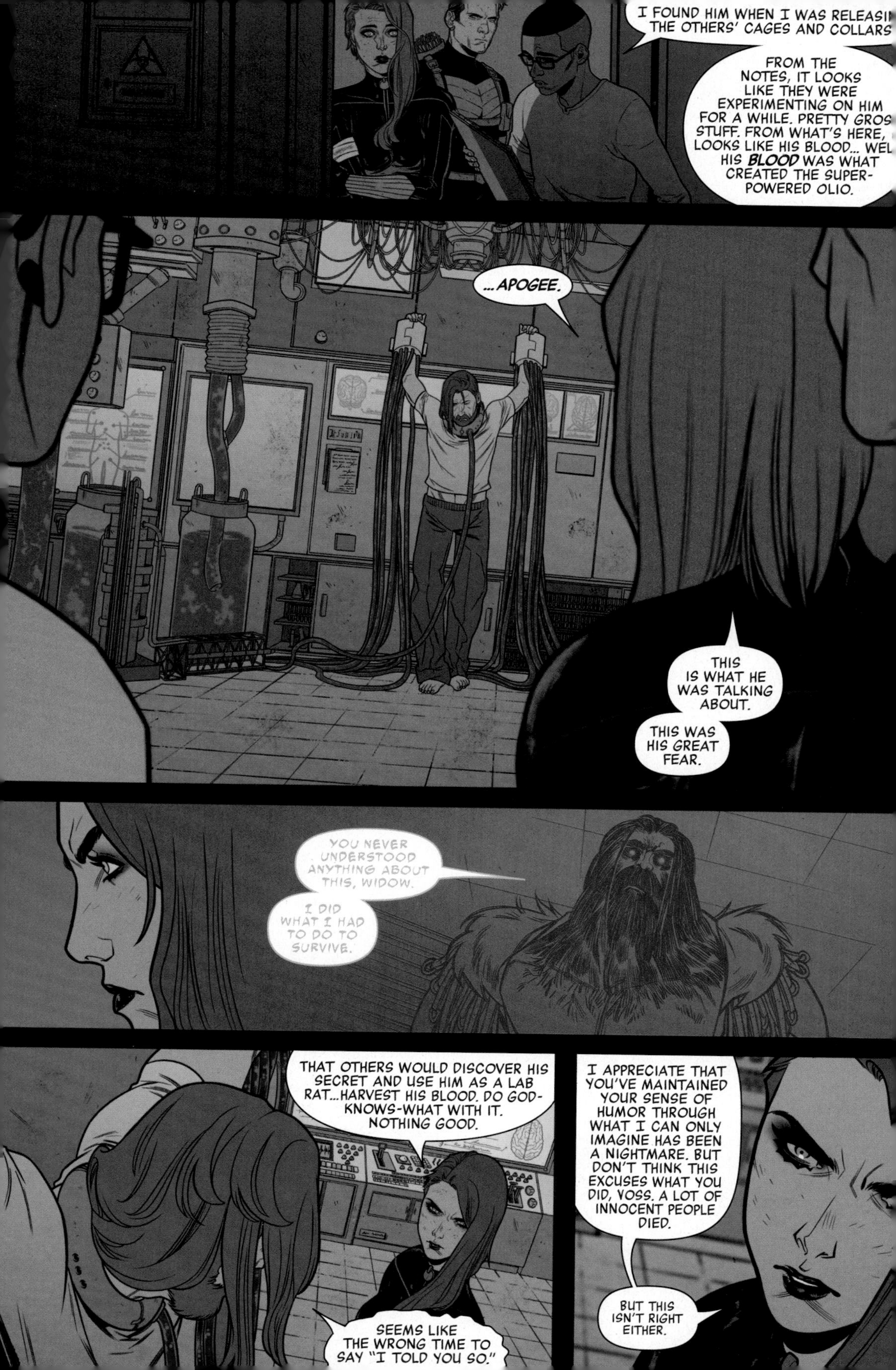
I FOUND HIM WHEN I WAS RELEASI
THE OTHERS' CAGES AND COLLARS
FROM THE NOTES, IT LOOKS LIKE THEY WERE EXPERIMENTING ON HIM FOR A WHILE. PRETTY GROS STUFF. FROM WHAT'S HERE, LOOKS LIKE HIS BLOOD... WEL HIS BLOOD WAS WHAT CREATED THE SUPER-POWERED OLIO.
...APOGEE.
THIS IS WHAT HE WAS TALKING ABOUT.
THIS WAS HIS GREAT FEAR.
YOU NEVER UNDERSTOOD ANYTHING ABOUT THIS, WIDOW.
I DID WHAT I HAD TO DO TO SURVIVE.
THAT OTHERS WOULD DISCOVER HIS SECRET AND USE HIM AS A LAB RAT...HARVEST HIS BLOOD. DO GOD-KNOWS-WHAT WITH IT. NOTHING GOOD.
SEEMS LIKE THE WRONG TIME TO SAY "I TOLD YOU SO."
I APPRECIATE THAT YOU'VE MAINTAINED YOUR SENSE OF HUMOR THROUGH WHAT I CAN ONLY IMAGINE HAS BEEN A NIGHTMARE. BUT DON'T THINK THIS EXCUSES WHAT YOU DID, VOSS. A LOT OF INNOCENT PEOPLE DIED.
BUT THIS ISN'T RIGHT EITHER.

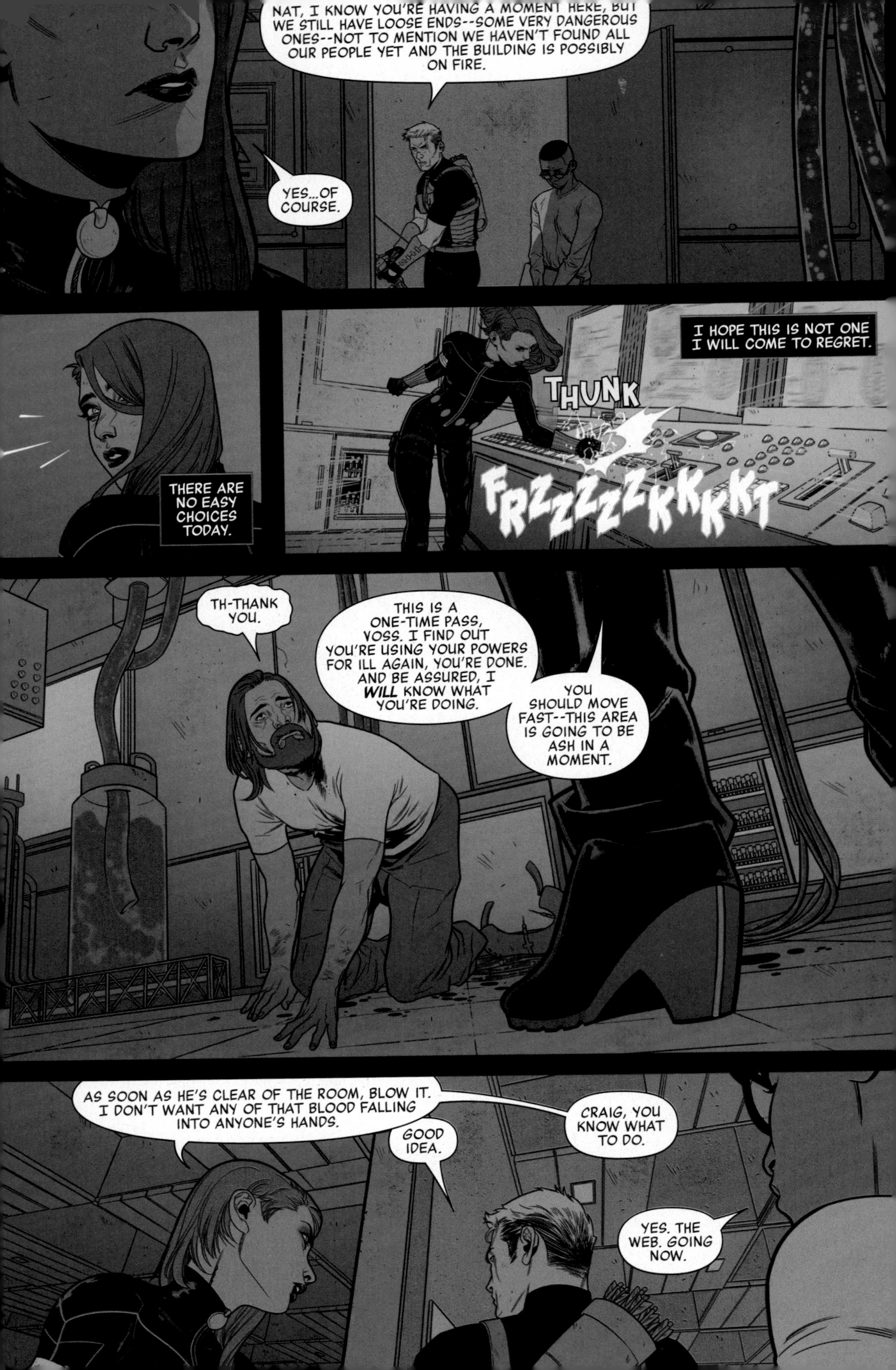
NAT, I KNOW YOU'RE HAVING A MOMENT HERE, BUT WE STILL HAVE LOOSE ENDS--SOME VERY DANGEROUS ONES--NOT TO MENTION WE HAVEN'T FOUND ALL OUR PEOPLE YET AND THE BUILDING IS POSSIBLY ON FIRE.
YES...OF COURSE.
THERE ARE NO EASY CHOICES TODAY.
I HOPE THIS IS NOT ONE I WILL COME TO REGRET.
THUNK
FRZZZZZKKKKT
TH-THANK YOU.
THIS IS A ONE-TIME PASS, VOSS. I FIND OUT YOU'RE USING YOUR POWERS FOR ILL AGAIN, YOU'RE DONE. AND BE ASSURED, I WILL KNOW WHAT YOU'RE DOING.
YOU SHOULD MOVE FAST--THIS AREA IS GOING TO BE ASH IN A MOMENT.
AS SOON AS HE'S CLEAR OF THE ROOM, BLOW IT. I DON'T WANT ANY OF THAT BLOOD FALLING INTO ANYONE'S HANDS.
CRAIG, YOU KNOW WHAT TO DO.
GOOD IDEA.
YES. THE WEB. GOING NOW.

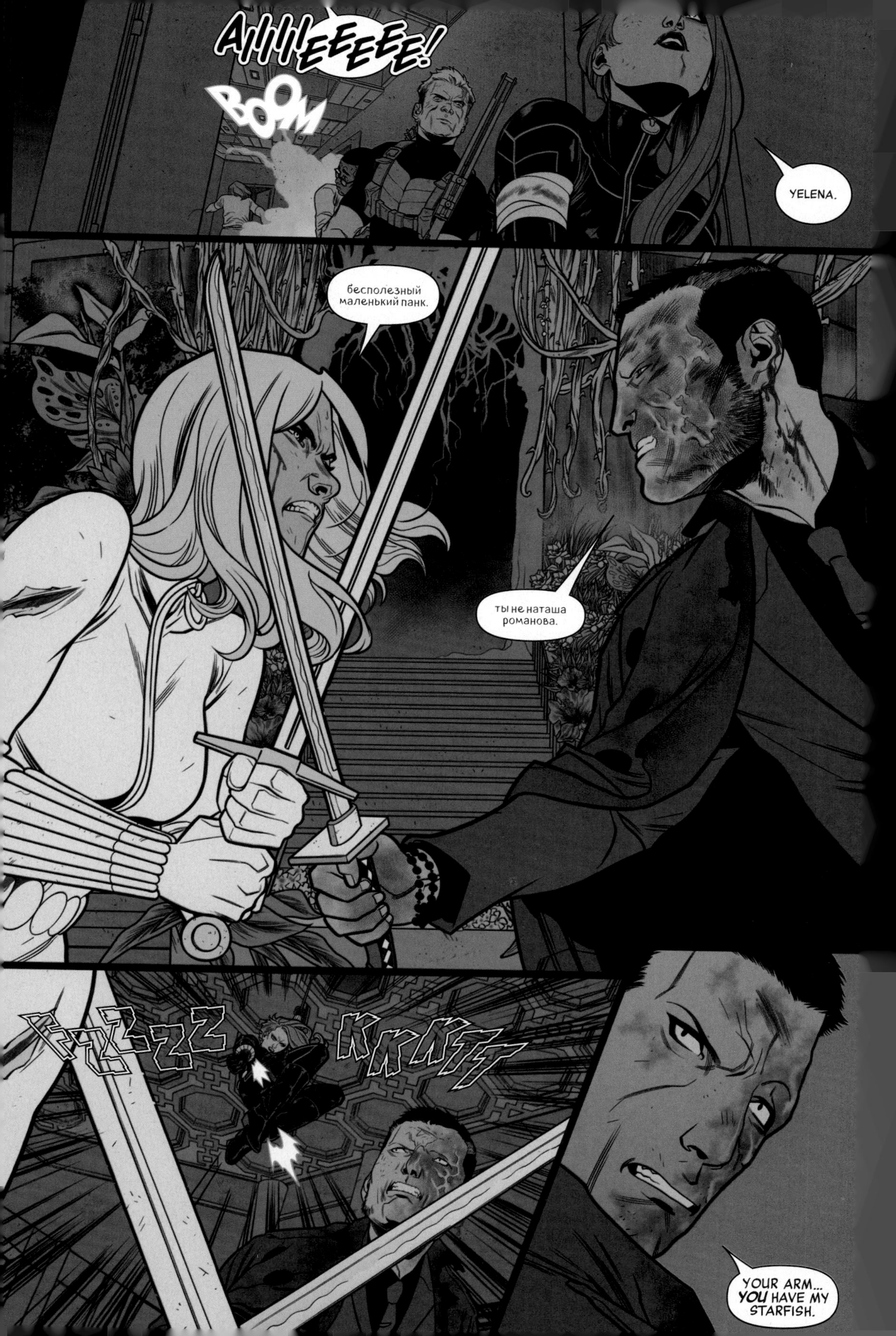
AIIIEEEEEE!
BOOM
YELENA.
бесполезный маленький панк.
ты не наташа романова.
YOUR ARM... YOU HAVE MY STARFISH.

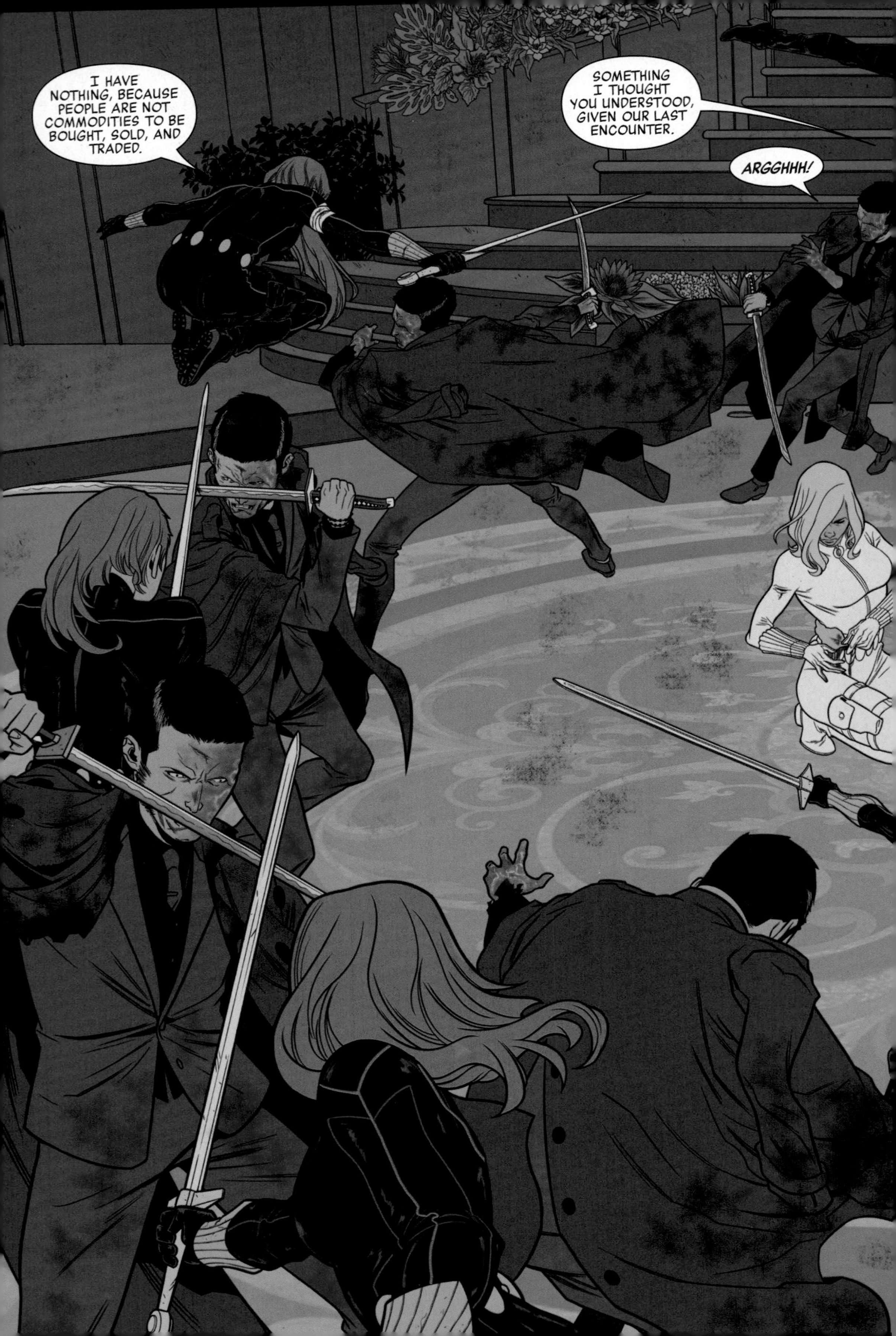
I HAVE NOTHING, BECAUSE PEOPLE ARE NOT COMMODITIES TO BE BOUGHT, SOLD, AND TRADED.
SOMETHING I THOUGHT YOU UNDERSTOOD, GIVEN OUR LAST ENCOUNTER.
ARGGHHH!

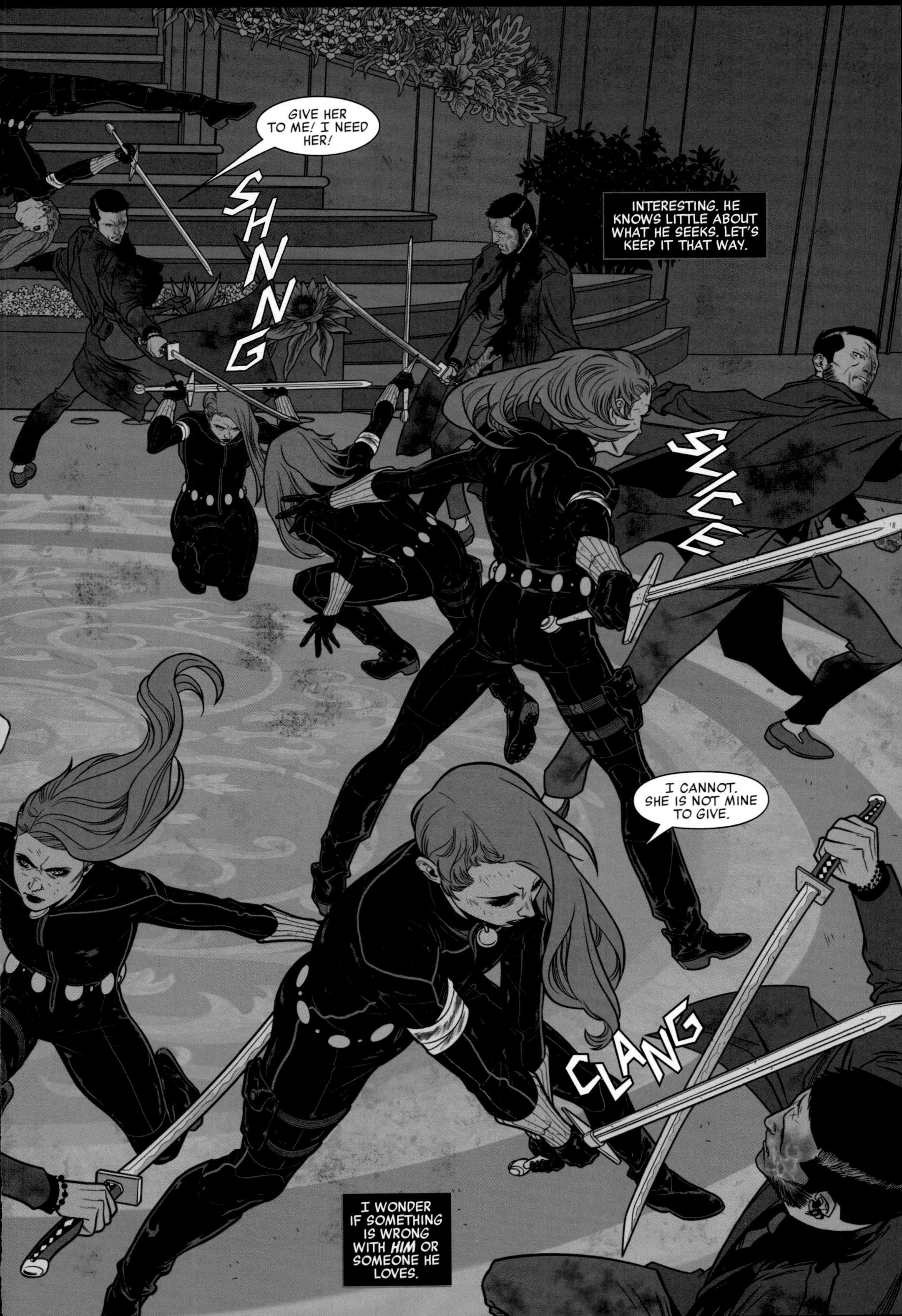
GIVE HER TO ME! I NEED HER!
SHNNG
INTERESTING. HE KNOWS LITTLE ABOUT WHAT HE SEEKS. LET'S KEEP IT THAT WAY.
SLICE
I CANNOT. SHE IS NOT MINE TO GIVE.
CLANG
I WONDER IF SOMETHING IS WRONG WITH *HIM* OR SOMEONE HE LOVES.

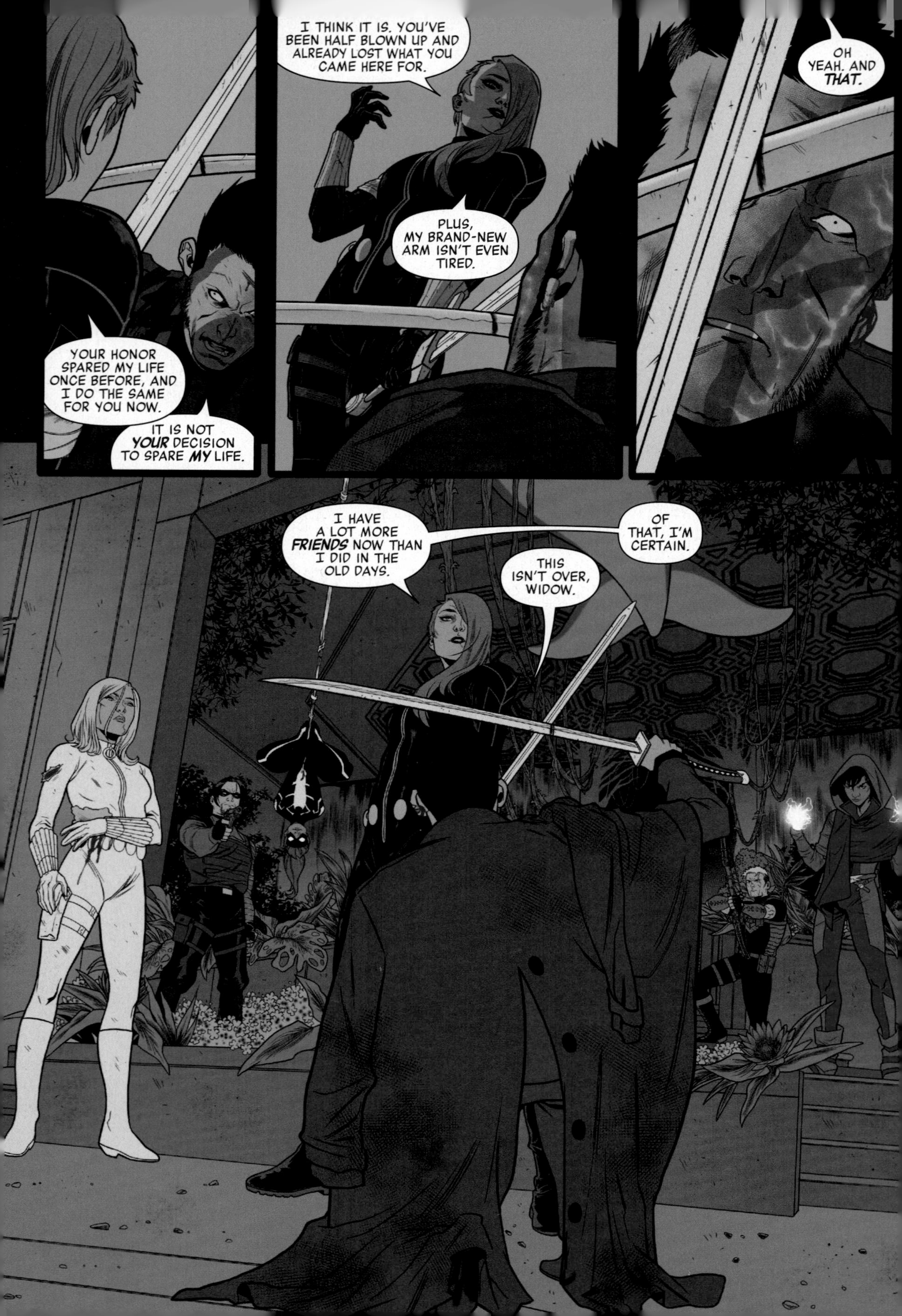
YOUR HONOR SPARED MY LIFE ONCE BEFORE, AND I DO THE SAME FOR YOU NOW.
IT IS NOT YOUR DECISION TO SPARE MY LIFE.
I THINK IT IS. YOU'VE BEEN HALF BLOWN UP AND ALREADY LOST WHAT YOU CAME HERE FOR.
PLUS, MY BRAND-NEW ARM ISN'T EVEN TIRED.
OH YEAH. AND THAT.
I HAVE A LOT MORE FRIENDS NOW THAN I DID IN THE OLD DAYS.
OF THAT, I'M CERTAIN.
THIS ISN'T OVER, WIDOW.

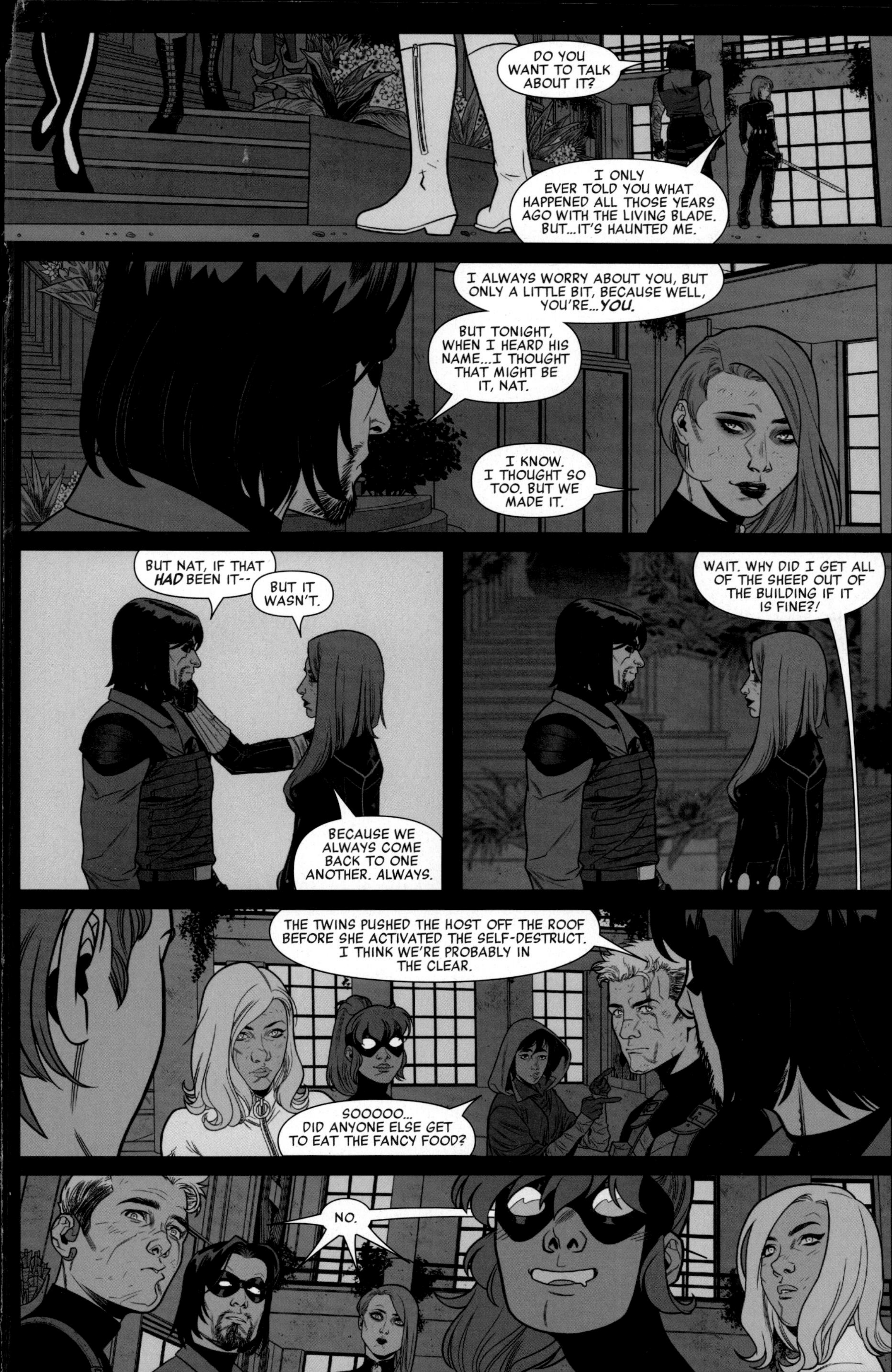
DO YOU WANT TO TALK ABOUT IT?
I ONLY EVER TOLD YOU WHAT HAPPENED ALL THOSE YEARS AGO WITH THE LIVING BLADE. BUT...IT'S HAUNTED ME.
I ALWAYS WORRY ABOUT YOU, BUT ONLY A LITTLE BIT, BECAUSE WELL, YOU'RE...*YOU.*
BUT TONIGHT, WHEN I HEARD HIS NAME...I THOUGHT THAT MIGHT BE IT, NAT.
I KNOW. I THOUGHT SO TOO. BUT WE MADE IT.
BUT NAT, IF THAT *HAD* BEEN IT--
BUT IT WASN'T.
BECAUSE WE ALWAYS COME BACK TO ONE ANOTHER. ALWAYS.
WAIT. WHY DID I GET ALL OF THE SHEEP OUT OF THE BUILDING IF IT IS FINE?!
THE TWINS PUSHED THE HOST OFF THE ROOF BEFORE SHE ACTIVATED THE SELF-DESTRUCT. I THINK WE'RE PROBABLY IN THE CLEAR.
SOOOOO... DID ANYONE ELSE GET TO EAT THE FANCY FOOD?
NO.

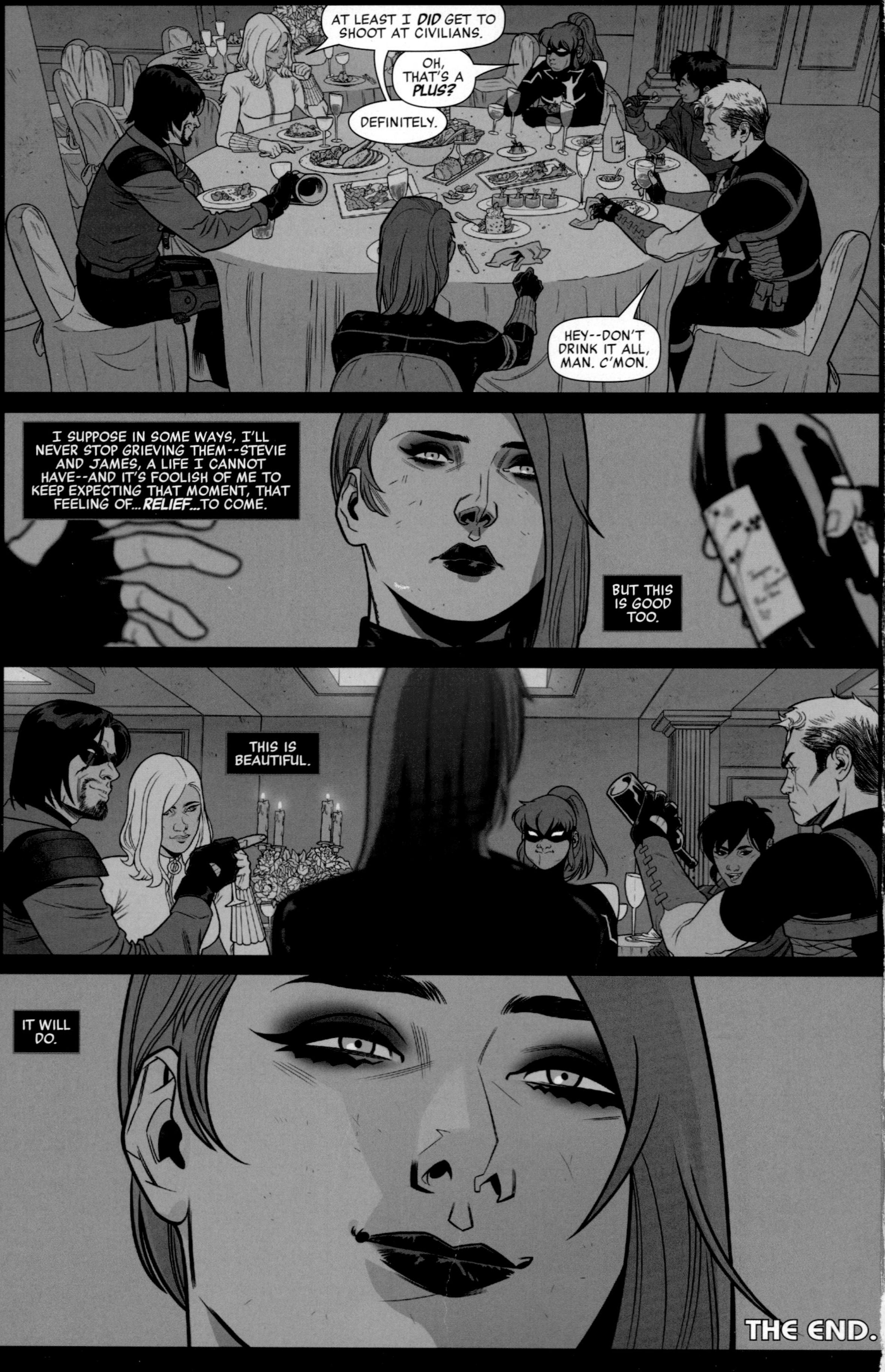
AT LEAST I DID GET TO SHOOT AT CIVILIANS.
OH, THAT'S A PLUS?
DEFINITELY.
HEY--DON'T DRINK IT ALL, MAN. C'MON.
I SUPPOSE IN SOME WAYS, I'LL NEVER STOP GRIEVING THEM--STEVIE AND JAMES, A LIFE I CANNOT HAVE--AND IT'S FOOLISH OF ME TO KEEP EXPECTING THAT MOMENT, THAT FEELING OF...RELIEF...TO COME.
BUT THIS IS GOOD TOO.
THIS IS BEAUTIFUL.
IT WILL DO.
THE END.